THE COMPLETE GUIDE TO

HOME SECURITY

THE COMPLETE GUIDE TO

HOME
SECURITY

How to Protect Your Family and Home from Harm

DAVID ALAN WACKER

BETTERWAY PUBLICATIONS, INC.
WHITE HALL, VIRGINIA

Published by Betterway Publications, Inc.
Box 219
Crozet, VA 22932
(804) 823-5661

Cover design and cover photograph by Susan Riley
Typography by East Coast Typography, Inc.

Library of Congress Cataloging-in-Publication Data

Wacker, David Alan
    The complete guide to home security : how to protect
your family and home from harm / by David Alan Wacker.
        p.   cm.
    Includes index.
    ISBN: 1-55870-163-X : $14.95
    1. Dwellings — Security measures.   2. Burglary protection.
    I. Title
TH9745.D85W33   1990
643'.16 — dc20   90-39097
                                                                    CIP

Printed in the United States of America
0 9 8 7 6 5 4 3 2

To Lora and Anna
for all their love and support.

Contents

Acknowledgments

My thanks to:

Jennifer Beedle for original illustrations
Larry Mack Sr. of Contract Security
U.S. Department of Justice
National Center for Missing & Exploited Children
National Fire Protection Association

I also wish to thank the following companies for providing photographs and illustrations:

Aritech-Moose Security Products
AutoPage, Inc.
Boat Sentry
Chronar Corp.
Kryptonite Corp.
Kwikset Corporation
M.A.G. Engineering & Mfg. Co. Inc.
Roll-A-Way Insulating Security Shutters
Schlage Lock Co.
Sentry Group
Ultrak, Inc.
Weatherguard Ornamental Iron

Introduction

Crime and the fear of crime in some way touches us all. You may not have been victimized by crime, but I'll bet you know someone who has — and with good reason. According to FBI statistics burglars hit 6 million of the nation's 93 million homes in 1988, or 65 out of every 1000 homes. One property crime occurs every 3 seconds, one burglary every 10 seconds, and one motor vehicle theft every 22 seconds. Over a twenty year period, three out of every four households is likely to be burglarized. The economic loss amounts to more than $1 billion annually with an average loss of $1000 per burglary. It's also safe. Burglars are seldom caught and stolen property is rarely recovered.

Regardless of where you live you're going to be affected by crime. Suburbia and rural America no longer afford a sanctuary from crime, with urban areas becoming more dangerous than ever. According to the FBI's "Uniform Crime Report, 1988 Crime in the United States" the top ten U.S. cities (based on crimes per person) hardest hit by burglary last year were: (1) Mobile, AL (2) Dallas, TX (3) Portland, OR (4) New Haven, CT (5) Tacoma, WA (6) Gulfport, MS (7) Hartford, CT (8) Atlanta, GA (9) Seattle, WA (10) Oklahoma City, OK. The ten cities least touched by burglary in 1988 were: (1) Fairbanks, AK (2) Laramie, WY (3) Watertown, SD (4) Aberdeen, SD (5) Juneau, AK (6) Green Bay, WI (7) Cheyenne, WY (8) Nashua, NH (9) Bloomington, MN (10) Sandy, UT.

If asked, most people would have certainly listed New York City, Los Angeles, Chicago, and Miami, among others, on the top ten list. The main point here is that no matter where you live you need to be concerned about security. Just because you've never had a problem before doesn't mean that you won't in the future. The biggest roadblock to improved crime prevention is the public's complacent attitude. I've found that most people pay little attention to security until after something happens either to them or to a neighbor. People think that crime only happens to the other guy. They think it can't happen to them, or that there is no way to stop a determined burglar from getting into their house — so why try? Both attitudes are wrong — it *can* happen to you, and you *can* do something to prevent it from happening to you.

Most crimes are crimes of opportunity. Take away the opportunity and you've significantly reduced your chances of becoming a victim. Prevention is the key to helping you remove the opportunity for crime. Studies have shown that a burglar will not complete his crime if delayed by as little as thirty seconds. If a burglar is confused about whether someone is home or not, cannot figure out how to break in easily, or has no place to hide while he breaks in, it's a good bet he will try to break in someplace else.

Ignorance, apathy, and a feeling of helplessness are the criminal's best allies. His worst enemy is an informed, alert, and security conscience public. You hold the key to reducing crime; with a little

TABLE 1: HOUSEHOLD BURGLARIES, 1973-82

Type of Burglary	Number	Percent
Forcible entry	24,251,000	33
Unlawful entry	32,956,000	45
Attempted forcible entry	16,100,000	22
Total	**73,308000**	**100%**

TABLE 2: TYPE OF STRUCTURE BURGLARIZED 1973-82

Type of Building	Percent
Dwelling:	**64**
House	33
Apartment	15
Mobile home	3
Hotel/motel	3
Group residence	5
Other	5
Non-Dwelling:	**36**
Garage	25
Other	11

TABLE 3: BURGLARIES INVOLVING PROPERTY THEFT OR DAMAGE 1973-82

Type of Crime	Total Entry	Forcible Entry	Unlawful Entry	Attempted Forcible Entry
Theft	62.9%	77.2%	81.9%	2.7%
Attempted theft	7.1	6.2	4.2	14.3
Property damage	41.7	72.6	7.1	66.0

TABLE 4: TYPES OF ITEMS STOLEN 1973-82

Type of Item	Percent*
Cash	22
Tools and building supplies	15
Television, stereo equipment, cameras	11
Bicycles/parts	11
Home furnishings	11
Jewelry, furs, silver	8
Food and drink	8
Clothing	6
Sporting goods	6
Motor vehicles/parts and equipment	5
Gasoline	4
Guns and ammunition	2

*Totals more than 100% because of multiple entries.

help you can fight back — and win! That help is now available in the pages of this book. In writing this book I have attempted to provide the general public with an up-to-date and complete informational resource that covers all aspects of residential crime prevention and security. I have identified the most common problem areas and provided easy to understand and affordable solutions based on the most current crime prevention information available and on my own experience as a police officer.

To help you to understand fully the scope of the burglary problem and the need for increased home security awareness I have included the following statistical information. This information was obtained from the U.S. Department of Justice's Bureau of Justice Statistics Bulletin entitled "Household Burglary," and from a national crime survey report issued by the National Criminal Justice Information and Statistics Service entitled "The Cost of Negligence: Losses from Preventable Household Burglaries."

HOUSEHOLD BURGLARY

The U.S. Department of Justice defines three types of burglary: forcible entry, in which force is used to gain entry; attempted forcible entry, in which force is used in an attempt to gain entry; and unlawful entry, in which someone with no legal right to be on the premises gains entry even though force is not used. During the ten year period of 1973-82, 73 million incidents of forcible entry, attempted forcible entry, and unlawful entry took place. Unlawful entry accounted for 45% of all burglaries, forcible entry made up 33%, and attempted forcible entry accounted for 22% of all burglaries (Table 1). The high rate of unlawful entries indicates that many burglars are opportunists looking for doors and windows left unlocked by careless residents. By simply locking up you will greatly decrease your chances of being burglarized.

The type of dwelling that you live in has a bearing on your probability of being burglarized. The most frequently burglarized types of dwellings are houses 33% followed by apartments 15% (Table 2). That translates to 24,191,640 houses and 10,996,200 apartments burglarized between 1973

and 1982. As you can see burglary is everyone's problem — not just the other guy's.

The vast majority of all forcible entries and unlawful entries involve property damage and actual or attempted theft of household property (Table 3). The type of items stolen (Table 4) indicates which property burglars prefer to steal. It's no surprise that cash is number one; many burglars are specialists - stealing only specific items — but all burglars will take cash whenever they find it. The moral to the story is: Don't keep a lot of cash in your house!

Burglaries occur more often in the warmer months than in the colder months, with July the most active month. A possible explanation for the seasonal fluctuation is the greater tendency to leave windows and doors open during warm months. Another possible reason is that burglars don't like to be out in cold weather any more than anyone else does.

It should be no surprise that 35% of all burglaries occur during daytime hours (6 a.m.-6 p.m.) since most people are at work during the day. Nighttime burglaries account for 38% of all burglaries with most occurring between 6 p.m. and midnight, the remaining 27% occurred at an unknown time. From my experience the afternoon and early evening hours, especially right after dusk, are the prime times for home burglaries. This is because burglars can use the cover of approaching darkness to conceal them and to identify targets — a dark house is usually an unoccupied house.

One of the greatest fears that people have concerning burglary is the possibility that a burglar may inflict physical harm on a household member who happens to be present during the incident. Statistics indicate that these fears are well-founded. A substantial proportion of the violent crimes that occur in the home are committed during household burglaries (Table 5). A household member was present during only 9% of all forcible entries, 14% of all unlawful entries and 17% of all attempted forcible entries. However, in these cases a violent crime was committed during a third of the forcible entries, during almost two-fifths of the unlawful entries, and during one-seventh of the at-

TABLE 5: VIOLENT CRIMES COMMITTED DURING HOUSEHOLD BURGLARIES 1973–82

Type of Violent Crime	Total Number of Burglaries	Forcible Entry	Unlawful Entry	Attempted Forcible Entry
Rape	281,000	34.8	62.5	2.7
Robbery	786,000	33.8	60.5	5.9
Aggravated Assault	623,000	21.8	56.0	22.2
Simple Assault	1,071,000	20.8	64.5	14.7
Total	**2,761,000**	**26.1%**	**61.3%**	**12.6%**

tempted entries. As you can see, most burglaries occur when no one is at home, but the ones that happen when someone is home often lead to violence. This means that you need to take precautions when you're home as well as when you're away.

The statistics in the preceding tables are not mere numbers. They represent ordinary, everyday people — like you and me — who probably thought that it wouldn't happen to them, too. I want to impress upon you that it can happen to you, but also that you can do something to prevent it from happening. You must take action now — today — before you become a statistic.

Remember. Crime is not inevitable — it is preventable!

1
Getting Started

Completing a thorough security survey of your home is the first step on the road to increasing your home's security. I know, you're thinking to yourself, just what is a security survey anyway? Put simply, a security survey is a critical on-site examination and analysis of your home to ascertain its present security status, to identify deficiencies, and to determine protection needed.

Many local law enforcement agencies provide free home security surveys as a public service. To determine the availability of this service in your area call the police or sheriff department's crime prevention officer. If this service is unavailable in your area, you can do the survey yourself. A word of caution: Many security providers such as alarm companies, locksmiths, and security door/window sellers often advertise "free" security surveys. This is simply a gimmick they use to get their foot in the door. It's better to have an unbiased professional inspect your home then someone who is going to try to sell you a product or service.

It often helps when you're doing the survey to put yourself in the burglar's shoes. Looking at your home from a burglar's perspective will help you spot problems that you may otherwise have overlooked. Try thinking to yourself, "How would I go about breaking into my house?" If you can find an easy way to get in, so can a thief! It may also help to have a trusted friend accompany you when checking your house. You're so accustomed to your own home that you may overlook problems which are immediately obvious to someone unfamiliar with your house.

Use the security survey checklist provided in this chapter to help you in identifying your home's potential problem areas. To use the checklist begin at the top of the survey and go down the list checking every item that applies to your home. Check the appropriate yes or no box and write down any problems you find in the "Notes" section of the checklist. After completing the survey turn to the appropriate chapter to find detailed solutions and possible alternatives to the problems that you found during the survey.

THE "LIVED IN" LOOK

After you've completed a thorough security survey of your home you're now ready to begin taking the steps necessary to protect your home and family. Having a secure home does not mean that you must spend large sums of money. On the contrary, most home security measures can be easily implemented with little or no cost. First, we'll cover some simple and often overlooked crime prevention measures that you can put to use right away.

What Does the Burglar See?

Start where the burglar does — from the outside. A burglar's first view of your home is usually from the street. What he sees will often determine whether he attempts entry. When casing a neighborhood, burglars look for homes that appear unoccupied. Making your home appear occupied when you're away is the most important part of an effective home crime prevention program. If the burglar thinks that you're home he will go onto the next house until he finds a good target.

For clues on what to avoid watch your neighbors' houses when they're home and away. It's usually very obvious when they're home and when they're not, and it's just as obvious to a burglar casing your neighborhood. Then take a look at your home. Do you close the shades whenever you're gone, then open them up when you get home? Is the newspaper lying in the driveway and advertising circulars hanging on your door when you get home in the evening? Do you come home to a dark house when the rest of your block is lit up? Do you let your pets out only when you're home? When you're away is the carport empty?

Most of the measures that give your home a lived-in look are common sense ones. Once you get into the habit of doing them you will significantly increase your home's security. Likewise you need to break any bad habits you have that compromise your home's security. Bear in mind that all the ploys described in this chapter are intended to "fool" the thief and keep him away from your house. If he is confused about whether someone is home, cannot figure out how to break in easily, or has nowhere to hide while he breaks in, it's a good bet he will try somewhere else.

Some of the things that make a house appear lived in are: an open front door; the water sprinkler on; tools left by unfinished yard work; the stereo or television playing; vehicles parked in the carport or in front of the house. Obvious signs that indicate no one's home are: a house that is closed up tight, especially during the summer; shades pulled down tight; morning newspaper lying in the driveway; no cars in the carport or garage; a phone ringing unanswered; no sounds coming from inside the house; and no lights on in the house in the evening, especially during the winter months.

A dark house is a good indication that no one is home, especially during the early evening hours. This problem is at its worst during the winter because less daylight equals more burglaries. You should also be extra cautious during the changeover from daylight-savings time to standard time when your house will be dark for an hour or more before you get home from work. You can solve this problem by using light timers set to come on at dusk. Your best bet is to buy a timer with a photoelectric eye that automatically adjusts for the changing moment of sunset every evening. But don't just put a timer on one 25-watt bulb in your living room. Burglars read that as an indication that nobody's home.

Instead have two, three, or more rooms, such as the kitchen, dining room, family room, or a bedroom, lit up. That's the way your house looks when you're home, which is exactly what you want a prowler to think.

Light timers start at about $10 and up, and are available at your local hardware store, building materials store, or general merchandise discount store. More sophisticated home control systems that are capable of controlling all of your lights and appliances are available for $50 and up. X-10 (U.S.A.), Inc. manufactures a complete line of inexpensive home control/automation systems which are installed by simply plugging them into an existing wall outlet. The simpler home control systems can be found at the same retail outlets that carry light timers. (For more information on lighting see Chapter 5: Landscaping and Lighting for Security and for home automation systems look in Chapter 6: Home Security Systems. For a complete listing of lighting and home automation manufacturers look in the Appendix under Manufacturers of Security Products.)

When away for the evening, removing objects from the exterior of the house serves one purpose but giving the outside a barren appearance serves another. Scattering a few objects about the yard gives an "at home" appearance, even when there's no one home. For example, a small tricycle left out front, a small barbecue grill left in back, or a few flower pots at the side of the house gives the illusion that someone is at home. However, don't leave the same things out all the time, as this forms a pattern which decreases the effectiveness of this tactic.

Be sure to pick up your newspapers and ads. If you're going to be away, arrange to have a neighbor pick them up for you. A pile of papers or uncollected ads will alert anyone who happens by that you're not home. This is hard to do if you normally leave home before the paper is delivered. But if anyone, even your children, is home when the paper is delivered it should be his or her responsibility to bring the paper in. These same rules apply to your mail box. An overflowing mail box is one of the best indicators that no one is home, since most people pick up their mail daily, whereas they may not always pick up the newspaper every day.

Never leave notes on your front door or mail box indicating your absence. Likewise don't advertise a pending absence to anyone but trusted friends or neighbors. Burglars read newspapers, too. Don't include your address when placing a classified advertisement. Announce social events and vacations after they happen, not before. If there's a death in the family, arrange for a house-sitter on the day of the funeral. If you're frequently away from home ask a trusted neighbor to keep an eye on your home whenever you're out. The neighbor who is normally home when you're not and who has an unobstructed view of your house is the best person to watch it when you're gone. Be sure to return the favor by watching his house when he's away.

Don't put your name (not even your last) on your mail box, front door, or anyplace else that can be viewed from the street. This only helps a burglar casing your home, as he can use your last name (obtained from the mail box or door) and address to look up your telephone number. He can then call your home from complete safety to check if anybody is home. Some apartment and condominium complexes may tell you that you have to put your name on the complex directory and mail box in order to get mail delivery. If you must use a name on either the directory or mail box then use only your last name and then get a non-published phone number. If the mail box number isn't the same as your apartment number there is less danger that your security will be compromised.

Whenever you're away turn the bell on your phone way down low. That way a burglar won't be alerted to your absence by a ringing telephone. It's also a good idea to use an answering machine or voice mail to keep your phone from ringing unanswered. An unanswered phone call is almost a sure sign that no one is home. This tip is even more effective if you consistently use your answering machine — especially when you're home. That way if a burglar calls casing your home he'll be unsure whether you're home or not.

Don't signal your absence by closing your drapes when you're gone and opening them up when you're home. You might as well put out a sign that says "Gone for the day come in and take what you like." But you do want to draw the drapes at night, especially on the bedroom windows. This prevents people looking inside and casing your house. Drawing the bedroom and bathroom drapes will also give you added protection from peeping toms.

You need to make sure that your drapes actually obstruct a would-be intruder's view into your home. To do this you should check all of your windows both during the day and again at night. Daylight works in your favor because the glare off the windows helps keep people from seeing inside. But at night the opposite is true; someone outside can see inside better than you can see out. For this reason it's very important to check your windows after dark. Turn on the lights and have someone stand in the room near the window while you go outside. If you can still see into the room with the shades down you'll need to either replace your drapes with heavier ones or add a room darkening shade. There are many attractive styles of shades and draperies on the market which effectively protect you from prying eyes.

Keep your yard well maintained, grass mowed, bushes trimmed, and leaves raked. During the winter don't forget to shovel the sidewalks and driveway, or at least make tracks in and out of the house and garage. Virgin snow still on your driveway or sidewalks several days after a storm is a dead give-away that the house is unoccupied. If you're going to be gone for extended periods during the winter have a neighbor shovel your walk and driveway.

Watering your lawn gives the impression that someone is at home to move the water. To do this put a manual type water sprinkler in your front yard and hook it up to a timer. To make the most of this tip, alter the start and stop time, as well as the running length and area watered each day. You can buy a reliable programmable water timer at your local hardware store for about $35 to $45. This ploy works because people without automatic sprinkler systems don't normally water the lawn unless they're home to move the sprinkler. As with any other trick it will lose its effectiveness if you follow the same pattern every day.

Having empty trash cans or no trash cans set out on collection day is another indication that you're not home. The best solution is to put your garbage out in plastic trash bags. That way once they've been picked up there are no empty trash cans left out to tip off burglars casing your neighborhood. If you must use trash cans either have a neighbor put them away for you or build a trash can holder curb side (if allowed) so that your trash cans are always out. If you're gone on trash day have a neighbor put out one of his trash cans in front of your house so that it looks like you're home.

Dogs as Protection

Burglars will likely bypass a house where they think a dog lives because they're usually not willing to tangle with a big dog or to have its barking alert neighbors. A large dog which has a menacing bark but doesn't bite is your best bet. A barking dog is just as effective because its barking will alert the neighbors and scare away intruders. Liability is another reason for not keeping a vicious dog for protection. Although having a dog for protection is an effective crime prevention measure, they're neither foolproof nor inexpensive.

If you don't want to or can't afford to own a dog but still want the protection afforded by one, make people think you have a dog – a big one. You do

this by putting up "Beware of Dog" signs. Give the signs credibility by putting out a large dog dish filled with dog food, or by building a large dog house in the back yard. To add more believability you can install a barking dog alarm which makes a sound like a barking dog when someone approaches the monitored area. The Barking Dog Security Alarm from Heath Zenith uses a passive infrared motion detector (PIR) to detect intruders. The Barking Dog Alarm from The Progressive Energy Corp. is similar in function but is noise activated.

The Ram Radar Watchdog is a new portable barking dog alarm from The Ram Company of Beverly Hills, CA. This system uses electronic radar and a new technology that detects motion through solid walls, doors, glass, and metal. This system has no outside sensors that can be detected, tampered with, or subjected to vandalism. When an intruder steps into the detection area, it makes the loud barking sound of a large dog. As the intruder moves, Watchdog tracks the movements and continues to bark, sounding more frenzied as the intruder moves closer to the unit. Once the intruder stops moving or leaves the area of detection the unit stops barking and automatically resets itself. The Watchdog is available in AC-powered or battery-operated models. The detection range is adjustable from zero to 30 feet and The Barking volume is also adjustable. The unit wholesales for $79 and is available only through professional security dealers.

NEIGHBORHOOD CRIME PREVENTION

A good neighbor is the best crime prevention device ever invented. When neighbors look out for each other, crime often goes down. Meet with your neighbors; get to know them and their children. In short, become friends, because friends are more likely to watch out for each other than are strangers. Exchange work and vacation schedules, home and business telephone numbers and addresses. Make arrangements to watch each other's homes and property when you're at work or on vacation. Everyone in the neighborhood should be on the

Sign for a neighborhood watch program.

lookout for suspicious activities or persons and report them to the police immediately. This is easier when you know your neighbors and know who belongs and who doesn't.

You can either do this informally or by forming a neighborhood watch group sponsored by your local police department. If you're interested in starting a neighborhood watch in your area contact your local police or sheriff's department. Most police and sheriff's departments sponsor neighborhood watch programs. They will send a crime prevention officer to your neighborhood meeting to help you set up a neighborhood watch program. They will offer tips on home security, self-protection, and what to report to the police. They will also put up Neighborhood Watch warning signs in your neighborhood. The only drawback to this program is that the police department requires that a majority of residents in the affected area participate in the program.

Many people have observed a crime in progress

without realizing it until it's too late. If you observe a suspicious activity or person in your neighborhood whose intentions you are uncertain of, call the police immediately. Don't try confronting suspicious persons or checking out suspicious activities on your own — that's a job for the police. To help you know what to be on the lookout for I have included descriptions of typical suspicious persons and activities. Keep in mind that many such occurrences could be completely innocent, but this is something the police should determine.

Many burglars use vehicles, often stolen, in the commission of their crimes. So you need to be on the lookout for suspicious vehicles. But what is a suspicious vehicle? Basically you should be suspicious of any unfamiliar vehicle in your neighborhood, especially if it is doing any of the following: Parked vehicles containing one or more persons, especially significant if at an unusual hour. The occupants could be lookouts for a companion who is burglarizing nearby homes, or they could be involved in the use or sale of drugs. Slow moving vehicles, especially if driving without lights, following an aimless or repetitive course. Burglars often cruise slowly through neighborhoods looking for potential targets. A vehicle parked in a neighbor's driveway being loaded with valuables, even if the vehicle looks legitimate, especially a moving van. If you've taken the initiative to get to know your neighbors, then you will know if they are moving or if the people removing items from the house belong there or not.

You also need to watch for: Property in vehicles, especially if at night or if property is household goods or appliances such as stereos, TVs, guns, cameras, bed sheets or pillow cases filled with unknown items. Many burglars wrap up their loot in pillow cases or sheets so that they can carry away more of your stuff. Abandoned vehicles either new or old, with or without license plates, may be stolen and could have been used in the commission of other crimes. Apparent business transactions conducted from a car around schools, parks or in quiet residential neighborhoods are a sign of possible drug sales. If you see persons being forced into a vehicle, a kidnapping or rape may be taking place.

Suspicious People and Activities

You also need to watch for suspicious persons. What is a suspicious person? A suspicious person is anyone, male or female, young or old, shabbily or well dressed, who does not live in your neighborhood, especially if he or she is engaged in any of the following suspicious activities.

- Strangers entering your neighbor's house when the neighbor isn't home.

- Someone going door-to-door in your neighborhood, especially if a companion waits out front or a car follows close behind. Don't assume that he or she is a legitimate door-to-door salesman; that's exactly what burglars hope you will think.

- Someone trying to force entry into a home, even if he's wearing a repairman's uniform. A legitimate repairman is not going to break into your home if you're not there.

- Persons shortcutting through yards. They may have just burglarized your neighbor's house and are making a getaway.

- Persons carrying property that is not boxed or wrapped, especially if the person is running or gets into a vehicle that hastily leaves the area.

Other suspicious activities to watch for are:

- Persons loitering around or removing mechanical parts or accessories from parked cars, especially at night.

- Open doors, broken doors or windows, or other signs of forced entry to a neighbor's house.

- Property being removed from a house or building; if residents are at work, on vacation, or known to be absent.

- Unusual noises, like a scream, breaking glass, pounding noises, or explosions.

If you see or hear anything suspicious, call the police immediately. Give them a physical description of the person and the license plate number and description of suspicious vehicles. Even if nothing is wrong, they'll thank you for your alertness.

During my police career I have responded to countless reports of suspicious people or crimes in progress where an eyewitness could only provide a generic description of the suspects or their getaway vehicle. Vague descriptions and generalities are of little help to the police and sometimes they are worse than no description at all. The more accurate the information is that you supply to the police, the easier it will be for them to make a quick arrest. To assist you in obtaining accurate descriptions of persons and vehicles follow the guidelines below, which are listed in order of importance.

Describing Suspicious Persons

- Sex
- Race (white, Black, Oriental, Hispanic, etc.)
- Build (short, tall, thin, fat)
- Dress (color and type of clothing)
- Unusual features or marks (facial hair, scars, tattoos)
- Hair color, length, and style
- Eye color
- Height
- Weight
- Age

Describing Suspicious Vehicles

- Color (top/bottom)
- Basic type (truck, van, motorcycle, etc.)
- Number of doors (2 door, 4 door, hatchback, etc.)
- Make (Chevrolet, Ford, Toyota, etc.)
- Model (Accord, Trans Am, etc.)
- Age (within 2-3 years of model year)
- Condition
- Year (exact model year)
- State of license
- Complete or partial license number

SUMMONING HELP

Do you know who to call in an emergency? Don't wait until an emergency arises to find out that you don't know who to call for help. If you're lucky you can dial 911 in order to get emergency help. But in many areas there is still one number for the police department and a separate number for the fire department and yet another number for the rescue unit/ambulance. You can eliminate any potential problems by calling the non-emergency phone number for your local police department. Give them your address and ask if they are responsible for the dispatching of police, fire, and rescue units to that address. If they are, find out what phone number to call in case of an emergency. If not, have them direct you to the proper agency, and then give that agency a call to verify the information and phone number.

Make sure responding emergency units can locate your house in an emergency. To do this your house number should be clearly visible from the street — day or night. Use numbers made of reflective materials or contrasting colors with the best combination being black numerals on a white background. The numbers should be at least 6 inches high and arranged horizontally. Horizontal numbers are easier to read than vertical or diagonal numbers. Avoid script letters for the numbers — they can cause confusion and delays. If your house is some distance from the road, post the number at the driveway entrance. If you live on a corner, make sure the number faces the street named in your address. Replace any broken or missing numbers so that your complete number is showing. Finally, make sure that your landscaping doesn't obstruct the visibility of your address from the street.

A very inexpensive way to make sure that your home can be easily found both day and night is to use a solar-powered yard address sign. The Digi-lite™ solar-powered address sign from Sunergy, Inc. can be either mounted directly onto your house or used as a yard sign complete with a theft resistant stake. The sign has a photoelectric eye which automatically turns on the light at dusk, and since the unit is solar powered there is no wiring, no electrical installation, no digging up the lawn, and no electrical costs.

You can help responding emergency equipment find your house more quickly by installing a device that flashes the porch or yard light during an emergency. I recommend the 911 Flash-lite from Consumer Engineering, Inc. which retails for less than $10. The 911 Flash-lite is simple and painless to install. You simply remove the light bulb in your fixture, screw the device into the socket and then install your light bulb into the device. Flipping the switch once (as you normally would to turn on a light) causes the light to remain on until the switch is flipped to the off position. To make it flash, flip the switch that controls the porch or yard light twice. This causes the light to flash rapidly. So, in an emergency, the flashing light will help the police, fire truck, or ambulance find your house. In this day and age of subdivisions, where all the houses look like they came out of the same cookie cutter, emergency vehicles can identify exactly where the emergency is on the street.

IF IT HAPPENS TO YOU

If you arrive home and suspect that a burglary has occurred, don't go in and don't touch anything. Go to a neighbor and call the police immediately — even a delay of five minutes can mean that the chances of catching the criminal have dropped significantly — then wait outside for them to arrive. If you confront a burglar, don't try to stop him. Run to a neighbor and call the police at once. If none of your neighbors are home run down the street yelling and screaming — do anything to attract attention. This may seem foolish and embarrassing to you now, but if this course of action someday saves your life it will be well worth any amount of embarrassment.

Never, never remain in your home while a burglar's inside. Get out as fast as you can, any way that you can — even if it means jumping out a second story window. If you remain, there is a very good chance (better than 50%) that you will become the victim of a violent crime: rape, robbery, assault, homicide. No possession is worth your life; if something is stolen it can be replaced —

Large house numbers that are easily visible from the street make it easy for responding emergency units to locate your house, even at night.

The Digilite solar powered house number light from Sunergy is an ideal location finder for police, fire, and delivery. Photo courtesy of Sunergy, Inc.

your life can't! The best thing for you to do is to get away and to try and get a good physical description of the suspect and any getaway vehicle and determine the suspect's direction of travel after he leaves your home.

If you've put off increasing your home's security because it wouldn't "happen to me" then now is a very good time to do it. It may be too late to prevent the burglary that has already occurred, but statistics show that homes that have already been burglarized face a better than 30% chance of being burglarized a second time. If you don't make changes now then whatever vulnerability it was that enticed the first thief to burglarize your home is still present to entice other criminals.

After the police have made sure that it is safe for you to enter your home the first thing you need to do is to check each room to find out what, if anything, is missing. Don't touch anything until the officer tells you to; you could inadvertently destroy valuable evidence. To make the police report a useful tool in the recovery of your property the officer will need a complete description of all stolen items, including serial numbers. This is why it is so important to have an up-to-date property inventory available (see Chapter 7). Without this information there is very little chance of your property being located and returned to you. Once you've made a police report, you need to obtain the case report number from the reporting officer. Your insurance company will need this number for you to file a claim.

HOME SECURITY CHECKLIST

Date _____

YES NO Check (✓) the appropriate box

DOORS (Chapter 2)

☐ ☐ Are all exterior doors of metal or solid wood construction at least 1¾ " thick?

☐ ☐ Do exterior doors close tightly and are they double locked?

☐ ☐ Are exterior door hinges protected from removal from the outside?

☐ ☐ Are there windows in the door or within 40 inches of the lock?

☐ ☐ If so, is the door secured with a double cylinder deadbolt lock?

☐ ☐ If there are no windows in the door, is there a wide angle viewer or intercom?

☐ ☐ Are the locks on all exterior doors of the deadbolt type with at least a 1-inch throw?

☐ ☐ Are there auxiliary locks on the doors?

☐ ☐ Are strikes and strike plates securely fastened with at least 3 inch screws?

☐ ☐ Can the door locks be reached through a mail slot, delivery port, or pet entrance?

☐ ☐ Are exterior entranceways equipped with steel security doors?

☐ ☐ Is there a screen or storm door with an adequate lock?

☐ ☐ Are all exterior entrances lighted?

☐ ☐ Can entrances be observed from the street or public areas?

☐ ☐ Are front and back doors kept lighted in evening?

☐ ☐ Does the porch or landscaping offer concealment from view from the street or public area?

☐ ☐ If the door is a sliding glass door, is the sliding panel secure from being lifted out of the track?

☐ ☐ Is the sliding door mounted on the inside of the stationary panel?

☐ ☐ Is a charley bar or key-operated auxiliary lock used on the sliding glass door?

☐ ☐ Are all entrances to living quarters from the garage and basement of metal or solid wood construction?

☐ ☐ Does the door from the garage to the living quarters have auxiliary locks that are operated from the living quarters side?

☐ ☐ Is the automobile entrance door to the garage equipped with a locking device or garage door opener?

☐ ☐ Is the garage door kept closed and locked at all times?

☐ ☐ If your car is in the garage, are the doors locked and the keys removed?

☐ ☐ Is the outside utility entrance to the garage as secure as required for any ground floor entrance?

☐ ☐ Are all garage doors lighted on the outside?

☐ ☐ Is there a door from the outside to the basement?

☐ ☐ If so, is that door adequately secure for an exterior door?

☐ ☐ Is the outside basement entrance lighted by exterior lighting?

☐ ☐ Is the basement door concealed from the street or neighbors?

☐ ☐ If padlocks are used, are they high quality?

☐ ☐ If hinges and hasps show, are the screws and hinge pins of the type which cannot easily be removed?

WINDOWS (Chapter 3)

☐ ☐ Do all windows have key-operated locks or a method of pinning in addition to the regular lock?

☐ ☐ If windows are kept open for ventilation, can they be locked in the open position?

☐ ☐ Do all windows have screens or storm windows that lock from the inside?

☐ ☐ Are ground floor windows secured with steel security window guards?

☐ ☐ If so, are bedroom window guards equipped with quick release fire escape mechanisms?

☐ ☐ Do any windows open onto areas that may be hazardous or offer special risk to burglary?

☐ ☐ Are exterior areas of windows free from concealing structure or landscaping?

☐ ☐ Are the window air conditioners bolted to prevent removal from the outside?

☐ ☐ Do any upper floor windows open onto porch or garage roofs or roofs of adjoining buildings?

☐ ☐ If so, are they secured as adequately as if they were at ground level?

☐ ☐ Are trees and shrubbery kept trimmed back from upper floor windows?

☐ ☐ Are shrubs and trees trimmed low, below window level?

☐ ☐ Are skylights well secured, that is, not easily removed from the roof?

☐ ☐ Are all basement windows secured against entrance?

☐ ☐ Are garage windows secured adequately for ground floor windows?

☐ ☐ Do window coverings prevent someone from seeing inside?

GENERAL HOME SECURITY (Chapters 4, 5, 6, 7)

☐ ☐ Do you have a burglar alarm?

☐ ☐ If so, do you use it consistently when you're away?

☐ ☐ If you have a wireless security system have you checked the batteries in your sensors recently?

☐ ☐ Are there stickers on your windows and doors, stating that your property is protected by an alarm system?

☐ ☐ Do you have a yard alarm warning sign?

☐ ☐ Are trees and shrubs pruned so a potential intruder cannot work concealed from view?

☐ ☐ Does a privacy fence let a potential intruder operate out of view?

☐ ☐ Are bicycles, garden equipment, and other items kept indoors and locked?

☐ ☐ Do you have a locking mailbox?

☐ ☐ Can an intruder remove your clothes dryer's vent and reach inside and unlock a door or window?

☐ ☐ When you retire or leave, do you check doors and windows to be certain they are locked?

☐ ☐ Do you keep a spare house key hidden outside?

☐ ☐ Do you avoid handing out duplicate keys indiscriminately?

☐ ☐ If you park your car in a public lot, do you separate the car keys from the house keys?

☐ ☐ When repairmen and utility company representatives come to your door, do you request identification?

☐ ☐ Is valuable property inventoried, periodically updated, and the list secured?

☐ ☐ Is the list of serial numbers of those items which have been recorded kept off the premises?

☐ ☐ Are valuable items marked with a scriber and an identifying number?

☐ ☐ Do you have photos or video tape of your valuables?

☐ ☐ Are emergency telephone numbers memorized and also prominently displayed near the telephone?

☐ ☐ Do you avoid keeping cash in the house?

☐ ☐ Are valuables secured in a safe?

☐ ☐ Do you keep your important papers in a fire resistant safe or file cabinet?

☐ ☐ Are ladders stored out of sight?

☐ ☐ If you have weapons, are they secured?

☐ ☐ Do you have adequate homeowner's insurance?

☐ ☐ Is your home adequately lighted on all four sides?

☐ ☐ Are all outside lights working?

☐ ☐ Are selected inside lights controlled by timers?

☐ ☐ Is your address visible from the street — day and night?

☐ ☐ Has your local police or sheriff's department crime prevention officer been to your home to conduct a free security survey?

2
Securing Doors

Burglars gain entry into homes through the front door more often than all of the other possible entry points *combined*. That's why it is so important to have good security on all exterior doors, especially your front door. When checking your doors, don't forget garage, cellar, patio, or other doors that lead through storage areas or spare rooms — you can be sure the burglar won't. Are the door and frame in good condition and is the appropriate type of door used? A hollow core door is little better than no door at all. Does the door have adequate locks? A good door with poor or nonexistent locks is a burglary waiting to happen. Make sure these doors are strong, in good repair, equipped with good locks, and always locked. If doors and locks delay a burglar for as little as two to three minutes he'll get discouraged and leave.

Start by taking a good look at your doors and how you use them. Do you keep them locked? Many a burglar has entered through an unlocked door (45% of all burglaries required no forced entry). Keep your doors locked at all times, even when you are home. If your doors are unlocked an intruder can easily enter your home before you have a chance to lock the door or call for help. A locked door gives you that extra time you need to escape. If you are outside keep all doors locked except the ones within view. Many burglaries have occurred when people have left their front or back door unlocked while they were occupied in another part

of the house or outside in the yard. Don't hide a spare key outside; burglars know all the hiding places. It is better to give a trusted neighbor a spare key in case you ever lock yourself out. Remember, always use your locks. Even a five minute trip to the store is long enough for a burglar to enter your home.

Your doors are more vulnerable than you think. Most doors can simply be "kicked in" by any would-be burglar, even a juvenile. Kick-in attacks are the most commonly used method to gain forced entry, and the easiest to defend against. Even though your door and locks look formidable

Typical door damage resulting from a kick-in burglary. The homeowner lost over $400 worth of valuables in this unsolved burglary.

the door jamb is the weak point. Take a close look at the door jamb in the area of the strike plate. You'll find that the door jamb is most likely made from 1 × 4 inch pine. When the deadbolt was installed a bolt hole was drilled through the jamb as close as ½ to ¾ inch from the inside edge of the jamb. The strike plate, which is made of very thin metal, is attached to the door jamb by two ½ inch wood screws, which are only long enough to anchor to the jamb itself.

This situation, which is common to most door installations, is very weak. When someone kicks the door, the force of the blow is transferred through the door to the lock, then to the strike plate and jamb. The entire force of the blow, and it doesn't take much force, is applied to the weakened section of the door jamb where the strike plate is attached. The security of your door is relying on the strength of a ½" × ¾" section of the pine door jamb. Without reinforcement the jamb is easily broken with minimal effort.

Sophisticated burglars use a variety of other methods to attack your door besides the standard kick-in attack. You need to keep these techniques in mind when you're analyzing the security of your doors and locks. "Drilling the lock" is a technique where the burglar uses a power drill to drill out the door locks pin tumblers which then allows the door to be unlocked. Another technique used to gain forced entry is to deform or remove portions of the jamb and thereby disengage the bolt from the strike. This is known as "jamb peeling." With "jamb spreading" burglars often use a car jack or two large screwdrivers to spread the frame and force the door open, usually in less than a minute. "Jimmying" is a technique where a pry bar is used to pry the jamb away from the edge of the door a sufficient distance to disengage the bolt from the strike. A burglar using a thin, flat, flexible object such as a stiff piece of plastic which is inserted between the strike and the latch bolt to depress the latch bolt and release it from the strike is using a technique known as "loiding." "Wrenching the lock" is where either locking jaw pliers are used to grip and then twist off the cylinder guard ring exposing the locking mechanism.

Each type of residential door construction — hinged doors; sliding glass doors; garage doors — requires its own special security measures. Consult the appropriate section for detailed information on which security measures should be implemented for your type of door.

HINGED DOORS

Hinged doors are used extensively in modern residential construction and remodeling. Unfortunately these types of doors are very vulnerable to forced entry. The good news is that you can easily reinforce these doors to prevent unauthorized entry. Hinged doors should be either solid core wood or insulated metal doors that are at least 1¾ inches thick (no hollow core doors). The thickness of the sheet metal used in the construction of a metal door should be no thinner than 18 gauge. The door should fit its frame tightly, with no more than ⅛-inch clearance between the door and frame. If not, either replace the door or install an L-shaped metal strip on the outside of the door casing on inward swinging doors. This makes it tough to jimmy your lock.

The door should open inward so that the hinge pins are protected from tampering. If your door opens out either redo the door so that it opens inward or "pin the hinge." The open space between the door jamb and studding should have a solid wood filler extending not less than six inches above and below the hinge plate and solid wood filler extending not less than twelve inches above and below the strike plate. The strike plate and hinge plates, when attached to wood, should be secured with not less than No. 10 by 3-inch wood screws. Strike and hinge plates, when attached to metal, should be secured with not less than No. 10 machine screws. Door glass should be at least 40 inches away from the lock. This is to prevent someone from breaking the glass and reaching in to unlock the door. To secure a door with glass you can replace the door with a solid core one, replace the glass with unbreakable glass, install a security door, or use a double cylinder deadbolt lock (one that requires a key to open it from both sides).

If you have a double cylinder dead bolt be sure to keep the key handy in case of an emergency where you need to get out of the house quickly. If you don't have a door window install a peep hole with at least a 180° view in your front door so that you don't have to open the door to see who is there. Check the panels on your doors. Many are very thin and can be easily removed, allowing the burglar to reach inside and unlock the door. You can remedy this situation by either replacing the door or installing a steel security door. If you have a mail slot in your front door, install a hood over the slot on the inside of the door. This will prevent someone from looking or reaching through it but will not interfere with mail deposits.

The strike plate that comes with your standard deadbolt lock is very vulnerable to attack and should be replaced with either a high security strike plate or a strike box. If the strike plate is attached with small screws, the frame will break with one good kick, or lunge against the door. A high security strike plate is a larger strike plate attached with four to six heavy duty wood screws. A strike box is similar to the high security strike plate but has a metal box incorporated into the design for complete protection of the bolt. To install a strike box unscrew the old deadbolt strike plate, use a chisel to enlarge the slot in the jamb to accommodate the box of the new strike, and set the strike in the jamb to check its position; the bolt of the lock must slide into the box without binding. To set the dimensions of the new plate recess, trace around the plate, then chisel a recess within the outline so that the strike plate lies flush with the surface of the wood.

A steel door and frame, available as a unit, is probably the strongest physical barrier to forced entry you can obtain. But ordinary wooden doors can be made almost as batter- and pry-resistant as steel doors. The first step in reinforcing a solid-core wood door is to install metal reinforcement plates. Reinforcement plates are wide U-shaped pieces of hardened steel that fit over the edge of the door and around the knobs to strengthen these areas against kicks, hammer blows, prying, and attempts at sawing through the door to remove the lock. UNI-FORCE and INSTALL-A-LOCK from

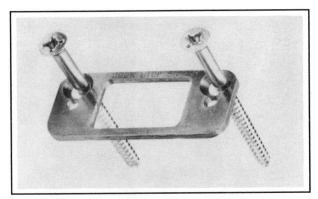

Schlage Lock Company's strike and door frame reinforcer. Photo courtesy of Schlage Lock Company.

M.A.G. Engineering are two of the most effective door reinforcers available. Door reinforcers are even more effective when used in combination with a high security strike plate/box such as the STRIKE 3 from M.A.G. Engineering.

An alternative that is more difficult to install, but will further discourage sawing through the door and at the same time increase its resistance to impact, is to embed steel rods horizontally in the sides of the door. To do this, drill long holes in the door's edges. You will need an electric drill, a ¼-inch diameter drill bit at least 10 inches long, and a drill guide to ensure that the holes are parallel to the faces of the door.

Starting at least 1 inch from any plates surrounding the locks, drill about half a dozen holes above the highest bolt and about the same number below the lowest. Space the holes approximately 2 inches apart. Between the bolts, drill as many holes as will fit, using the same spacing. Make each hole the same depth, at least 8 inches. When you are finished, clean out any sawdust, then insert lengths of ¼-inch diameter unthreaded steel rod, cut about ½ inch shorter than the length of the holes. You may want to treat the rods with silicone lubricant or powdered graphite to make them slide in more easily; you may also need to tap them into place with a hammer. Use a nailset to tap them in the final ½ inch. Finally, plug the ends of the holes with dowels. Besides installing rods along the latch edge of the door, it's also wise to install them on the opposite side, surrounding the hinges.

Despite the protection of a deadbolt lock, one well-placed kick can batter in a door, lock, and frame. M.A.G. Engineering manufactures security reinforcement hardware to guard against kick-in attacks. Bottom photo, left to right: UNI-FORCE® to reinforce a deadbolt or key-in-knob lock; INSTALL-A-LOCK® door reinforcer; and STRIKE-3®, a deadbolt and frame reinforcer. Photo courtesy of M.A.G. Engineering & Manufacturing, Inc.

If necessary, reinforce the jamb to prevent it from being pried away from the door. This is especially important on the latch side, where prying against the frame can free the bolts from the strike plates or boxes. To reinforce a jamb, remove the indoor casing (molding) from around the door frame. This exposes the sides of the frame and the studs of the rough opening. Then, where the strike plates and hinges are installed, pack the spaces between the frame and the studs with strips of plywood or other solid blocking cut to the width of the door frame and extending at least 12 inches above and below the hardware.

To make one shim assembly you need a 4″ × 6″ filler of ¼-inch plywood and two pieces of standard door shim, one of which has 3 inches trimmed from its thin end. Insert the plywood filler behind the jamb, leaving space for the thick end of the untrimmed shim. Push the shim into the gap between the filler and the stud, then tap the trimmed shim into the opening, thin end first, until the shims are snug. Install one shim assembly behind each hinge and behind the deadbolt strike. Use two fillers separated by a gap for the box of a high-security strike. To secure the fillers, replace short hinge screws with No. 10 by 3-inch strikeplate screws and drive pairs of identical screws above and below the strike plate.

Outward-swinging doors are usually more vulnerable to forced entry than inward-swinging doors because their hinge pins are exposed. However, there is a way to prevent outward-swinging doors from being opened even if the pins are withdrawn. First, remove one screw on the frame side of each hinge. Then remove the screw opposite it on the door side and replace it with the largest double-headed construction nail, screw, or threaded bolt that will fit the hole in the hinge leaf. Enlarge the hole in the leaf opposite each nail by reaming it with a drill bit slightly larger in diameter than the nail head. At the same time, deepen the holes in the frame so that the door will close. With the nails installed, the door cannot be pried away from the frame on the hinge side. The nail heads prevent the leaves of each hinge from sliding past each other. As long as the door remains locked it cannot be moved except by breaking it.

You can reinforce any hinged door by putting security surface sliding bolts at the top and bottom of the door on the inside. When both bolts are slid into position, even if the lock is completely destroyed, the door will not budge. This method can be effectively used on your front door when you can exit through an inside garage door. Even if you can't use the bolts when you're away they still provide valuable protection from intruders breaking in when you are home. A Jimmy Guard is another security product which can be used to help strengthen your doors against attack. This device consists of a pair of interlocking metal plates made of heavy duty steel which are installed on the door and jamb on in-swinging doors. The metal plates overlap to help prevent the jimmying or prying of the bolt.

To secure double doors, one of the doors must be made stationary (inactive) by concealed flush mounted header and threshold bolts. The active door should be secured to the inactive door by a deadbolt lock. Dutch doors should have a concealed slide bolt interlocking the upper and lower halves of the door, unless separate deadbolt locks are used to secure both halves of the door.

If you've discovered that your entry door is substandard you basically have two options: buy a replacement door or install a steel security door. If you opt for a replacement door some of the very best replacement doors are manufactured by Pease Industries, Inc. Their Ever-Strait entrance and patio doors are very attractive doors that have a lot of nice features including a deadbolt with an 1½ inch throw (1 inch on patio doors), heavy duty strike plate, extra long screws for the strike plate and hinges, 120° door viewer (in doors without windows). They also make a fire-rated garage-to-house door that is constructed of steel, with a wood interior. This door provides fire-safety, high-security, and increased energy efficiency. I highly recommend these doors for their built in security features and they look good as well.

SLIDING GLASS DOORS

Sliding glass doors are even more vulnerable then hinged doors because they're usually hidden from

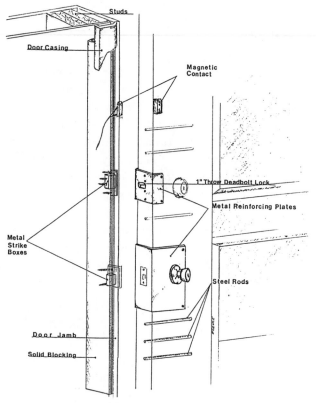

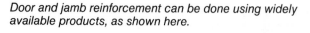

Door and jamb reinforcement can be done using widely available products, as shown here.

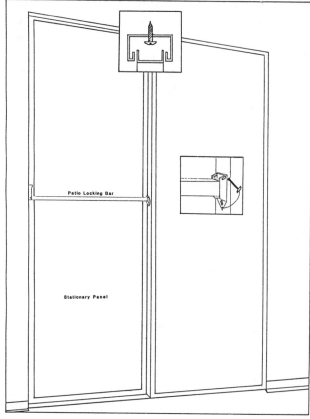

To secure your sliding glass patio doors, use a patio locking bar, also known as a charley bar. TTo prevent the door from being lifted off the track, install several screws into the upper track. Screw them in just far enough to allow the door to operate.

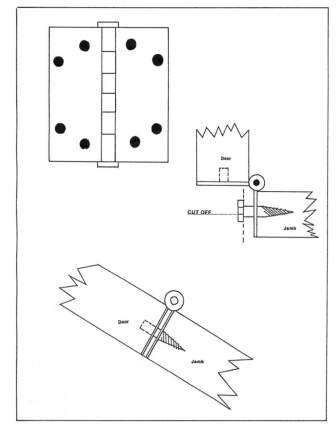

Pinning the hinge secures out-swingong doors against would-be intruders who remove the hinge pins.

view on the side or rear of your house. To make matters worse the locks on most sliding glass doors are very easy to jimmy, and the door itself can be easily lifted off its track using just a screwdriver. Burglars, who know all the tricks, like sliding doors because of their vulnerability. In spite of these inherent weaknesses sliding glass doors are fairly easy to protect.

To start, make sure that the movable door panel is located on the *inside* of the fixed panel. Secondary devices such as pin locks or charlie bars should be installed with the mounting screws inaccessible from the outside. To "pin the door" you drill a hole through the inside frame and part way through the sliding door and insert either an eyebolt or a locking pin which comes with an attached chain, so that the pin doesn't get lost. You can also install a "charlie bar" available at hardware stores and home building centers. The bar is mounted about waist level between the door frame channel and the sliding door. The bar swings down and connects with a hook that is attached to the end of the sliding door. This locks the sliding door closed and the hook keeps the bar in place.

The Burglar Bar from Churchill Mills is designed to keep the movable window or sliding door from being forced open by sliding the bar either in the track of the sliding glass door or window, or placing it over the movable window. To operate the bar, open the bar to the exact distance of the travel of movement of the door or window. Then, pull the bar out $1/16$ inch larger than this opening. Line up the holes in the bar and insert the metal pin. Then, gently force the bar into the opening. The bar is equipped with rubber tips to prevent it from scratching the surfaces where it is placed.

To prevent the door from being lifted off its track, you can adjust the rollers so the door cannot be pushed up enough to lift it off the track, insert a flexible pipe or dowel into the upper track, or install several screws in the upper track to keep the door from being lifted off. When you insert the screws leave enough room for the door to slide, but not enough space to lift the door out. You can protect the entire door by installing a security door, but this is the most expensive solution. Any

of the above inexpensive alternatives will adequately secure your sliding glass door.

GARAGE DOORS

Don't forget your garage doors — a burglar won't. Your garage is very vulnerable to forced entry because builders usually cut corners when it comes to garage door security. You're ahead of the game if your overhead garage door is already equipped with an electronic door opener. A garage door opener makes it virtually impossible to forcibly open the overhead door.

Overhead tracking garage doors can be protected by drilling a hole through the track above a roller, then inserting a pin or padlock in the hole. This prevents the door from being lifted past the padlock, which is blocking the track. Since counterbalanced garage doors have no tracks they should be secured with two case-hardened padlocks and hasps. Bolt a padlock onto each side of the garage door. With double out swing garage doors one of the doors must be made stationary with heavy duty slide bolts mounted on the inside of the door. A case-hardened hasp and padlock can then be bolted on to secure the active door to the inactive door.

Interior access doors from the garage need to be as secure as other entrance doors, and they should be kept locked when you're away. Yard access doors are also very vulnerable because they're often hollow core doors with large windows and no deadbolt. You should replace any such door with a good solid core door that conforms to the standards for entry doors as previously outlined. Don't forget garage windows. They need to be secured as well (see Chapter 3 for more).

Check the panels on your garage door. Are they loose, damaged, or inadequately secured? If a burglar can force open a panel he can climb in without having to open the door. Panels thinner than ¼ inch should be reinforced with either plywood, metal straps, or metal screen bolted across the panels. Caution: If too much weight is added to doors counterbalanced with springs, new springs might have to be added to counterbalance the new weight.

Steel security patio gates provide excellent security for sliding patio doors. Photo courtesy of Weatherguard Ornamental Iron.

Steel security storm doors provide your home with increased security as well as weather protection. Photo courtesy of Weatherguard Ornamental Iron.

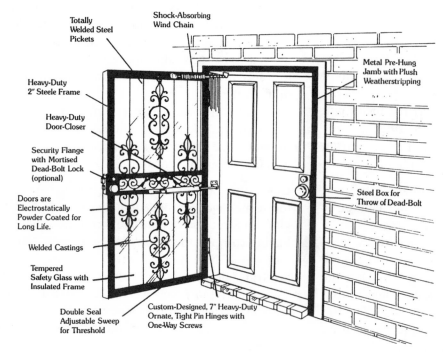

Totally Welded Steel Pickets

Shock-Absorbing Wind Chain

Metal Pre-Hung Jamb with Plush Weatherstripping

Heavy-Duty 2" Steele Frame

Heavy-Duty Door-Closer

Security Flange with Mortised Dead-Bolt Lock (optional)

Doors are Electrostatically Powder Coated for Long Life.

Welded Castings

Tempered Safety Glass with Insulated Frame

Steel Box for Throw of Dead-Bolt

Double Seal Adjustable Sweep for Threshold

Custom-Designed, 7" Heavy-Duty Ornate, Tight Pin Hinges with One-Way Screws

Courtesy of Weatherguard Ornamental Iron.

All the security in the world won't do you any good if you leave your garage door open. Even if you're home make sure that you keep your garage door closed at all times unless you're actually working in the garage or front yard. An open garage door is an irresistible invitation to a quick thief. He can be in and out again in as little as a few minutes with your tools under his arm or riding your expensive racing bicycle. At the very least you're flaunting your valuables for one and all to see.

STEEL SECURITY STORM DOORS

A good alternative for increasing the security of your exterior doors is to install a steel security/storm door. A good quality steel security/storm door will start at about $400 and go up from there, but it is worth the extra expense in the long run if it prevents only one burglary. Remember, the average loss per burglary is $1000, which would more than pay for a good security door or two. You can get security doors made to fit any door you have including double doors and patio doors. I suggest that you price several local dealers in your area using the criteria listed below to find the best product at the best price. You have to be careful when selecting the security door; many so-called security doors are nothing more than glorified screen doors that will not offer you any increase in security. Installation is also very important, as a poor job of installation will render even the best product worthless. Installation is usually built into the price of the door although you can buy the door and install it yourself to save a few dollars.

A top quality steel security/storm door should have the following features: A heavy duty 2-inch steel frame with steel pickets and castings that are fully welded for strength. Glass should be tempered safety glass mounted in an insulated weather-tight frame. A mortise-type 4-way double cylinder heavy duty deadbolt lock with at least a 1″ throw. The deadbolt should be secured in a steel lock box with a steel tamper lip to protect the deadbolt from prying. The frame should be prehung on a metal jamb that is installed into the entryway with heavy duty non-removable screws or bolts and insulated with plush weatherstripping. Hinges should have non-removable hinge pins and be secured with one-way hinge screws which make the hinge difficult to remove. For extra protection the door should also be equipped with vault-type hinge pins. The pins automatically insert into the frame upon closing, making it virtually impossible to remove the door even without the hinges.

A quality door will also have a heavy-duty pneumatic closure, shock absorber, wind safety chain, and a double-weatherstripped adjustable sweep for a better threshold air seal. As always make sure that there is a warranty on parts and installation.

I recommend that you consider using security doors on entrances that are favored targets for burglars such as front entrance doors, sliding patio doors, and doors that are concealed from view such as basement and garage doors. Weatherguard Ornamental Iron is one of the premier national manufacturers of steel security/storm doors and windows. They custom manufacture the security doors sold by national retailers such as Sears and Hugh M. Woods. There are also numerous local iron shops that custom build security doors and windows. Local manufacturers often offer several variations for the basic security door such as steel jambs, welded hinges, and automobile weatherstripping. But the basic function of the door is still the same, the variations being only selling points to differentiate them from the national manufacturers.

YOUR LOCKS ARE THE KEY

A good lock is just as important as a good door. It's the combination of a good door and a good lock that gives you adequate security. You need to check your locks to make sure that they're up to the job. Chances are your locks were installed with economy — not security — in mind. Many houses and apartments have only inexpensive key-in-knob locks or inadequate deadbolt locks. All exterior doors, including the garage access door, should be equipped with a quality deadbolt lock or alternative lock.

As many as half of all burglaries take place without forced entry. In many cases, a key was used to gain entry. Be sure your keys don't fall into the wrong hands. Never hide your keys outside; burglars know all the hiding places. If you lose a key have your locks re-keyed by a locksmith. When you move into a new home or apartment have the locks re-keyed or changed. Don't give out keys to maintenance, car lot, or delivery people. Don't carry identification tags on your key ring or holder.

Deadbolt locks are the most widely used increased security locks. Most lock sets come with templates which make installation easy. Look for the following characteristics:

- A 1-inch throw. (The bolt extends at least 1 inch beyond the edge of the door.)

- A case-hardened steel, tapered, freely rotating cylinder guard.

- The cylinder should have a minimum of five pin tumblers and should be connected to the inner portion of the lock by connecting screws at least ¼-inch in diameter.

- The cylinder is set in a tapered or loose, spinning steel sheath to prevent wrenching.

- A removeable cylinder to allow for quick re-keying.

- UL listed, to make sure that the lock meets testing standards.

Double cylinder deadbolt locks are for use on doors with windows or glass panels. These need a key to open the lock from both sides. Keep the key near the door but not reachable from the window. That way intruders can't get in, but in case of a fire or emergency you and your family can get out quickly.

For everyone who has ever lost, misplaced, or forgotten keys, one answer is the KEY 'N KEYLESS Electronic Lock by Schlage. Simply turn the doorknob left and right (much as you would a combination lock) to enter your 2-, 3-, or 4-digit access code. When the correct access code is entered, just turn the lock collar to draw back the deadbolt. Without the correct code, however, the collar spins freely, resisting attempts to wrench or pry it open. It's that easy. The KEY 'N KEYLESS Lock comes with a 1-inch throw deadbolt that is bolstered by Schlage's exclusive strike plate reinforcer, anchored to wall studs with heavy-duty 3-inch screws.

The KEY 'N KEYLESS Lock comes with two other standard features unique to Schlage — a built-in security alarm and a temporary access control. The lock has two alarm settings available to scare off intruders when they rotate the knob or try to guess the code. With the access control feature you can give maids, plumbers, baby-sitters, or visitors their own temporary access code — separate from your personal code — to get in. Simply flip a switch to activate the temporary code, and change it as often as you like. Forget about juggling schedules or keeping track of extra sets of keys: they're a thing of the past.

According to the manufacturer, the KEY 'N KEYLESS Lock is an ideal choice for new construction or renovation, because it fits conventional 2⅛ inch lock holes. Simply remove the old lock set and slide in the KEY 'N KEYLESS lockset and attach its other components as indicated by the concise instructions provided in each box. In most cases, little or no door preparation is necessary, and the unit can be installed with simple tools — no special tools or wiring required.

Life safety officials stress the use of residential locks that allow "safe egress." The interconnected lock offers a deadbolt lock combined with a knob lock to give the safety of a "panic-proof" exit. A turn of the inside knob retracts bolt and latch simultaneously. They can be ordered with a non-locking latch to hold the door closed when the bolt is not in use or with key-in-knob lock to give two lock convenience and security.

CAUTION: Check local building codes for double cylinder restrictions on new construction. The double cylinder deadbolt with a key on both sides of the door can be a treat to life safety. In a panic situation, such as a fire or earthquake when every second can be vital, the unlocking of a deadbolt with a key, or the operation of a combination of locks, might cause confusion which could be fatal.

A double cylinder deadbolt should be used ONLY when the house is to be unoccupied. When someone is in the house, the key should be left in the inside keyway for immediate exit if needed.

A deadbolt rim lock is easy to install but hard to jimmy. The lock is attached to the surface of the door with machine screws that should go completely through the door. The locking device on the door fits into the strike plate mounted on the frame. When the key is turned strong steel bolts slide into the strike. Rim locks come in single and double cylinder models, the same as deadbolt locks.

Don't rely on a chain lock — even one with a key. Almost anyone can break through a chain lock by kicking the door, ramming it with a shoulder, or cutting it with wire cutters. A Door Guard is a solid metal device similar to a chain guard but with a solid bar instead of chain. Key-locking chain guards can be locked and unlocked from outside, providing chain guard protection when away from home. Some guards add protection with a 1″ steel bolt.

The Police/Buttress Lock is a metal bar bracketed against the inside of the door at an angle with one end in a hole on the floor and the other hooked into a bracket on the back of the door. It prevents a burglar from jimmying the lock or kicking down the door. Although this type of lock will never be aesthetically pleasing it provides good security for basement, garage, and other highly vulnerable doors.

The double-bar high-security lock is designed mainly for doors that open outward. It utilizes the strength of long steel bars that run horizontally along the inside face of the door and slide into strike plates anchored to the vertical studs on each side of the door. The bolts are secured to the door with brackets and are moved by a rack-and-pinion mechanism that is operated by an exterior keylock and an inside thumb turn set in the center of the door. Another high-security lock is the multi-point locking system which uses hardened steel deadbolts on the top, bottom, and both sides of your door for maximum burglary protection. All the rods travel concealed within the door and are equipped with simultaneous locking and retraction features.

Padlocks provide dependable, portable security that won't break your budget. They are categorized by locking mechanism, shackle, and case types. A high security padlock will have a disc or pin tumbler, a hardened steel shackle, and a laminated or solid case. Look for drain holes in high security padlocks you intend to use outdoors. The holes allow dirt and sludge to be flushed out of the lock. One lock that was conceived to take on the elements is the Environmental Padlock from Sargent & Greenleaf, Nicholasville, KY. The lock resists corrosion, moisture, freezing, physical attack, and picking. Instead of springs or pins, the lock uses a disc and spacer design with a rotating action for opening. Space is allowed in between the discs so that dirt and contamination can fall away from the locking mechanism.

Padlocks are typically used for gates, sheds, and workshops. They're usually easy to cut or saw through, and some can be simply yanked open. To discourage tampering, look for a thick laminated body (identified by a layered or grooved surface) with a double locking ⅜-inch case-hardened steel shackle. A padlock is only as good as the hasp it is mounted on. The hasp should be case-hardened and weather-resistant, and it should have a loop at least as thick as the shackle on the lock. The hasp should be secured with bolts that are concealed when the padlock is locked.

Schlage deadbolt locksets with patented door frame reinforcer are another effective choice for improving door security. Photo courtesy of Schlage Lock Company.

Schlage's KEY 'N KEYLESS high security electronic lockset and deadbolt means no more lockouts. Photo courtesy of Schlage Lock Company.

Kwikset's Model 880 heavy-duty deadbolt lockset provides the average homeowner with increased security at a reasonable cost. Photo courtesy of Kwikset Corporation.

For increased fire safety, consider installing interconnecting locksets. They open with just one turn of the door knob, even when the deadbolt is locked.

3
Securing Windows

Now that you've adequately secured your doors against forced entry, don't forget your windows. After doors, windows are a burglar's next obvious target. Windows are a problem because many are never closed, at least not during warm weather, and many others are closed but not locked. Even if you close and lock your windows, many window locks are inadequate and can be easily opened. Protecting your windows can be as simple as adding a couple of well-placed screws or as complex as installing steel window guards or shatterproof glass. As with your doors, the more difficult you make it for a burglar to get in through a window, the more you increase his chances of being caught, and the less likely he is to bother you.

Many burglaries are committed by simply breaking or cutting out the window glass and reaching through to unlock the window. Still other burglaries are accomplished by inserting a thin, stiff object between the meeting rails or stiles to move the latch to the open position, or by inserting a thin stiff wire through openings between the stile or rail and the frame to manipulate the sash operator of pivoting windows. Another popular burglary method involves lifting sliding windows out of the track by using a screwdriver to lift the window up past the top of the bottom track. Each type of window has its own special security problems and solutions. The different types of windows typically found in residential construction are discussed as follows.

TYPES OF WINDOWS

Double Hung Windows

Double hung windows consist of two windows which slide up and down. Most standard double hung windows have a small thumb lock for security. Don't rely on these locks alone. A knife blade or screwdriver inserted between the two frames will quickly open the lock, or it can be easily opened by reaching through a broken pane. To increase security replace the standard thumb lock with a heavy duty keyed sash lock. If you opt for key-operated locks, have them all installed and keyed at the same time, so that you need only one key to open all of them. Make sure the window putty is in good condition. Dried-out putty can be easily and quietly removed so the glass lifts free from the frame.

An easy, inexpensive way to secure your double hung windows is the pin-in-the-sash trick. Drill two angled holes through the top frame of the lower window and partially into the frame of the upper window. As you drill, angle the holes downward. Drill the holes in the extreme corners of the window — even if a burglar breaks the glass, he may not be able to reach the pins. Insert an eyebolt or common duplex nail that is at least ¼ inch in diameter into each hole. The window can't be opened until the eye bolts are removed. The eye bolts won't bend and they provide strong resistance against jimmying. Make a second set of holes

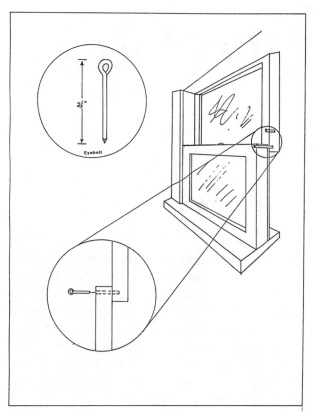

Pin-in-the-sash method of securing double-hung windows.

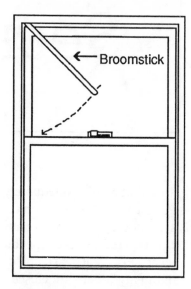

Broomstick cut to fit sash channel of double hung window.

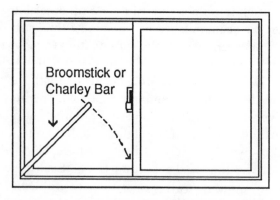

Broomstick or charley bar secures sliding window.

4 inches above the first set of holes. This will allow the window to be opened for ventilation without compromising security. An alternative is to drill the holes into the side channels instead of the sash.

Ventilating wood window locks are the manufactured version of the pin-in-the-sash. Wood window locks use a bolt to lock or unlock the window in either the closed or ventilating position. They're also available with a keyed lock for extra protection in case the window is broken or cut. Another alternative is a window sash lock, which is a tamper-proof screw-type lock for wood windows. This device secures the upper and lower sash together with a screw which can only be unlocked with a special key. A very inexpensive option is to cut two wedges out of scrap lumber and insert them in between the side channel and the lower sash. The wedges will prevent anyone from opening the window. Or, you can increase security somewhat by cutting a broomstick to fit tightly in the sash channel. These methods are effective as long as the window isn't broken out.

Sliding Glass Windows

Sliding glass windows have the same weaknesses as sliding glass doors. The same solutions that apply to sliding glass doors applies to sliding windows. To prevent the window from being lifted off the track, insert several screws along the upper track of the window. Leave enough room for the window to slide, but not enough space to lift the window out. To protect the window from being pried open use track locks, pin-in-the-track, or a charley bar or broomstick. The most economical and simplest device for sliding aluminum windows uses a thumbscrew to secure the window in closed or ventilating positions. It can be used with either horizontal or vertical tracked windows. Also comes in a keyed version for extra protection in case the window is broken or cut.

The pin-in-the-track method is similar to the pin-in-the-sash method used on double hung windows. To pin the track drill a hole through the inside frame and part way through the metal window frame and insert an eyebolt, machine screw, or double-headed nail. For ventilation drill another

hole through the frame which allows the window to be opened no more then 4 inches. At the very least cut a broomstick which fits into the bottom track — make sure it fits tightly into the track. This will help prevent the window from being forced open, but only if the window is not broken or cut out.

Louvered Windows

Louvered windows present their own special problems. The panes of a louvered window can be easily and quickly removed from the outside. To help prevent this, glue the glass panels to the brackets with silicone sealer. For better protection, you should either replace the louvered window altogether or secure it by covering the glass with a metal grate or a steel window guard, neither of which is aesthetically pleasing. If the louvered windows are in a door, I recommend replacing the door with a good solid core wood or metal door.

Casement Windows

Casement windows are those windows which are opened and closed by the use of a crank. Casement windows are safest when they must be opened and closed with a removable crank. The crank should be removed and stored an arm's length away from the window. You can remove the crank on most casement windows simply by loosening the retaining screw and pulling the handle straight off. If your windows operate by pushing and pulling rather than cranking, replace the window's handle with one that has a keyed lock. Remember, do not leave the window open more than 4 inches even with the crank removed. Burglars have been known to climb through windows with as little as 6 inches of clearance.

Basement Windows

Basement windows are another problem area. Normal basement windows have very little security value, making these windows a favorite target for burglars. If your basement windows are not used for ventilation you should replace the windows with glass blocks. Glass blocks let the light in, are aesthetically pleasing, and are almost impossible to break. If the basement is used as a living space, breakable or unbreakable plastic window well covers can be installed; these cannot be easily removed. Another alternative is to install steel window guards. Whichever option you choose, at least one window should be accessible as a fire escape route.

Another alternative is to secure all of your windows with screws. You drill a hole through the frame and into the window, then insert a screw. You then simply tighten down the screw, making it impossible for a burglar to open the window. This is a good alternative to use on windows that you do not use for ventilation. It is also a good suggestion for the times when you are away for extended periods. DO NOT, however, screw any window shut that is used as a fire escape exit. No matter which of the security measures you use it is very important to remember to leave your fire escape routes easily accessible.

Don't forget to check your window air conditioning units. If not properly secured they can be easily pulled out of the window from the outside. You can secure the air conditioning unit by attaching an iron bar to the unit and anchoring the bar to the studs on each side of the window with non-removable screws or bolts. If the unit does not take up the entire window opening, close the remaining portion off with ¾ inch plywood braced by 2 × 4 studs and anchored with good heavy gauge wood screws at least 3 inches long.

For especially vulnerable windows — those on street level or hidden from view — consider installing steel window guards, security screens, security shutters, or glass blocks. Each solution has its good and bad points, but it comes down to how much you're willing to spend or how much of the work you can do yourself. If you're handy with tools, all of the security methods and products detailed in this chapter can be a do-it-yourself project. If you're all thumbs, then you will need to have the work done by someone else, which increases the cost of the project.

SHATTERPROOF GLASS

Different types of glass break differently. How much resistance to breakage a particular type has and how it breaks should be considered when planning perimeter protection. Here are four common types: *Annealed glass* breaks relatively easily. Once broken, its typical break pattern includes long sharp splinters. Annealed glass is the type that you most likely have in your home. *Wire glass,* which usually is annealed glass with embedded wire mesh, also breaks easily but the wire holds much of the fractured glass in place. Wire glass is usually used in industrial applications. *Tempered glass* is several times stronger than annealed glass. When broken, the glass crumbles into small particles with few pieces remaining in the frame. This type of glass is most commonly found in retail store fronts. *Laminated glass* includes interlayers of various polyethylene materials for strength. Glass fragments usually adhere to the plastic instead of falling out of the frame after breakage.

Some security glass and glazing products are UL-listed. Typically, burglary-resistant polycarbonate or acrylic plastic glazing material will resist blows that would shatter and destroy most glass. This type of material also resists heat, flame, extreme cold, hammers, picks, and axes. Plastic is less expensive and lighter than laminated glass, but many types are more easily scratched and defaced. Consider using plastic glazing products on windows above ground level where they won't be subject to damage and everyday abuse. Most burglary-resistant glass, which may consist of two layers of glass held together by a layer of polyvinyl butyral, usually is indistinguishable from ordinary glass. One such product available for home use is Monsanto's Saflex home-security glass which has a plastic interlayer that does not shatter when struck by heavy objects, making it a great deterrent to home break-ins.

You don't always have to start from scratch by removing and replacing glass panes. Depending on the existing type of glass and the threat you're trying to avert, security film applied to windows may adequately harden the window against attack. Scotchshield™ from 3M is an excellent product

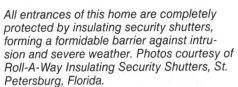

All entrances of this home are completely protected by insulating security shutters, forming a formidable barrier against intrusion and severe weather. Photos courtesy of Roll-A-Way Insulating Security Shutters, St. Petersburg, Florida.

ShutterPrime from Roll-A-Way is energy efficient, durable, and secure — an ideal aluminum window replacement system. Photo courtesy of Roll-A-Way Insulating Security Shutters, St. Petersburg, Florida.

perfectly suited for home use. Security film not only guards against break-ins but it also protects your windows from breakage caused by severe weather and accidents. Window security film has the added benefit of being invisible protection unlike security bars or screens. Different types of security glass and glazing materials serve different purposes, so be sure your application is correct. Manufacturers of security glass, glazing, and related materials are your best source of application and installation information. They can put you into contact with a local glass company that sells and installs their product. Unless you're an experienced glazier you shouldn't attempt this project yourself.

Be sure the security glass you install doesn't degrade existing electronic detection. Security glass often has different properties than the common annealed and tempered glass found in many homes. Don't assume that the on-glass glass-breakage sensors and audio discriminators you have will work effectively with security glass. Check with the sensors' manufacturers to verify that the devices will work properly on specialty glass and glazing materials.

SECURITY SHUTTERS

Coastal residents know the benefits of using security shutters. For years they've used security shutters to protect their homes from hurricanes. Security shutters have been proven to offer increased security for your home. In addition to improved security you also gain increased energy savings by installing insulating security shutters. They're especially effective in securing vacation homes, as well as your primary home. Security shutters provide total home protection by protecting not only windows but doors as well. When the shutters are in their closed and locked position they form a virtually impenetrable barrier. A burglar would have to force his way past the shutters, which is not an easy task, then he would have to contend with the door or window before gaining access. Remember, the more difficult that you make it for a burglar to get in, the more likely he will go elsewhere.

Security shutters come in several different styles — roll-away, folding, and hinged. Roll-away security shutters are similar in principal to the roll down shutters used by businesses to protect their stores, but they're much more attractive. They come in manual and remote controlled electric models. Roll-away shutters come in several different styles including models that can be hidden under the eaves then rolled down when needed to completely cover all your doors and windows. Folding shutters are mounted on tracks installed above and below your window and opened and closed manually. They're less versatile than the roll-away design but they still provide extra security. The last type of security shutter is the hinged shutter. Hinged shutters are the typical old style of shutter either hinged horizontally or vertically. They're operated manually and require a locking bar and padlock to adequately secure them. Hinged shutters are more practical for vacation homes than everyday home use because they're time consuming to operate.

STEEL WINDOW GUARDS

Steel window guards, also known as burglar bars, can be an effective deterrent to burglary, but be careful when shopping. Purchase only quality products. They may cost more up front but you will be money ahead in the long run. Fire safety is a major consideration when shopping for window guards. People have died during fires because they became trapped inside by the very security bars that were meant to protect them from burglars. All bedroom windows and at least one window on each floor should have window guard fire exits, including the basement. A good fire exit window guard will provide excellent security combined with a means of quick escape in case of fire.

Window guards should have a steel frame with steel pickets and castings that are fully welded for strength. The window should be anchored to the house with heavy duty, non-removable screws or bolts. Hinges should have non-removable hinge pins and be secured with either one-way hinge screws or by welding the hinge in place. The fire

CLOSED

Inside Release Button.

OPEN

Outside Locking Device.

Emergency quick-release for window guards. Photo courtesy of Weatherguard Ornamental Iron.

escape release should be a quick release mechanism which can be easily operated yet is strong enough to withstand a break-in attempt. Use window guards on all first floor windows, garden level windows, and on windows which are hidden from view.

Burglar Bars from Sterling Hardware offer a do-it-yourself alternative to professionally installed steel window guards. Burglar Bars have adjustable steel bars which are mounted to the inside of the window frame, and come with several different locking options — bolt and nut, padlock, fixed, and a quick release option so you can use the window as a fire exit. Burglar Bars are not as burglar resistant as steel window guards, but they're less expensive and are easy for the do-it-yourselfer to install. Burglar Bars are available at most hardware and building suply centers.

Accordion grates, also known as "scissors grates," are another practical form of protection for windows, normally found only in inner city tenement and apartment buildings along the East Coast. Accordion grates are not very attractive to look at but can be effective security for vulnerable windows. They can be opened and folded back quickly to provide an escape route in case of fire. If you have accordion grates, make sure that they're in good working order and are firmly attached to the frame by non-removable screws at least 3 inches long. The grate should be secured with a high security padlock — keep the key handy to unlock the padlock during an emergency.

A more aesthetic alternative to window security than iron bars is the security screen. Security screens are effective in stopping break-ins and vandalism because the screen protects the window from projectiles. Although they are not as ugly as bars they do somewhat restrict your view. I recommend using security screens on your more vulnerable windows, or on all of your windows if you live in a high crime area. When considering security screens look for the following features:

- Screen made from tough, stainless steel wire cloth

- Reinforced steel frame

- Concealed locking system

- Compression guards on concealed hinges

- Concealed wire support system with built-in shock absorber units

- Opens from the inside so you can get at the screen and window for cleaning and maintenance; also allows the window to be used as a fire escape

- Installed with non-removable security screws

If you have basement window wells large enough for someone to climb into you should protect them with a steel guard. Window guards made especially for window wells are available and are similar in construction to the window guards described above. Quick release fire escape devices are available as an option on quality window well guards. All basement bedrooms must have at least one fire escape in each one of the rooms. Even if you rarely use the basement you should have one of the window well guards equipped with a quick release fire escape device. When buying window well guards look for the same features as described for window guards.

4
Securing Your Valuables

To protect valuables such as jewelry, coins and stamps, and important papers I suggest a safety deposit box. The major drawback to safety deposit boxes is their limited accessibility. You have to plan ahead if you want to get something out. A good alternative is to have a home safe for your valuables and a fire-resistant container for important papers.

HOME SAFES

When considering the purchase of a safe the first question you need to ask yourself is, am I looking for fire protection or protection against theft? If the former, perhaps for documents and the like, I suggest you purchase a fire-resistant cabinet rather than a fire-resistant safe. A locked safe may attract a thief's attention even though little of value is contained inside, and important documents may be destroyed.

If theft protection is your primary concern then you need to follow a few guidelines when selecting a safe. At a minimum, the safe should have side walls made of ½-inch solid steel with a 1-inch thick door. The door should be opened with a handle that operates locking bolts. The combination lock should have a re-locking device that freezes the bolt mechanism in the locked position if someone tries to punch a hole though the lock. Another spring-loaded re-locking device should shoot a separate bolt from the safe's door into the wall if the lock is compromised.

The safe should be installed in an inconspicuous location and securely anchored to, or built into, the floor or wall. It does no good to have a good quality safe only to have a burglar wheel it out of your house to work on it at his leisure. When buying a safe, bear in mind that your current capacity needs are more likely to grow than shrink, so buy a safe that will offer you room for growth. Consider only Underwriters Laboratories (UL) labeled safes, fire-resistant safes, and storage containers. That way you are assured that the safe has been thoroughly tested and that it meets certain minimum standards for theft and fire protection. Quality safes start at about $300 and up, with the best safes in the $1000 to $3000 range. There are plenty of cheaper safes available, but the problem with those units is they can be easily pried open with a crowbar. While virtually any safe can be opened by a burglar with sufficient time and tools, in most cases these are scarce commodities during a robbery. The ideal safe will be so difficult to break into that the common burglar won't even try.

For fire protection you need to look for a fire-resistant container that has been UL tested to ensure that the interior temperature remains safely below 350° F. (450° F. is the point at which paper

One of Sentry's line of FIRE-SAFE safes — ideal for storing vital documents, jewelry, cash, and other valuables. Sentry safes are UL tested for one hour up to 1700 ° F. Fire Endurance Test, Fire Impact Test, and 2000° F. Explosion Hazard Test. Photo courtesy of Sentry Group.

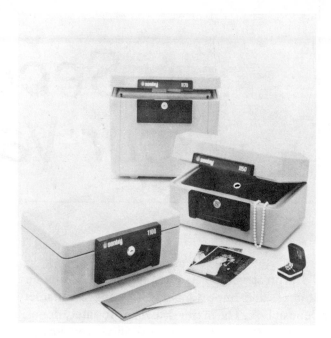

These portable security chests from the Sentry Group provide up to five times the fire resistance of ordinary insulating metal boxes for your insurance policies, personal records, and family keepsakes, and they're more convenient and less expensive than a bank safe deposit box. Photo courtesy of Sentry Group.

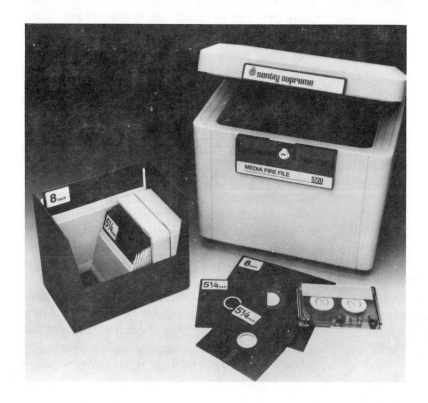

Sentry's Media Fire File provides protection for sensitive computer tapes and diskettes, against damage from fire, heat, and humidity, in a locking chest. Photo courtesy of Sentry Group.

chars) while being subjected to 1550° for one-half hour. Sensitive computer tapes and diskettes have special storage needs. They can lose data or become inoperative at temperatures as low as 125° F. at 80% humidity. The Sentry Group offers a complete line of home/office fire-safe security files, chests, office files, media storage, and safes to protect your important papers and other valuables from fire, with retail prices starting at $35 to $40 for their portable Sentry Fire-Safe Security Chest up to their Sentry Professional Quality Fire Safes floor standing models for about $300. Sentry also offers two unique items for the home office, the full-size Sentry Fire-Safe 2-drawer Office File at about $465 and the desktop Fire-Safe Media Chest for about $320 that protect sensitive computer software and disks. Sentry U.L. fire rated safes and containers are sold through the Sears catalog, K-Mart, hardware and housewares stores, locksmiths, office supply stores, mass merchants, and other retailers nationwide.

Here is a checklist of important documents or irreplaceable possessions that should be kept safe from fire. How many do you currently have stored in a fire-safe container?

- Insurance policies
- Tax returns, records, receipts
- Marriage/birth certificates
- Automobile titles
- Stock and bond certificates
- Bank records
- Passports
- Warranties
- Video storage media
- Legal contracts
- Deeds and appraisals
- Armed service records
- Credit card data
- Gold or silver
- Family heirlooms
- Photographs
- Jewelry
- Computer software/disks

If you can't afford a quality safe, you should consider a wall vault. You can buy a small, easy to install wall safe that is designed to fit between two studs in the wall. The safe is anchored to the studs, making it very difficult for a burglar to remove. You still have a problem with prying, but the safe is easier to hide than a larger stand-up model. The major drawback is that at about 420 cubic inches of capacity a wall vault doesn't have a lot of room for large items. You can find wall vaults at your local building supply store and from locksmiths. Wall vaults are fairly inexpensive starting at around $35-40 and they're fairly simple to install.

Covert safes are an even cheaper way to protect your valuables. Covert safes are disguised to look like ordinary consumer product containers or fake food items. They are weighted to feel authentic and each has a compartment for hiding your valuables. Carry the "shave cream" on your next trip. Store your "oil can" in the most conspicuous spot. Place your "bug spray" under the kitchen sink. A would-be thief will never find your valuables unless he decides to go through every can you have in your home. Another type of covert safe is the "book safe." It is similar to the consumer products described above except the safe is made out of a real book. The inside is hollowed out to provide storage space which is ideal for jewelry, keys, cash, or anything else you want safe from prying eyes.

THE SECURITY ROOM

Every home should have at least one room converted into a security room. This room acts as a second line of defense should an intruder get past your outside security, and it can protect you long enough to allow you to summon help. The master bedroom is the most logical place, since that's probably where you will be if a burglar breaks in late at night. An alternative to the master bedroom is to convert an unused closet or unfinished basement into a security room for storing your valuables. Line the interior of the closet with fire retardant/resistant material and replace the door with a good solid core fire resistant door that is equipped with a good deadbolt lock. This is a good place to install a safe or wall vault because of the extra

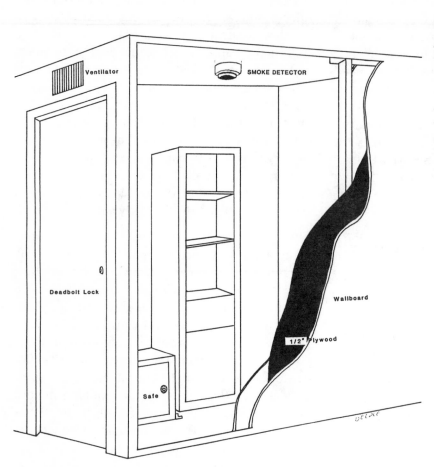

Ventilator

SMOKE DETECTOR

Deadbolt Lock

Wallboard

1/2" Plywood

Safe

A typical basement security room should have a solid core wood door with high security deadbolt lock, ½ inch plywood fire stopping in the walls, a fire-safe safe securely anchored to the floor or wall, and a smoke detector for early warning in case of fire. If you have a home security system, the door to the security room and the safe should be alarmed.

protection provided by the security room. The more barriers that a thief has to get through before getting to the safe, the more likely he will give up and leave empty-handed.

In order to convert your bedroom into a security room you should replace the door with a good quality solid core wood door equipped with a deadbolt lock. The door and locks should be the same quality as on your front door to provide the extra protection you need. For added fire protection I recommend you consider using a 20 minute fire-rated door. A fire-rated door will keep you safe during a fire longer then an ordinary door will. In case of a fire or other emergency the room should have at least one escape route other than the door.

Sleep with your bedroom door closed and locked. You won't have time to close and lock the door if something should happen during the night. To give yourself advance warning consider using a doorknob alarm. The Watchdog doorknob alarm which retails for about $10 is available from Kalglo Electronics Co. Inc., Bethlehem, PA. You simply hang this device on the inside doorknob and turn it on. The built-in alarm sounds whenever the outside knob is touched. This added warning could make the difference between life and death.

You should also have a telephone near your bed with the local emergency number easily available. A flashlight, preferably a rechargeable one, and a fire extinguisher should be also kept nearby. A fire escape ladder should also be available if your bedroom is on the second story or higher. If you keep a firearm for protection it should be loaded and accessible but kept out of reach of children. A good choice is to keep the gun in a holster which is attached to the back of the bed's headboard. If you have an alarm system a keypad with panic button should be installed in the room. This enables you to activate the system in case of an emergency.

PROTECTING BICYCLES, FIREARMS, AND JEWELRY

Bicycles are a frequent target of thieves. They're often stolen off of front lawns, porches, or out of unlocked garages. School yards and playgrounds are also popular targets for bike thieves. Don't make it easy for a thief to steal your bike. Practice the following crime prevention tips for safeguarding your bicycle. Don't leave bicycles on the lawn, the porch, or in an unlocked garage — especially at night. If you must leave your bicycle unattended anywhere, it should be secured to a solidly fixed rack, streetlight, or tree with a good quality chain and lock. The chain should be looped through the frame and both wheels. Encourage school and recreation authorities to provide secure bike racks located where they can be seen by employees of the facility. Register your bicycle with your local police agency and engrave your state's two letter abbreviation followed by your social security number on the frame and all removeable parts. This will assist in the recovery of the bike if it is ever stolen.

Firearms, especially handguns and semi-automatic assault rifles, are another favored target for burglars. All firearms (except the one that you use for personal security) should be stored unloaded and secured with a trigger lock. Your firearms should be kept locked up in a hidden storage area with the ammunition stored separately. Don't keep your firearms in a gun cabinet as this only attracts attention to them and gun cabinets are not secure. Likewise, don't keep your guns stacked in the bedroom closet. Everyone seems to do this, a fact that hasn't gone unnoticed by criminals. Closets are the first place they go when looking for

The K4 bicycle lock from the Kryptonite Corp. provides your bicycle with more protection than provided by ordinary bicycle chains. Kryptonite also has a tire-frame lock available for motorcycles. Photo courtesy of Kryptonite Corporation.

guns. Consider buying and installing a steel home security gun cabinet. These gun cabinets are securely mounted to wall studs or other solid surfaces and should be equipped with anti-drill locks. If you have a security system be sure to wire your gun storage area into your interior security zone. (See Chapter 6: Home Security Systems for more detailed information on security systems.)

As with firearms, jewelry is a frequent target, with some burglars specializing in only stealing jewelry. Jewelry is a hot item as it is easily concealed and hard to trace. Secure your expensive jewelry in a home safe, safe deposit box, or hide it in fake food containers or under furniture. It's a good idea to keep your costume jewelry in a jewelry box in your bedroom — and leave it out in plain view. This way if a burglar does get in he'll likely take the jewelry box and not bother to look any further, completely missing your good stuff. If you have a lot of expensive jewelry I also recommend a home security system in addition to any other measures you've already undertaken. Make sure that you have a rider on your homeowner's insurance to cover your jewelry. The average homeowner's policy limits coverage to a relatively small sum.

Secure your valuables, especially jewelry, before workmen or cleaning people arrive and be sure you're at home during the work. Before you admit workmen you are not familiar with, be sure to verify their authenticity with the home office. When they're working don't allow the workers to wonder around the house unattended. Being left alone gives them the opportunity to commit a crime. If they think that they're being closely watched they're not as likely to try something. After they leave check your valuables and make a report to the police and their employer immediately if you discover anything missing.

PROTECTION FOR COMPUTERS AND HOME ELECTRONICS

Computer equipment theft has grown in direct proportion to the increased popularity of the personal computer. If you own a personal computer you need to take extra security measures to safeguard your system. First, don't advertise that you have computer equipment. Don't throw the shipping boxes out with the trash when you get a new piece of equipment. Never put your home address on classified advertisements when selling equipment. Likewise if you operate a computer business out of your home don't include your home address on business cards or advertising; use a post office box instead. Your equipment will be a lot safer.

One alternative is to buy and install home computer security equipment and locks which anchor your computer hardware to fixed objects in your home such as wall studs, the floor, or large furniture. Computer anchoring equipment is available at most computer stores and from specialty mail order catalogs. If you own a lot of expensive computer or electronic equipment I recommend that you consider installing a good home security system. Again, be sure that you have a rider on your homeowner's insurance that will cover your computer in case of theft.

Televisions, microwaves, and stereo equipment have been popular items with thieves for a long time. If a burglar manages to get into your home, there is nothing to prevent him from just picking up your TV or stereo and walking out the door. But now there is a new product that provides increased security for VCRs, CD players, camcorders, or other electronic components. FlexLok from the Rokan Corp. works like this: Steel plates attached to your equipment are connected to nearby wall studs using vinyl sheathed steel cables with brass cylinder locks. With this system in place it will be much more difficult and time consuming for a burglar to remove protected items. The only other preventive measure that you can take is to make sure that your electronic equipment is completely and accurately recorded on a property inventory form.

PROTECTING YOUR CASH, CREDIT CARDS, AND CHECKS

Everyone knows that you shouldn't keep a large amount of cash in the house. Yet many people still keep cash hidden in obvious places — the cookie jar, in the pockets of clothes, under the mattress. Thieves know about all the usual hiding places and go straight to them. Either get a good home safe or keep your money safe at the bank. Protect your checks as you would your cash. Secure unused checks in a safe place with the boxes sealed. Many burglars look for checks they can steal and then forge. They will usually remove a check from the middle of an unused book so that you won't miss the check until after the forgery has been committed. If the boxes are sealed it will be easier to tell if a check has been stolen.

When you are out in public don't carry large amounts of cash or valuables with you, and carry the cash you do have in several separate places. If you are robbed, surrender your valuables but refuse to go into an alley with a robber — you may not come back out. Don't carry your house keys in the same place as your ID. That way if you lose your keys anyone who finds them will not know your address; likewise if you lose your ID your house keys will be safely with you. Don't carry your wallet in an unbuttoned hip pocket unless you have no other choice. A better location is your purse, the breast pocket of your suit jacket, or a front pants pocket.

Don't carry a long, full-sized billfold. Look for a small folding one that is easier to hide. Try not to let people know where you carry your wallet. Don't give pickpockets any clues by unnecessarily handling or displaying your wallet. Carry your cash and credit cards in separate places. A money clip is a good, safe way to carry cash. Keep it in a pocket or someplace other than in your wallet or purse. If you need to carry a large amount of cash you should use a money belt. Bring "emergency" change for cab fare, bus fare, or a telephone call. Be alert. If you are jostled or bumped in a crowded place grab your wallet and watch to make sure that they stay where they belong. Be particularly alert when leaving a bank, automatic teller machine (ATM), or other location where people frequently obtain money.

Don't carry credit cards around that you rarely use. Sign your cards. If a thief signs them for you, he can run up charges more easily. Be certain that all charge slips are completely filled out and totaled before you sign them. Keep a copy of all your charge slips (ask for the carbons if that type of slip is used) and compare them with your monthly statement. Always determine that the credit card being returned to you after a purchase is *your* card. Be sure to destroy old credit cards and your carbons. Keep a list of your card numbers and the phone numbers to call to cancel stolen cards.

When you pay with a credit card, the clerk often asks you to write your address and phone number on the credit slip. Asking for this information is more than just an invasion of privacy; it opens you to the possibility of becoming a victim of credit card fraud, which is expected to hit a record $175 million in 1990. Under rules established by Visa, MasterCard, and American Express, a merchant cannot refuse to charge a sale to your card on the sole ground that you won't reveal your address or phone number. In fact, starting January 1, 1990, New York state made it generally illegal for merchants to force customers to put that information on a credit card slip. What should you do when the cashier tells you to add your address and/or phone number to the credit card slip? Some customers dodge the issue by writing illegibly. Others enter false information when asked for this information.

If you refuse to fill in the blanks and a clerk makes a stink, take your case to the manager. Should that fail, consider filing a complaint with the creditcard issuer.

Limit, as much as possible, the number of signatures you have in your wallet: The more signatures, the better schooled a forger will be in how you sign your name. Consider carrying your checkbook and ledger in a separate wallet from your cash and credit cards. Pickpockets aren't likely to pull both from a purse or pocket — and you will minimize your loss. If someone calls to say they've found your wallet, be sure they're legitimate. Thieves may do this to stall you from reporting card losses — while they're running up charges on your account. Never keep your personal identification number (PIN) with your ATM card and don't let anyone watch you make a withdrawal from an ATM machine.

According to the U.S. Department of Justice, nationwide automatic teller bank loss from fraud during 1983 was estimated to be between $70 and $100 million, with the average loss to account holders (where claimed losses are denied in full by the bank) of $255 per incident. Where account holder liability was limited, the average loss was still $74 per incident. The vast majority of incidents in which both the account holder and the bank sustained loss involved Federal Regulation E. Federal Regulation E provides that account holder liability is limited to $50 (if the card is reported missing within two days of discovery) or $500 (if the card is reported missing more than two days after discovery). It therefore is very important to keep records of your credit card and ATM card numbers plus the phone number to call to cancel each card. This information should be kept in a fire-safe chest or safe.

The Department of Justice study indicated that 25% of stolen ATM cards were lost or stolen in the home, 20% were taken from retail establishments, 18% from cars, 12% from places of employment, 8% on the street, and 7% from schools. Where cards were stolen, approximately two-thirds were taken as the result of a theft of a purse or wallet (purse snatching). Cards were also the specific object of a theft in 26% of cases and were taken as part of a more general theft of personal belongings 8% of the time. The personal identification number was recorded and kept near the card (typically in the purse or wallet) in 72% of the incidents. PINs were actually written on the card in 6% of the incidents and were written and kept separate from the card or purse in 7%. In 15% of incidents, the account holder claimed that PINs were not written down.

Don't carry your wallet in a purse without a clasp or zipper closure, and keep your purse closed at all times. Women should not carry a purse — consider carrying valuables in a pocketbook instead. If you do carry a purse buy one with short straps and carry it close to your body with your hand over the clasp to make the purse harder to grab and therefore less inviting. Avoid wrapping a purse strap around your wrist or arm. You might be injured if a purse snatcher struggles for the purse and you can't free yourself. Wear clothes and shoes that give you freedom of movement. Don't burden yourself with too many packages.

Be conscious of the security of your purse at all times. Don't make yourself a "mark" by displaying a lot of money or leaving your purse open so that money and valuables are plainly visible. Don't put your purse down and allow your attention to be diverted from it. While shopping keep your purse on your person at all times. Do not leave it in a shopping cart unattended. Keep your purse off the floor when using public rest rooms or fitting rooms. When carrying bags, packages or other items, carry your purse between these items and your body. Do not leave packages unsupervised for even a short time.

If you're attacked, remain calm, and try not to panic or show any signs of anger or confusion. If the attacker is only after your purse or other valuables, don't resist. You don't want to escalate a property crime into a violent confrontation. Make a conscious effort to get an accurate description of your attacker: age, race, complexion, body build, height, weight, and type and color of clothing. Call the police immediately, identifying yourself and your location. If you see a crime being committed,

call the police immediately and stay with the victim until they arrive. Don't be afraid to become involved. How would you feel if you needed help and no one volunteered?

MAIL SECURITY

You have to be on guard against crime in everything you do, even when mailing packages. The Postal Service doesn't like to admit it but some of their own employees steal items from the mail. The primary targets are parcels containing jewelry, firearms, cash, and other items with a high "street value," which are easily concealed. A package's appearance may make the difference between a safe, anonymous journey and theft by a pilferer at the Post Office or private parcel delivery service. Carton size, labeling, and sealing are the three most useful "flags" to a thief. Any one of them can alert him to the possibility that the package contains desirable merchandise.

The pilferer can be denied the clue of size if the shipper over packs small packages containing valuable merchandise in larger cartons. Cartons of shoe box size or larger generally face fewer risks from theft or damage than smaller packages. This is because the larger the carton, the more difficult it is for the thief to conceal it or its wrapping. Labeling is the most obvious flag to a package thief. Shippers sometimes write the value or contents on the package itself, possibly hoping to encourage special care in the handling of their package. More likely, these markings will encourage a pilferer to break into the package. The way a carton is sealed is the third flag to the observant thief. Cartons swathed in reinforced "pilferproof" tapes are immediately conspicuous. The carton must be securely closed, but you should use common packaging tape or staples. Too many pilferages begin with a carton that has popped a flap or lost its tape, exposing the contents to temptation and opportunity.

If you receive a package that appears to have been tampered with, you should notify the carrier and the shipper of the package immediately and in that order. Too often, the carrier doesn't learn of the problem in his system until a loss claim is filed. By then it may be too late to develop information that, had the problem been brought to his attention sooner, may have resulted in the identification of a thief. To recap, when shipping valuables you should use cartons that are shoe box size or larger, labeled and marked as anonymously as possible, and sealed securely, yet conservatively.

5
Exterior Security

Exterior security involves protecting all aspects of the security of your home. Landscaping can be effectively planned both to eliminate places for intruders to hide, and to keep those potential intruders away. Lighting should be used for the same reasons: to protect the residents inside or approaching the home and to keep prowlers away.

LANDSCAPING FOR SECURITY

Residential security through landscape design is a very practical alternative to metal bars and expensive alarm systems. Unlike security bars and threatening signs, strategically deployed plants do their jobs unobtrusively. They don't advertise possessions worth defending. They don't provoke vandals. Instead, sentinel species beautify as they fortify, which means money spent on an outdoor upgrade does double duty. Thoughtful landscaping, including security-conscious plants, can enhance the perceived size of your yard as it secures the property. Anything you can do to change the appearance of your home so it doesn't look like an easy target will help keep burglars out. While landscaping can help you restrict access to your home or yard, it can also help a burglar if it is not designed properly.

To avoid getting caught, intruders look for property they can get into and out of quickly. A burglar's ideal target is a house surrounded by large hedges, shrubs, and tall fences, which obstruct visibility from the street and neighbors' houses. They look for no or few obstacles blocking quick exits, and public access on at least one side of a property fence. If the only way into your property is also the only way out, a potential burglar may choose to move on. Corner lots and homes next to schools, drainage ditches, along green belts, and next to parks are among the most vulnerable. They're also among those that can best use security landscaping.

Overgrown plants are the worst landscaping offenders. If a bush obscures your view of key areas or could offer cover to a lurking assailant, plan to cut it back as soon as its proper pruning season comes around. Prune tree branches that could help a burglar climb in a second story window. Prune or remove tall shrubs near doors and walkways. Thin out overgrown foliage on large shrubs to expose branch structure. If you can see through your shrubs no one can hide behind them. Trim back trees or shrubs if they're blocking your street address. Prune shrubs so that you have an unobstructed view from your windows. Planting open and low-growing shrubs will allow for better visibility without the need for constant pruning.

Say you want to discourage anyone from sneaking around your house on that windowless side. A thick carpet of ivy or lush stands of ornamental grasses create an ankle-engulfing barrier of foliage. Or use gravel paths next to bedroom windows. This will alert you to the presence of prowlers. Protect vulnerable windows by planting

Can you spot what's wrong in this picture? The tree in front of this house is completely blocking the window and half of the front door, providing a perfect hiding place for a would-be burglar while he breaks in.

climbing roses in front of the window. Train the roses up a trellis installed in front of the window to form an impenetrable barrier. Of course, you shouldn't place trellises where they can be used as ladders to second floor windows. While you want to restrict access from the outside, you don't want to restrict egress — your ability to get out of a home through a door or window — in case of fire. Thorny bushes planted below windows will also discourage the most determined intruder.

Shrub Rustlers

Protecting your trees and shrubs against theft is another important consideration when planning your landscaping. Nocturnal shrub rustlers in New York are forcing homeowners to chain bushes together, to anchor trees to buried cinderblocks, and to plant flowers so uninteresting nobody wants to steal them. Some of the thieves are crack addicts or other desperate people who steal flowers and sell them on the street. Most appear to be landscapers who use the plants themselves or thieves who know exactly what to steal, how to steal it, and where to fence it. You can protect your landscaping by planting valuable trees and shrubs in your backyard and by illuminating the area with outdoor lighting.

Evergreen trees are frequently cut down or topped off by a Scrooge searching for a cheap Christmas tree. Spraying your evergreens with an obnoxious mixture of skunk odor and fox urine is a good

alternative to protect trees located in remote areas. This mixture has been used for several years by some Colorado cities to protect their public parks' evergreens, which were being stolen regularly every Christmas. The mixture's stench is so strong that no one would possibly use the tree. The smell wears off naturally after several weeks and does not harm the tree. The mixture is being produced commercially but on a small scale and may be difficult to obtain.

Fences

Fences are a very important part of your home's overall security. Fences define property boundaries and help keep intruders out. But you must be careful. A 6-foot privacy fence not only provides you with privacy but also provides privacy for an intruder. Fencing such as chain link, split rail, and picket provide very little security. A good alternative to the typical privacy fence is a steel barrier fence. These fences keep people out, children and pets in, and they don't obstruct the view of your house from the street or your neighbors. Steel fences offer other advantages as well: they come in a wide variety of styles and color; no maintenance painting is required; they won't burn, rot, or blow down like wood fences. They are also more difficult for intruders to climb than other types of fences.

The typical teenage burglar can vault the average fence in a matter of seconds with very little effort.

To help discourage intruders from climbing your fence, plant thorny shrubs or ground cover on the outside of the fence along the public accesses. Another alternative is to train spiny vines up and over privacy fences. The thorns will keep intruders out and the vines are more appealing than barbed wire, but are just as effective. Keep fences and shrubbery low along the property front to provide clear views from both the street and the house. No matter what type of fence you have, be sure to keep side and back gates locked by using high security, weather-resistant padlocks and hasps.

Do you have a neighbor who keeps an eye on your home when you're away? If so, walk over and take a look at your house from his vantage point to make sure he has a clear view. Secure ladders in the garage or a shed. Secure your trash cans inside the garage or secure them outside by using a good chain and padlock. This is to prevent a burglar from using the cans as a ladder to climb in a second story window. Don't store firewood or scrap lumber next to the house. Not only is it a fire hazard but it could be used as a hiding place or as a ladder to climb onto the roof or in a second story window.

Security-Conscience Plants

Any plant with thorns or spines large enough to inflict pain when touched qualifies as prowler proof. Make sure the plant you choose will eventually cover the entire area you want to protect or plant more than one. Start them close enough to the house or fence so that no one can hide behind them once they've matured. Listed below are some of the best plants to use when planting for security. Which specific plants you choose depends on your climate. Ask your local nursery for suggestions.

BARBERRY — Woody, thorny shrubs that vary widely in size, color, habit, etc. Both deciduous and evergreen forms offer pretty flowers and berries birds love.

HOLLY — Stiff-branched evergreen trees and shrubs of varying habit. Many have multi-taloned leaves. All attract wildlife.

ROSES — Sharp-thorned deciduous shrubs cultivated into a broad, beautiful spectrum of hues, forms, and fragrances. Hardy, old-fashioned, long-blooming types like *Rosa rugosa* make the best sentries.

HAWTHORN — Long-spined deciduous shrubs and trees found in several distinctive forms. All offer spring bloom, autumn color and winter fruit.

FIRETHORN — Wood-thorned, waxy-leafed, most evergreen shrubs. Some varieties can be trained up walls. All produce spring flowers and colorful wildlife-luring berries.

BRAMBLE — Includes raspberry, blackberry, and loganberry. Low growing deciduous shrubs with long, loppy, prickly canes. All produce delicate flowers and delicious fruit.

CURRANT — Including black and red currant and gooseberry. Especially winter-hardy and prickly deciduous shrubs that follow delicate flowers with tasty fruit.

FLOWERING QUINCE — Highly ornamental deciduous shrubs with wine-red thorns and leaf tips.

LOCUST — Deciduous trees wickedly thorny even as sprouts and prunable into a staunch natural fence.

DEVIL'S WALKING STICK, DEVIL'S CLUB, HERCULES CLUB — Small, summer-flowering trees with large leaves, exotic fruits (not for humans), and nasty thorns.

OTHER PLANTS TO CONSIDER — Oregon grape, bougainvillea, citrus, Natal plum, pyracantha, cactus, spine-tipped yuccas.

SWIMMING POOL SECURITY AND SAFETY

Homeowners with swimming pools and hot tubs should take extra precautions to protect themselves and their property. Trespassers, often juveniles, frequently sneak into your back yard for a midnight swim. In a new fad popularized in California, trespassers use the drained swimming pool of a vacant home or one where the owners are on vacation as a skateboarding arena. In either case theft or vandalism of your property is likely. You also have a substantial liability if one of these trespassers should be injured while on your property. Swimming pools are also a safety hazard, especially for young children. Too many young children drown in backyard swimming pools each year.

The good news is that the recommended security measures described below are also good safety measures which should be implemented even if security isn't your first concern. First and foremost, all pools and hot tubs should have covers which can and should be kept secured in place when the pool is not in use. Pool covers should be made from a sturdy material that can support the weight of an adult without collapsing. The cover should form a tight fit and be securely anchored when in place. I recommend a motorized pool cover because you're more likely to use it than one that you have to operate manually. I also recommend that you use several good outdoor padlocks to secure the cover in place, especially if you're going to be away for extended periods.

The pool area should be completely surrounded by a fence that is at least 3 feet high, I recommend a 6-foot fence for added protection. All gates should be kept closed and secured with a high security weather-resistant padlock. This is a very important safety feature that is a must for families with small children. Even if you don't have small children you should have a fence if there are children in the neighborhood. Many localities require that pools be fenced by law. Leslie-Locke, Inc. manufactures decorative metal pool fencing which comes in 4-, 6-, and 8-foot lengths that are 3 to 6 feet high. To discourage intruders from climbing the fence you can plant thorny bushes along the outside perimeter of the fence.

I also recommend installing motion detector floodlights arranged to cover the entire pool area. This way you will be alerted to the presence of trespassers in the pool area after dark. Solar-powered lighting is the easiest type of outdoor lighting to install. With solar-powered lights you don't have to worry about laying wire or increased electric bills. There are also models available that come with a plug-in chime alarm that sounds whenever the motion detector is activated.

For additional safety and security you should purchase a pool alarm. Waterproof self-contained pool alarms float in the pool and a loud built-in siren is activated if anyone causes waves in the pool. This is a good backup safety device for alerting you in case your child accidentally falls into the pool. The alarm would also help to scare off trespassers who may have penetrated your other security measures. Pool alarms are available from the following manufacturers: Electronic Control Corp., Optex (USA) Inc., and Remington Products, Inc. A complete listing is available in the Appendix.

If you have small children you should use some common sense safety precautions in addition to the ones already discussed. First, never leave small children unattended near a pool — even an empty one. Get a cordless telephone or an answering machine so that you don't have to leave to answer the phone. Don't leave toys in or around the pool as small children may accidentally fall in while trying to get the toys. Teach your children to swim at an early age and to respect the danger potential of water. You and your spouse should take a class on CPR and water rescue. Set rules covering the use of the pool and be sure that your child knows and follows these rules. You should include things such as no swimming without a parent present, no visitors without letting a parent know first — even if you're not going swimming, and no playing near the pool without supervision.

SECURITY LIGHTING

Outdoor lighting provides security at night by denying burglars, vandals, and other "perpetrators" the shroud of darkness they need to pursue their goals. If an intruder can be easily seen he is likely to pass you by. In addition to increasing security, lighting also enhances your home's livability and value. In most cases you don't need flood lights to illuminate your property adequately. Low-wattage lights strategically placed around your home can be just as effective. In most cases a 60-watt bulb should be sufficient. All entrances to your

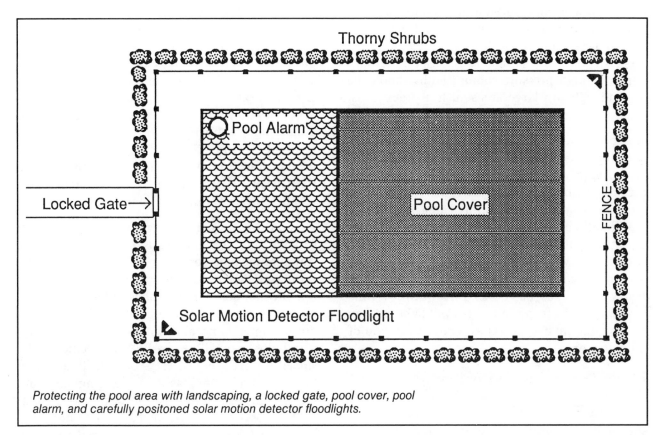

Protecting the pool area with landscaping, a locked gate, pool cover, pool alarm, and carefully positoned solar motion detector floodlights.

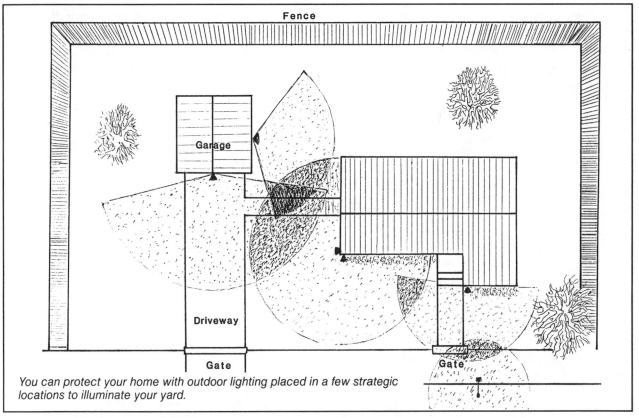

You can protect your home with outdoor lighting placed in a few strategic locations to illuminate your yard.

home, garage, and outbuildings should be well lighted. In addition to lighting all entrances you should install lights on all four sides of your home, especially dark corners and large bushes. Mercury vapor or high pressure sodium bulbs should be used to light up large areas such as backyards, remote parking areas, and alleys.

A good multi-purpose outdoor light is the motion detector floodlight. Motion detector floodlights use infrared motion detectors to monitor a specific area. The floodlights are activated when movement is detected in the monitored area. Unlike regular floodlights, which remain on all night, motion detector lights come on only when necessary — saving money on your energy bill. Motion detectors are ideal for lighting driveways, walkways, backyards, patios, and decks. Put one to cover the walkway to the front door. This will light the way for you and invited quests as well as warn you of uninvited ones.

Motion detectors are also available with an interior plug-in alarm feature which sounds an alarm if the motion detector is activated. I recommend solar-powered motion detectors such as the Solar Sentinel from Sunergy, Inc. because they're easy to install and inexpensive to operate. In addition to lights activated by infrared motion detectors, there are sound activated systems. Sound activated lights come on if any noise above the prescreened background levels is detected in the monitored area. If you use floodlights, don't point them away from the house, the glare can actually provide cover for an intruder. Instead, direct them downward from the eaves or upward from the ground toward the house.

Solar powered lights are an excellent choice when considering outdoor lighting. They're easy to install, inexpensive to operate, and provide lighting in hard-to-reach locations. The WalkLite from Sunergy has a built-in rechargeable battery that charges by day and lights up to seven hours per night on a single charge. You should make sure to light up your house numbers so that emergency personnel can find address more quickly. Digilite, a solar-powered house number light from Sunergy, is ideal for identifying your house to emergency response units as well as visitors. Digilite has 4-inch high numbers which are visible from 500 feet and can run all night on a solar charge of as little as ninety minutes. Sunergy, a subsidiary of the Chronar Corporation, is one of the leading manufacturers of outdoor solar lighting products.

A good way to increase the effectiveness of your existing outdoor lighting is to switch from the standard incandescent light bulbs to high pressure sodium (HPS) bulbs. HPS bulbs cost much less to operate than standard incandescent light bulbs, although the initial cost is higher. Since HPS bulbs are not interchangeable with standard incandescent bulbs you will need a fixture specifically designed for HPS bulbs. HPS bulbs will last years longer, reducing the hassle of changing burnt-out bulbs. For residential use 35-watt and 50-watt HPS bulbs are recommended. The light output of a 35-watt HPS lamp is slightly more than a 100-watt standard incandescent light bulb. The light output of a 50-watt HPS lamp is comparable to two 150-watt floodlights. High pressure sodium (HPS) bulbs are identical in color to street light.

For more information contact the National Lighting Bureau. The National Lighting Bureau offers a free pamphlet titled "Lighting and Security," which describes how proper outdoor lighting can deter burglars, improve safety, and provide other benefits. They also have a booklet "Lighting for Safety and Security" available for $5 per copy. Although this latter publication is aimed at businesses, it contains valuable information for the homeowner. The above titles can be ordered from the National Lighting Bureau, 2101 L Street N.W., Suite 300, Washington, DC 20037 (202) 457-8437.

To provide dusk to dawn outdoor lighting, simply install First Alert®'s Automatic Light Control in a standard light socket. The unit's photocell automatically turns the light on at dusk and off at dawn. Photo courtesy of BRK Electronics, Div. of the Pittway Corporation.

The Solar Sentinel is designed for security lighting or convenience lighting in your yard, at your garage, around your carport, or wherever security lighting is required at night. The unit is controlled by a patented passive infrared motion detector that detects activity up to 75 feet away. When activated, the Solar Sentinel throws a flood of light into the target area for up to three minutes or as long as there is movement in the area. Photo courtesy of Sunergy, Inc.

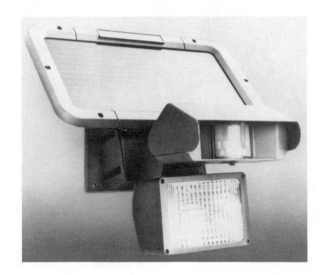

Walklite from Sunergy gives you all the benefits of outside lighting for patios and decks, gardens, yards, walkways, and driveways without the expense of installation, wiring, and utility costs. Photo courtesy of Sunergy, Inc.

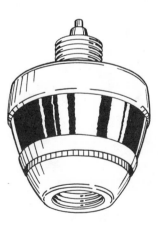

First Alert®'s Sensor Switch is an infrared motion detector light socket for inside your home. Sensor Switch automatically turns the light on as you approach and turns it off after you leave. Sensor Switch is great for garages, basements, attics, walk-in closets, and fire escape routes. Photo courtesy of BRK Electronics, Div. of the Pittway Corporation.

6
Home
Security Systems

Your best defense against burglary is a professionally installed alarm system. An alarm system lets you rest easy when you're home and eliminates worry when you aren't. When you buy an alarm system, you're purchasing a lot more than electronic components; you're buying the services an alarm company provides. More important, you're gaining peace of mind. Generally, a professionally installed system is more reliable then a homeowner-installed system. The reason is a professional system is sold by a trained salesman and installed by a trained technician. The professional knows the type of break-ins occurring in a community and will customize the choice of components and the placement of equipment to maximize protection.

ALARM SYSTEMS

Alarm systems have come a long way in the past decade. Where once they were only used by the affluent who could afford the hefty price tag, affordable systems are now available designed and priced for the average homeowner. The best systems include fire and medical emergency features integrated into one system along with the tradition burglar alarm. Roughly 7% of U.S. households have a security system. Yet more people might consider such an investment if they knew that convicted criminals say alarms are the most effective deterrent to theft.

- 85% of police officials believe that security systems decrease chances of homes being burglarized

- 99% of all alarm owners say their home alarms are effective

- 98% of alarm owners would recommend a home security system

- 96% of potential alarm owners think a home alarm is effective

- The average loss from a residential burglary in 1987 was $1,004; from a non-residential burglary it was $914

In a study called "The Business of Crime: The Criminal Perspective" (Table 6), 589 imprisoned property offenders were asked what prevention measures were most effective in preventing burglary, breaking and entering, and grand theft. Monitored burglar alarm systems topped the list of fifteen items the inmates rated from not effective to very effective security measures. Offenders who plan crimes in advance say monitored systems are 95% effective in protecting a residence. Other top methods the felons consider effective are electronic sensors visible in windows, closed circuit television cameras in stores, and private security patrols. Local burglar alarms scored lower with a rating of 0.83 on a scale of zero (not effective) to two (very effective).

TABLE 6: FELONS RATE ALARM EFFECTIVENESS

The following question was asked of 589 convicted property offenders: "How effective is each of the following likely to be in preventing burglary, breaking and entering, and grand theft?"

Monitored burglar alarms	1.51
Electronic sensors in windows	1.35
Closed circuit TV cameras in stores	1.31
Private security patrols	1.14
Dog in house	1.11
Weapons in home	1.10
Guardhouses protecting homes	1.07
Random police foot patrols	1.05
Better exterior lighting	1.02
"Neighborhood Watch" programs	0.98
Safes/strong boxes	0.83
Local burglar alarms	0.83
Deadbolt locks	0.79
Timed interior lights	0.78

0	1	2
Not Effective	Somewhat Effective	Very Effective

Source: "The Figgie Report Part VI — The Business of Crime: The Criminal Perspective." Figgie International, Inc., 1988.

Above: alarm system keypad. At right: the Z100E Residential Security System from Aritech-Moose is typical of professionally installed hard-wired home security systems. Photos courtesy of Aritech-Moose Security Products.

Alarm systems do more than detect intrusions. They also deter burglars. Put yourself in the burglar's shoe for a minute. Pretend you're casing your neighborhood, looking for a house to burglarize. As you walk up the sidewalk, you see a yard sign that says: "Protected by . . ." When you reach the porch, you see a window decal. It says: "Professional Protection Installed By . . ." Think about it, would you break into a house with a professionally installed alarm system? Probably not. You'd move on to an easier target.

There are many good reasons to have an alarm system but the most important reason is your own peace of mind. If you will sleep better by having an alarm system protecting you and your home, then you should have one. You should also consider a security system if you live in an isolated area or if you keep valuable property in your home. By using the information contained in this chapter, and by shopping around, you will be able to select a cost effective security system that meets your needs.

According to *Security Distributing & Marketing*, an alarm industry trade journal, the average price for an installed home alarm system was $1672 and the average monthly monitoring fee was $18.76. The average system cost ranged from a high of $1957 in the northeast to a low of $1567 in the west. The west had the highest monthly monitoring fee, a steep $20.82 to the north central's low of $16.77.

In Denver monthly monitoring fees vary between $11 a month to over $25, so it pays to shop around before buying.

While the industry's average home security system price is $1672 you can buy basic installed hard-wired systems for as little as $200. Companies selling these systems are actually losing money on the equipment and installation, but they make it up by locking you into a multi-year monitoring contract for $20-$25 a month. These systems are also very basic, with the average system consisting of three perimeter sensors, one interior sensor, and the control unit. Additional equipment is available but your total cost goes up quickly once you start adding on. In addition to owning your security system outright, there are companies which offer leased systems and others that offer leases with an option to buy. You should consider one of these options if you are unsure whether an alarm system is for you. By renting a system before you buy, you can try out the system without becoming locked into a long term commitment.

THE TYPICAL SECURITY SYSTEM

All alarm systems consist of three essential components: the control unit, sensors, and siren. The control unit is the "brain" of the alarm system. With it, you arm and disarm the system. The control unit monitors the sensors, and when it receives signals that indicate an alarm condition it sounds the siren and relays the alarm to the central monitoring station.

Alarm systems can be set up to provide three levels of defense: perimeter protection, space protection, and point protection. Perimeter protection means equipping exterior doors and windows with sensors to detect unauthorized entry. For space protection, motion detectors or other types of sensors are installed inside the home as a second line of defense to guard specific hallways or rooms. Point protection is used for guarding specific objects or storage areas. The most effective alarm systems usually combine comprehensive perimeter protection with some space protection in areas an intruder is most likely to pass through. Point protection is normally used only in homes that have especially valuable objects, such as expensive artwork or other collections, or potentially dangerous items like guns.

The primary device used in perimeter protection is the magnetic contact switch. Each switch has two parts: One is mounted on the inside of the door or window jamb and the other on the door or window sash. When the system is armed, the alarm will sound if contact between the two parts of the switch is broken. For ventilation you can mount an additional half of a magnetic contact elsewhere on the jamb so that the contact on the sash will align with it in the open position.

Recessed magnetic switches are useful when protecting doors, windows, sliding doors, hinged skylights, gun and china cabinets, file cabinets, and drawers containing valuables such as silverware and jewelry. Plunger-type contact switches are used for tamper-control, to protect against unauthorized access to a control panel enclosure. Roller-plunger switches can be used under vases, sculptures, and movable safes to detect the movement of the protected object. Cable switches are used to protect non-stationary items like motorcycles, bikes, RVs, and trailers that are stored outside near the home.

Wired screens, which activate the alarm when they're tampered with, are another option for homeowners who like to keep their windows open. Alarm screens look like any high-quality, fiber-glass type screen, but offer a detective ability. Once the system is plugged in, an alarm will be activated if the screens are tampered with from the outside. Small wires are woven vertically through the screens at 4-inch intervals. Once connected, these wires form a protective barrier. They fit any window, even louvers.

Inertia shock sensors are designed to detect a forced entry before the intruder has gained entry to the protected area or building, not after the penetration has been accomplished. All inertia shock sensors detect the impulse generated by an attempted forced entry. Some of the different materials that shock sensors can be mounted on are: glass, brick, wood, drywall, and sheet metal. The most popular application is for glass. One benefit in using a shock sensor is that it can be mounted on the frame — not necessarily on the glass itself. By frame mounting, the sensor will protect windows that open, without the use of unsightly take-offs or door cords. One sensor can protect multiple panes of glass, which makes it cost effective as well. Some of the very best shock sensors on the market are manufactured by Ultrak, Inc.

The Ultrak design incorporates a lighter mass and higher contact pressure, which gives greater stability because the lighter mass does not react as easily to low-end irritations such as trucks, trains, wind, etc. However, the ability of the Ultrak design to detect the breaking of material as a result of a forced entry is equal to or better than any detector in the world. The end result is higher reliability and superior overall performance on the job.

False alarms have become a very serious problem for the security industry, the police, and the end user — you, the homeowner. As more homes and businesses install alarm systems, the number of emergency dispatches increases. Nearly 99% of all alarms turn out to be false, according to police agencies. Cities all over the United States have turned to false alarm legislation and fees in their frustration over this continuing problem. To help solve the problem of false alarms you should consider two-way audio-verification systems. Listen-in systems come in two detection formats: sound-activated and motion-activated.

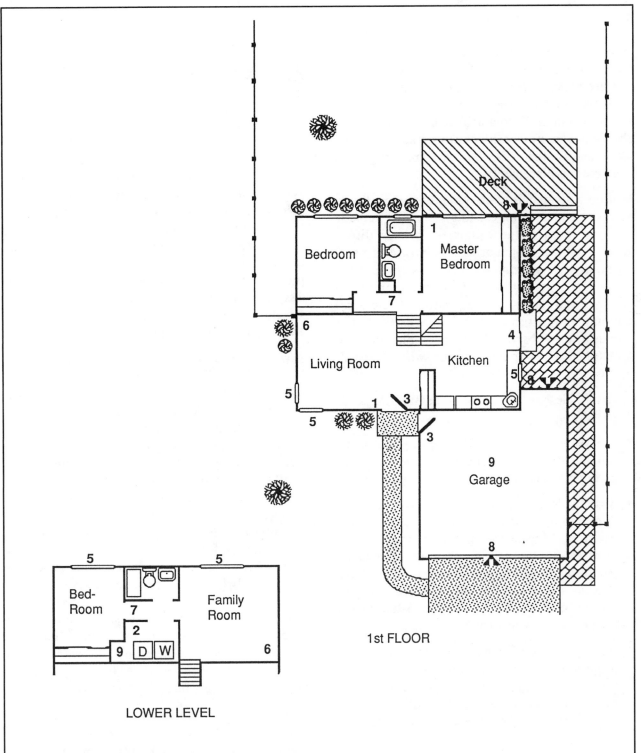

Deck

1

Bedroom

Master
Bedroom

7

6

4

Living Room

Kitchen

5

5

3

1

5

3

9

Garage

8

1st FLOOR

5   5

Bed-
Room   Family
                    Room
7

2

9   D W   6

LOWER LEVEL

*Components of the typical security system: 1: Keypad. 2. Control panel (installed in the basement).
3. Magnetic door contact. 4. Sliding glass door sensor with glass-break detector. 5. Magnetic window
sensor or shock sensor. 6. Passive infrared motion detector. 7. Smoke detector. 8. Passive infrared
motion controlled floodlights. 9. Rate-of-rise heat sensor.*

A sound-activated installation relies on special microphones used as sound sensors. Their sensitivity is set to let the monitoring center hear into the premises if a noise rises above a certain ambient level or if selected sound discrimination frequencies are present. However, noise from airplanes, some trucks, motorcycles, and thunder will activate the system. Sound-activated systems generally do not interface with existing traditional systems unless there is extensive rewiring and equipment replacement.

Motion-activated listen-in system components can be easily added to an existing system to make it two-way, even if the equipment brands differ. When a contact switch or passive infrared sensor, for example, triggers an alarm, the system operates like a hands-free intercom between the protected premises and the monitoring station. The central station operator receiving the signal listens to the sounds at the subscriber's premises. Based on the sounds heard, the operator decides whether to call the police.

For a reliable, easy-to-use security system, look for these features:

- Entry and exit delays. These give you time to arm and disarm the alarm system, without triggering it, when you leave and enter your home.

- Switchable instant and delay circuits. Most door and window sensors should be on the circuit that triggers the alarm instantly. You'll want to set the main entry doors on a delay circuit when you're not at home so you have time to get in and out of the house, but you should be able to switch them to instant alarm for protection when you're at home.

- Automatic cutoff and reset features. Your neighbors will appreciate an alarm system that turns off the siren after sounding it for a preset period. But after turning itself off automatically, the system should rearm itself to maintain security.

- Battery backup. Systems connected directly to house wiring should have the capability of switching to battery operation if the AC power fails. When the AC power is restored, it should

switch back. In addition, the batteries should be rechargeable to ensure that power is available when needed.

CHOOSING THE RIGHT TYPE OF SYSTEM

Once you've decided on a security system you need to choose the type of system that is best for you. There are two main types of security systems, hard-wired and wireless. If you choose a wireless system you must then decide on either a supervised system or an unsupervised system. A hard-wired system is one where the systems components, i.e., sensors, control box, siren, etc., are all connected together by electrical wiring. There are far fewer problems with hard-wired systems than with wireless ones. A hard-wired system is the best type of system that you can buy. It is also the most expensive, but its benefits outweigh the higher price.

A wireless system is where all the components are battery powered, and the alarm signal is transmitted to the control unit via radio waves. Wireless systems are fairly cheap and easy to install, which accounts for their popularity. There are, however, several problems with wireless systems. The radio signal from the sensors to the control unit is difficult to align properly, and if not aligned, the signal may not reach the control unit. Environments change, which can affect a system's operation. For example, the addition or removal of metal cabinets or appliances, foil wallpaper or mirrors can block or reduce radio frequency transmission range. Another disadvantage of the wireless system is that the sensors that transmit signals to the control panel are powered by batteries. If a homeowner forgets to change them, his protection is compromised. Some of the newer units, however, signal when the battery starts to get low. If you buy a wireless system get one that is supervised.

A supervised system is electromechanical insurance in any protective system that the system is in a state of good operational readiness. A warning is given if the system is not ready. A transmitter which is fully supervised checks in with its receiver every one hour and twelve minutes (the most frequent interval allowed by the Federal Communi-

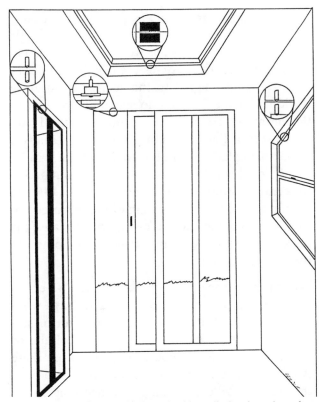

Some of the typical installation locations for magnetic contact switches — recessed switches for doors, windows, and gun cabinets; rolling-plunger switches for sliding glass doors; surface mount switches for protecting skylights.

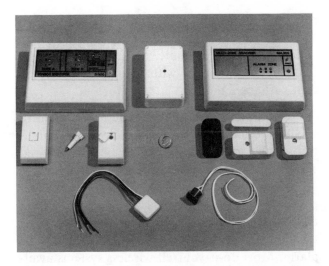

Inertia shock sensors are designed to detect a forced entry before the intruder has gained entry, not after the entry has been accomplished. Shock sensors work by detecting the impulse generated by an attempted forced entry. Photo courtesy of The Ultrak Group.

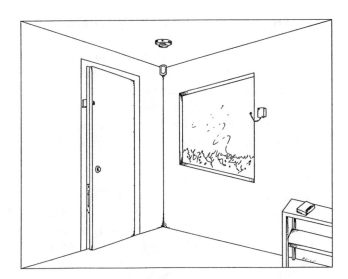

Some of the most basic wireless security devices — smoke detectors, contact switches, glass break detectors, and passive infrared motion detectors — come with battery-powered built-in short-range radio frequency transmitters for fast and easy installation.

cation Commission). It reports opened and closed status of the sensor, tamper condition, and battery status. Without this hourly report, a wireless system can fail unnoticed with no one the wiser, except perhaps a burglar.

An alarm system without any built-in system to check automatically the status and working condition of the sensors is known as an unsupervised system. With this type of system a manual battery check must be done monthly and the batteries replaced at least once a year. If you forget to check the batteries and one goes dead any break-in at the location of the dead sensor will not activate the alarm. Most do-it-yourself wireless systems available at your local hardware store are unsupervised systems.

A system in which the alarm signal is heard and/or seen only in the immediate vicinity of the protected area is known as a local alarm system. You simply cannot rely on a neighbor to make a timely call to the police should he hear your alarm going off. Monitored alarm systems are the preferred type of system. The alarm signal is transmitted to a 24 hour monitoring station which in turn calls the appropriate agency to dispatch emergency units (e.g.,police, fire department, ambulance). Monitoring is an ongoing expense, but one that is well worth it.

An alarm system that has a telephone link to a central station provides the most reliable protection. For a monthly fee, the central station monitors your alarm system — 24 hours a day, seven days a week. Whenever the alarm is activated, the system's control unit automatically places a call to the monitoring station, alerting it to a possible problem. Typically, if the homeowner sets the alarm off by accident, the central station will telephone the home and ask if everything is all right. If you say yes and then give them your secret password, this assures them that it is not a burglar answering your phone, and it doesn't go any further. Systems employing automatic telephone dialers should have a dedicated phone line or cellular backup so that the central station will be notified even if the household phone lines are tampered with.

Your alarm system is only as good as its weakest link. The telephone connection box on the outside of your house is one such weak link. This is because most security systems use telephone lines to send the alarm signal to the central monitoring station. Cut the line and no signal can be sent to the monitoring station. To protect yourself you can install a line interrupt alarm which sends a signal through the phone line to the central station. If the signal is interrupted an alarm is sounded at the central station. The drawback to this is that the station has no way of knowing where the interruption is. This could lead to false alarms because the lines are down somewhere between your home and the central station.

You can also back up your phone line with either a cellular phone connection or a mid-range wireless radio transmitter. The central monitoring station will have to be equipped to receive cellular or the wireless radio for you to be able to use these two alternatives. A cheaper alternative is to have the alarm installers relocate your incoming phone line so that it isn't accessible to tampering. You should leave a dummy line where the old one was so that a burglar will be fooled into thinking that he has disabled the alarm when in fact it is still in operation.

PICKING AN ALARM COMPANY

Finding a professional alarm company isn't difficult. Check the Yellow Pages under "Burglar Alarms" for an idea of how many firms serve your area. Also ask friends and business associates who have alarm systems for their recommendations. Then check the alarm company's credentials by asking for references. Employee training is an important criterion for judging an alarm company. Ask how employees are trained. The more employees who have successfully completed training courses — such as the National Burglar and Fire Alarm Association's National Training School — the better.

The membership roster of your state alarm association is a good place to start looking for a reputable alarm company. Although not all alarm companies are association members, membership indicates a commitment to industry standards and professionalism. To obtain a free list of state and regional associations, send a self-addressed, stamped envelope to: Association List c/o John Sanger, Box 681011, Schaumburg, IL 60168-1011. Two free brochures will help you understand how alarm systems work and how to select a reputable alarm company: "Considerations When Looking for a Burglar/Fire Alarm System," from the National Burglar and Fire Alarm Association, Box 3110, Bethesda, MD 20814 (301) 907-3202. "Plain Talk About Home Burglar Alarm Systems," from the National Crime Prevention Institute, School of Justice Administration, University of Louisville, Shelby Campus, Louisville, KY 40202 (502) 588-6987.

Police departments usually won't recommend specific alarm installing companies, but a call to the police will get you some basic information. You can find out if alarm companies must be licensed in your state or city, for example. If so, ask for a list of licensed companies — and deal only with those firms. An alarm company's membership in a local, regional, or national alarm association usually indicates a commitment to professionalism.

You have to be careful in selecting the appropriate system and the company you buy the system from. As with any major purchase you need to check out the company and the product to make sure that you are dealing with a reputable organization that is going to install the system correctly and be around to give you service down the road. Once you have decided upon the type of system you want and pre-screened several alarm companies, have a salesman come out and give you an estimate. You're better off getting each company's stated best offer and then choosing the best one to continue negotiations with. Never pay the first price quoted; you can usually get a better price if you have patience.

If you are thinking about installing your own electronic alarm system, the following books can help save you money, time, and frustration. These books are available in most public libraries:

The Complete Watchdog's Guide to Installing Your Own Home Burglar Alarm, by David Petraglia (1984, Prentice-Hall, Inc.)

Security: Everything You Need to Know About Household Alarm Systems, by Tom Lewin (1982, Park Lane Enterprises)

Security Systems: Considerations, Layout, and Performance, by William J. Cook, Jr. (1982), Howard W. Sams & Co.)

SPECIAL PURPOSE ALARMS

A new device for detecting an earthquake and triggering an alarm or other device is being developed by Earthquake Protection, Inc. of Mill Valley, CA. In the event of an earthquake, the device will alert people through an alarm and/or voice chip. It also can be configured to shut off gas and/or electricity, turn off computers, close doors, and activate any type of safety- or security-related equipment. These capabilities can prevent fires and explosions that might occur after an earthquake. The magnitude of an earthquake required to trigger the device can be selected for particular areas and the degree of risk the user wants to assume. Although this device is primarily for business use, the technology holds promise for residential use.

On the very inexpensive side are the stand-alone alarms which are usually a sensor of some type with a integrated audible alarm all enclosed in one unit. Stand-alone alarms are designed to cover a specific location such as a door, window, or hallway, and sound an alarm whenever the sensor is activated. The audible alarm is supposed to scare off any would-be intruder since these simple alarms do not have the capability of being monitored. Stand-alone alarms are a good and inexpensive early warning system when you're home, especially when asleep. They can alert you when someone is trying to get into your home. Security Force from International Consumer Brands Inc. is one such product, which sells for between $28 and $38 depending on the model selected. There is a table top/bookshelf infrared sensor/alarm unit which plugs into any existing electrical outlet and is designed to cover a room or hallway. Security

Force has an optional portable remote control available for about $10.

Honeywell's new Electronic Alarm & Lock Bar, priced at about $30, is a sliding door/window barricade bar with wireless alarm, which provides instant security in homes, dormitories, and hotel rooms. By simply setting the bar on the door tracks between the "free-sliding" door and the opposite frame, it provides an effective barrier against forced entry. At the slightest pressure from attempted forced entry, the bar flashes a bright krypton light and sounds a 90 decibel sonic alarm to scare off the intruder. Another type of portable alarm hangs on the doorknob on the inside of your door. If anyone touches the outside of the doorknob the built-in siren is activated. This device is ideal as a second line of defense for your bedroom or when you travel.

Stand-alone electric patio door and window alarms are also available at your local hardware store or building center. These battery-operated alarms can be used with the door or window closed or opened for ventilation. A 70 decibel alarm is triggered when unauthorized entry occurs. Another alternative is an electronic push button door alarm which sounds an 80 decibel alarm when the door is opened by an unauthorized person. This device uses 9V batteries, has visitor and alarm delay features, and is available in key-operated versions.

For secluded homes with long driveways a new product is available that gives you advanced warning of approaching vehicles. The Home Driveway Alert System is an infrared alert system which gives you advance notice of approaching guests, service calls, or intruders. Mounted on a tree or post, the infrared sensor detects the heat and motion of approaching visitors up to 40 feet away and sends a signal to the receiver inside the house.

Can't afford an alarm system? You can buy fake alarm key panels that you install by your front door along with window decals to make a potential thief think that you have an alarm system. Or you can buy window decals and yard warning signs just like the ones real alarm companies use. These ploys work because a big part of a security system's effectiveness is the advertising of the fact that the house is protected by an alarm. Many burglars see the alarm company's warning sign or window decal and move on to an easier target — without ever attempting to break in.

Fake electronic alarm systems are designed to simulate professionally installed alarm systems. They consist of a key-switch plate that is mounted next to the entry door, a fake window glass detector, and window decals. The key-switch plate has a battery-powered flashing LED lamp to indicate "System On." This is a good idea since burglars will normally bypass any house that they think is alarmed. The only problem with the simulated alarm systems currently on the market is that the type of switch plate they use is not used in real alarm systems and there is usually only one window detector. To be truly effective a fake system needs to be indistinguishable from the real thing.

HOME AUTOMATION SYSTEMS

Home management systems are designed as "behind the scene" systems; they operate the home for normal day-to-day activities without homeowner intervention while allowing quick and simple homeowner override for unusual circumstances. Home management systems provide personal and property security, manage climate control, and control lighting and appliances using reliable, affordable, and easy-to-use technology. They provide enhanced personal and property security, unparalleled comfort and efficiency, and complete control of electrical circuits based on personal schedules and/or events occurring in and around the home. Here are just a few of the things that a home management system can control: security, safety, emergencies, convenience, and energy efficiency.

The Home Automation System from Mitsubishi can control security, lighting, appliances, video and audio equipment, heating and cooling systems, and communications systems. A phone call from anywhere in the world is all it takes to turn these functions on or off. The Home Manager from Unity Systems Inc. is a fully integrated home control system providing room-by-room security

The Home Manager by Unity Systems controls heating, cooling, security system, lighting, and appliances from a single touch screen. Photo courtesy of Unity Systems, Inc.

and temperature control, as well as centralized scheduling and control of a home's lighting and appliances. The system uses a sophisticated computer and a wall-mounted touchscreen which displays the home's unique floor plan with simple, step-by-step instructions enabling homeowners to set up the home's actions to complement their lifestyle.

The Home Manager provides the ultimate in security capability, protecting up to 24 individual zones including fire and smoke detection devices. The homeowner may instantly assign separate pass codes for cleaning, repair, or delivery people, limiting their access to specific times, days, and security zones. Unity's Home Manager accepts most standard sensors including infrared, ultrasonic, microwave, mechanical, magnetic, vibration, pressure, and screen circuits. The touchscreen provides a log (location and time) of security zone activation and current status. Up to eight remote keypads can be included with each system for added convenience. The system has a backup power supply as well as a voice synthesizer and telephone interface for remote operation and control from a touchtone telephone or remote personal computer.

Unity's Home Manager is UL-listed for Household Fire, Burglary, and Process Management and can be installed in new or existing homes. A typical installed system costs between $6000 and $15,000 depending on the size of the home, options and installation specifications. Case studies of actual residences and buildings controlled by Home Manager have demonstrated energy savings of up to 60 percent over a year's time. Simple touchscreen operation, combined with virtually unlimited options in scheduling and room-by-room control, allow the homeowner to fully utilize his security and energy equipment.

VIDEO INTERCOMS

By combining both video and audio, a video intercom system lets users positively identify a caller through sight and sound without having to open the door. A video intercom has two basic parts: an outside entrance station with a closed circuit television camera and an intercom, and an inside station or video monitor with an intercom. A visitor presses a button, signaling his presence to the occupant. Inside the entrance station, the camera relays the image to the inside station. When a caller announces his arrival by pressing a button, the occupant sees and hears him at the same time. After identification, the occupant gives the visitor access by either opening the front door or by pressing a button on his unit, activating an electric door strike.

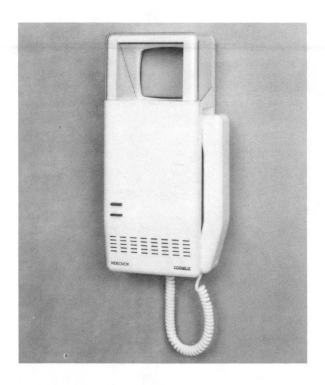

Video intercoms allow maximum security and convenience by providing positive visual identification of visitors before allowing them access to your home. The Videovox is a video intercom security system that works without coaxial cable. Photo courtesy of The Ultrak Group.

Video intercom systems were once used primarily for apartment complexes and commercial buildings. But they have found their way into residential use as more parents search for ways to protect their latchkey children. Young children alone while their parents are at work can inconspicuously identify callers at the front door without letting them know they're home. With multiple stations installed, the system becomes an extension of the parents' eyes. Systems with audio and visual capabilities in one package retail for $1000 and up. The Videovox system from Ultrak, Inc. works without coaxial cables which makes installation much simpler.

The Siedle-Vario letterbox system from Siedle IntercomUSA combines an intercom system with a security mail box. The letter box modules can be arranged horizontally or vertically, are free-standing, and come in flush-mounted or surface-mounted models. The security of your mail is guar-

anteed by an anti-removal guard which prevents anyone from reaching through the letterbox slot. And it is fitted with a heavy-duty safety lock with large-area barring.

SECURITY SYSTEM COMPONENTS

AUTOMATIC LIGHTING CONTROL — When the alarm sounds and during delay periods before you disarm the system, this control activates the lights instantly. It also turns on the lights during a fire to light your escape route.

BARRIER BARS — Barrier bars are spring-loaded plastic bars that are usually installed in hard to protect basement windows. An alarm is initiated if anyone attempts to remove the bar.

BATTERY BACKUP — The system should have an automatic-recharging battery backup for uninterrupted service during power outages. The system should automatically send a signal to the central station when the battery gets low.

CONTROL PANEL/PROCESSOR — The control panel is the brains of the system. All sensors send signals to the control panel via wire or radio-frequency transmitters. The control panel should be installed inside the house where it is protected from tampering. Typically it is installed in a furnace room or other unfinished portion of the house.

DIGITAL COMMUNICATOR — Also known as an automatic dialer, this device connects the alarm system via the phone lines to the central station and has on-line a seizure feature, which allows the alarm system to send a signal to the station automatically even if the phone is in use or disconnected.

FREEZE SENSOR — To avoid freeze up and bursting of pipes, this sensor alerts you to low temperatures that indicate furnace failure. It is usually installed in the basement on an outside wall, at the opposite end of the room from the furnace.

GLASS-BREAK DETECTOR — This sensor detects the sound of breaking glass. It is usually used for fixed-pane windows.

KEYPAD/ARMING PANEL — The panel is used to arm and disarm the system, as well as signal the alarm. A keypad is usually installed just inside the entrance door or doors that you most frequently use.

MAGNETIC SWITCH — A switch that consists of two separate units: a magnetically activated switch and a magnet. The switch is usually mounted in a fixed position (door jamb or window frame) opposing the magnet, which is fastened to the door or window. When the movable section is opened, the magnet moves with it activating the switch.

MICROWAVE DETECTORS — Microwave detectors use high frequency radio waves to detect intrusion. A transmitter sends and receives radio waves while the detector monitors the reflected energy. An alarm is initiated when the waves sent out have been distorted by someone or something moving in the protected area.

PANIC BUTTON — Panic buttons are used to sound alarms instantly. This gives you immediate protection if an intruder tries to break in while you're home. They can also be used for medical emergencies when you can't get to the phone. Hand-held transmitters can also be used to initiate an alarm. Because of their portability, they offer greater flexibility in your personal safety. These transmitters usually have a line-of-sight range of 100-150 feet from your house.

PASSIVE INFRARED DETECTORS — These detectors measure rapid temperature changes within a protected area. The sensor does this first by establishing a normal temperature for the area and then monitors it for slight changes. A burglar entering the protected area will give off enough body heat to initiate an alarm.

PHOTOELECTRIC BEAM DETECTORS — Photoelectric beam detectors use a beam of light projected between two points. Any interruption of the beam, such as an intruder passing through, sets off the alarm.

PRESSURE PAD — Also known as floor mat switches, these are weight sensitive devices that are installed under carpets, usually in front of a vault or other valuables. They are a series of thin metal strips separated by a non-conductive material. When enough pressure is placed on any one of the strips, the alarm circuit is closed and an alarm is initiated.

RADIO FREQUENCY MOTION DETECTION — A means for detecting the presence of an intruder through use of radio frequency generating and receiving equipment. Generally, it is an area detection type of system, where the area under protection is saturated with a pattern of radio frequency waves, any disturbance of which initiates an alarm signal.

RATE OF RISE HEAT DETECTORS — These send an alarm if the temperature rises more than 10° within sixty seconds, or the temperature exceeds the set upper limits on the unit. These are normally placed in the attic, by the furnace, and by the water heater.

SHOCK SENSOR — Actually two sensors in one, it detects the shattering of glass or the splintering of wood. Mounted on the frame of a window, it eliminates the need for a separate sensor on each pane of glass.

SIREN — A multi-tone siren should be included, and it should be loud enough to be heard outside the home. The siren should have an automatic reset after fifteen minutes as you will have a lot of unhappy neighbors if your alarm blares for several hours while your away. It should have separate and distinctive tones as to what type of emergency is occurring — police, fire, or medical. Prevention is what alarms are all about. If a would-be burglar knows that he has set off an alarm he is not going to stick around for long.

SONIC MOTION DETECTION — A system using audible sound waves to detect the presence of an intruder or any other disturbance of a sound pattern generated in a protected area.

SOUND DISCRIMINATORS — Sound discriminators, sometimes called audio detectors, are microphones which are sensitive to certain sounds and frequencies. They are tuned to pick out or discriminate for sounds of breaking glass and splintering wood while ignoring background noise.

TAMPER SWITCH — A device that secures an object or a door in a closed position and activates an alarm if the door is opened or the object is lifted off the switch.

TELEPHONE DIALER, AUTOMATIC — A device that, when activated, automatically dials one or more pre-programmed telephone numbers, (e.g., police, fire department) and relays a recorded voice or coded message giving the location and nature of the alarm.

ULTRASONIC DETECTORS — These detectors sense intrusion with sound waves by transmitting and receiving inaudible sound wave patterns. When these patterns are transmitted, they bounce off ceilings and walls finding their way back to the receiver. The detector compares the sound wave patterns transmitted to those received. An alarm is initiated when the patterns differ. Anyone entering the protected area will cause a change in the sound wave patterns.

7
The Property Inventory

A very important aspect of crime prevention that is often overlooked is that of keeping an accurate and up-to-date record of your valuables. Police property rooms all over the country are filled with recovered stolen property that will never be returned to its rightful owner because either the owner can't be identified or ownership cannot be proven. A lot of recovered property is sold at auction and criminal cases are lost simply because a victim didn't know the serial number of his stolen property. Keeping property inventory records will also make it easier for you to prove a loss to the IRS and your insurance company.

If you will take an hour or so right now to get everything you currently own properly recorded. You will be able to keep your property inventory records file up-to-date in as little as five minutes each time you make a new purchase. Be sure to keep the list in a safe place so that it won't be destroyed in a fire or stolen during a burglary. A fire resistant file cabinet is the safest and most convenient location for your inventory records.

ENGRAVING YOUR VALUABLES

An integral part of keeping good records is Operation Identification. Operation ID is a valuable program sponsored by most police and sheriff's departments. Your local department's crime prevention unit has engraving tools and property inventory forms that they loan out free of charge so that you can engrave your valuables. You should engrave all of your valuables with your state's two letter abbreviation followed by your social security number. Mark your items permanently in a place that is readily visible and difficult to remove. The police department may also provide window decals advising thieves that your property is marked. The window decals are important because you want a would-be thief to know that your property is marked, because he knows that marked property is difficult, if not impossible, to sell.

I recommend that you engrave all valuables that are likely to be stolen such as TVs, VCRs, cameras, stereo equipment, and anything else that does not have a serial number permanently stamped into the item. The serial number on many TVs, VCRs, and stereo equipment is located on a piece of tape which can be easily removed or altered. Sometimes it is not practical nor desirable to mark certain kinds of valuables. Jewelry is often too small to provide space for engraving, and the last thing that you want to do is to deface valuable artwork or antiques. These types of items should be well photographed and described instead of engraved. An alternative to engraving is to stamp your small items with Trace Mark from Microstamp. Trace Mark is a micro-marking system for permanent identification of articles. The device can be used on surfaces too small to mark by conventional methods.

PHOTOGRAPHING YOUR VALUABLES

In addition to engraving you should take photos of all your valuables especially jewelry, coins, stamps, and antiques. Photographs come in handy in the recovery of stolen items where a description alone is insufficient to identify the item. Film is relatively inexpensive, so take as many photos as are needed to completely show the item. This usually means taking a photo from all four sides of an object. In some cases one photo will suffice, but in others you may have to take more to depict the object accurately. You should have double prints made so that you can keep one set for your insurance company and save the other one for the police. Be sure to keep the negatives for your records.

For most common household items, TVs, VCRs, furniture, etc., you need only take one front view photograph. To document antiques and other unique items adequately you need to take photographs from all angles — front, back, sides, top, and bottom (if necessary). Be sure to take closeups of detailing such as handcrafting, painting, embroidering, etc. When photographing jewelry, coins, and other small articles it is best to use a macro lens, which allows you to take one-to-one closeups so that small details will show up clearly. Number your photos to correspond with your Property Inventory, so that you know which photo belongs with which description.

VIDEO INVENTORY

If you have a video camcorder you can use it to make very accurate records of your valuables. If you don't have a video camera you can borrow one from a friend, rent one, or hire a video inventory company to do the video inventory. A video inventory provides a more accurate visual description of your home and valuables than either still photos or written descriptions. Another advantage is that you don't have to send film off to be developed, which saves time and does not compromise your security.

Before you start taping, inventory your valuables and fill out the Property Inventory form. Them make a diagram of your house's floor plan showing the route you will take during filming. The next step is to prepare a narrative that describes what is being shown. Use the inventory to help you prepare the narrative and to make sure that you don't miss anything. What you want as a finished product is a detailed video "tour" of your home, inside and out.

To help you with the preparation of the narrative use the following example as a guide. Suppose that you're going to tape the family room next. First, look up the necessary information from the property inventory form. Then write that information down on the script in order of appearance. What you want to do is describe a particular item while it is being filmed. For example: While panning the family room the narrator says, "We are now moving into the ground floor family room. Located in the room is a Sony 19-inch portable color TV serial number XYZ 123 . . ." As you describe the TV you film the view from all four sides and taking closeups showing any detail (if necessary). You then move on to film and describe in order all the other valuables in the room. Follow this procedure for taping the rest of the rooms in your home.

A good filming diagram allows you to flow from one room to the next in a logical order. For example: Start outside, show the front of your house, including your address, then move around your house clockwise until you have video taped all four sides, including your garage and any outbuildings. Then move inside, start at the front door and tape all rooms starting from the front door and moving from room to room, either clockwise or counterclockwise making sure that you don't bypass any rooms. Complete all the rooms on each floor before going onto the next. To video tape a room, stand in the door and pan from one side of the room to the other so that you get a good overall view of the room. Always film each room the same way, if you start out panning from right to left continue to use this sequence with the rest of your room. This will make the tape consistent and easier to follow. Then move in for closeups of specific items. Be sure to get a good view from all four angles and a closeup of the serial number, model number, and make (if appropriate).

Once you have your script and diagram completed you're ready to start taping. Remember, not only are you recording your property to help the police in case of theft, but you're also making a detailed record for your insurance company. A good detailed permanent video record of your property will provide you with the necessary proof you'll need to file a claim in case your home is destroyed by fire or other natural disaster.

THE PROPERTY INVENTORY FORM

To help you keep accurate inventory records I have included a Property Inventory form that you can use to inventory your valuables. Just remove the form and make as many copies as needed. You can also obtain Operation ID property inventory forms from your local police or sheriff's department. For those of you with personal computers there are several special home inventory software programs available from software vendors. For a complete list of vendors see the Appendix.

The following guidelines will assist you in accurately completing the Property Inventory form found on page 78. The numbered descriptions correspond to the numbered sections on the property inventory sample shown below.

```
┌─────────────────────────────────────────────────┐
│            PROPERTY INVENTORY                    │
│                                                  │
│        Room _____(1)_____              │
│   Operation ID # _____(2)_____         │
│                                                  │
│  Make         (3)    Type          (8)           │
│                                                  │
│  Model        (4)    Serial #      (9)           │
│                                                  │
│  Color        (5)    Value $       (10)          │
│                                                  │
│ Video Tape/Film # (6)  Operation ID (7)  Date Purchased (11) │
└─────────────────────────────────────────────────┘
```

1. Room: The room (or rooms) in which the items on this page are located.

2. Operation I.D.#: Your state's two letter abbreviation followed by your social security number. Example: NY123-45-6789.

3. Make: The manufacturer's brand name, such as Sony, RCA, IBM, Canon, etc., or a description for items without brand names such as jewelry, artwork, and heirlooms.

4. Model: A number, product name, or combination of the two.

5. Color: Usually expressed as either the predominant color with a colored trim such as black with a white trim, or as the color top to bottom, such as black over white.

6. Video Tape/Film #: The corresponding identification number on the video tape or photograph.

7. Operation I.D.: A "Yes" if the item is engraved with your Operation ID number, "No" if it is not.

8. Type: Additional descriptive information, such as AM/FM Cassette Tape Player Recorder.

9. Serial Number: The number is either stamped into the body or printed on labels usually found on the back or bottom of electronic equipment and appliances.

10. Value: Purchase price, fair market value, or appraised value (as with expensive art or jewelry).

11. Date Purchased: The date you purchased the item or received it as a gift.

PROPERTY INVENTORY

ROOM _____

OPERATION ID # _____

Make		Type
Model		Serial #
Color		Value $
Video Tape-Film #	Operation ID	Date Purchased

Make	Model	Type
Model		Serial #
Color		Value $
Video Tape-Film #	Operation ID	Date Purchased

Make		Type
Model		Serial #
Color		Value $
Video Tape-Film #	Operation ID	Date Purchased

Make		Type
Model		Serial #
Color		Value $
Video Tape-Film #	Operation ID	Date Purchased

Make		Type
Model		Serial #
Color		Value $
Video Tape-Film #	Operation ID	Date Purchased

Make		Type
Model		Serial #
Color		Value $
Video Tape-Film #	Operation ID	Date Purchased

KEEP IN A SAFE PLACE

Page___of___

8
When
You're Away

Going away? An empty house is a tempting target for a burglar. Having a friend house sit while you're gone is the best solution. If that is not possible then you need to make your home appear lived-in to fool potential burglars into believing that someone is home. Before you leave — even for a short trip — make sure that you close and lock all doors and windows. Don't forget the shed and garage doors. If you have a security system be sure that it is in good working condition and that you activate it before leaving. Notify the monitoring station of your pending absence and provide them with a phone number where you can be reached along with the phone number of the person watching your home during your absence.

Store your valuables such as jewelry and firearms in a home safe, with a friend, or in a safe deposit box or vault while you're away. Advise your local law enforcement agency to put your home on their extra patrol list. Use automatic timers to turn the lights, television, or radio on and off at appropriate times. Turn the bell on your phone down low. That way a burglar won't be alerted to your absence by a ringing phone that goes unanswered. Leave your blinds, shades, and curtains in their normal everyday positions. Don't close them unless that's what you would normally do when you're at home.

Have a trusted neighbor or friend watch your house while you're away. Leave your vacation ad-

dress and phone number with him in case of an emergency. Have him pick up your newspaper and mail. It is not a good idea to stop deliveries as you have no control over who may get the word that you're gone. Ask your neighbor to park his car in your driveway occasionally. If you're leaving your car at home have him move it occasionally so that it looks like you're home. Before you leave, pay all your bills that will be due while you're away. Arrange to have your yard maintained, the grass mowed, leaves raked, and snow shoveled. This will give your home a more lived-in look.

Don't tell people about your pending departure or travel plans. Don't pack the car the night before; it tells a burglar of your pending departure. If you're leaving by cab, don't have them pick you up at your house. Instead have them meet you at the nearest corner. Don't put your home address on your luggage tags. Use a PO box or your work address. That way a dishonest airline employee won't be able to get your address off of the bags and send an accomplice to burglarize your home. Don't leave empty trash cans sitting outside, or no trash cans set out on collection day; both are indications that you're not home. Don't board your pets. Have a neighbor come in to feed and care for them.

For increased protection you may want to consider renting an alarm system. My Alarm Inc. rents alarm systems to residential customers while they are away from home. The systems are available from travel agencies, real estate firms, construction businesses, and cable television companies. The security system, which rents for about $5 a day and covers up to 4000 square feet, has a push-button two-way speaker-telephone, smoke detector, two passive infrared sensors, two audio discriminators for either windows or doors, and one temperature sensor. This alternative provides your home with increased security and you with peace of mind for a very reasonable amount.

Use the vacation checklist found on the next page each time you go away so that you won't forget anything. Be careful, not careless. Enjoy a carefree vacation.

SECURING YOUR VACATION HOME

Vacation homes by their very nature are extremely vulnerable to crime. They are usually unoccupied for extended periods of time and are often located in isolated areas or in developments with few year-round residents. Because of this isolation there are few if any neighbors around to alert the police, and in such areas police or sheriff's patrols are likely to be infrequent. This makes it very tempting for burglars because they know that their activities will probably go undetected for some time.

The first thing that you need to do is to complete a thorough security survey of your vacation property. At the very least you should make the doors and windows as secure as the ones on your primary residence. For extra security you should consider installing roll-down security shutters. Roll-down security shutters supplement your existing security and they make it much more difficult for an intruder to make entry. (See Chapter 3 for more information.) Security systems may be useful if your property is located in a vacation development with on-site management that can respond to problems. But for isolated properties alarms are neither practical nor cost effective.

Whether your vacation residence is a single family home, condominium, trailer, or cabin you need to take extra security precautions. It is not enough to have good locks because given time any lock can

be defeated. If possible you should never leave valuables in your vacation home when you're not using the residence. This includes appliances such as microwaves, televisions, and stereos. If it's impractical to remove and store such appliances, then make sure that they are anchored to the wall or other secure surface. (See Chapter 4 for more information on securing electronic equipment).

You should store all outdoor furniture, gas grills, and sporting equipment inside the building. If due to space limitations your outdoor furniture cannot be stored inside, consider permanently anchoring such items to your deck or patio. An alternative is to use high security chains and padlocks to secure anything movable that you can't bring inside. Drain and cover swimming pools and hot tubs because they are a safety hazard if left full and uncovered. Be sure to shut off the gas/propane, water, and electricity before leaving. Never store flammable liquids or anything that could be a fire hazard inside the residence when you're not there. Don't leave food in your cabin as it could attract wild animals, which could damage your property trying to get at the food.

Make sure that you complete and keep a current property inventory list of all items that you routinely leave in your vacation home. A large red "X" behind pictures might act as a deterrent to theft, and will alert you quickly if anything is missing. A floor plan showing the location of valuable items is also good in checking for losses. This is very important if you rent out your vacation home when you're not using it. It is also a good idea to find someone who lives in the area year round to look after your property when you're away. If necessary offer to pay them or hire a property management service. You'll be money ahead knowing that your property is being taken care of. Be sure to have enough insurance to cover your vacation home and its contents.

TRAVEL SECURITY WHILE ABROAD

Traveling abroad can be a very rewarding experience, but don't let your guard down. About one in every 2000 American tourists is victimized by crime. While there will always be some incidents

VACATION CHECKLIST

Dos

☐ Are all doors and windows closed and locked?

☐ Has the alarm system been armed, and is it in operating order?

☐ Do you have a neighbor watching the house while you're away?

☐ Does he have your vacation address and phone number in case of an emergency?

☐ Did you pay your bills before you left?

☐ Did you store your valuables with a friend or in a safe deposit box?

☐ Did you advise your local law enforcement agency to put your home on their extra patrol list?

☐ Did you arrange for a friend or neighbor to pick up your newspapers and mail?

☐ Did you arrange to have your yard maintained while you're gone?

☐ Do you have automatic timers on your lights, radio, or TV?

☐ Is the bell on your phone turned down low?

☐ Did you leave your blinds, shades, and curtains in their normal positions?

☐ Did you ask a neighbor to park his car in your driveway or move your car occasionally so it looks like the driveway is being used?

☐ Did you turn down the thermostat?

☐ Did you unplug appliances such as air conditioners, irons, and toasters?

☐ Did you properly store flammables such as cleaning fluids, paint, and gasoline?

Don'ts

☐ Don't tell people about your pending departure or travel plans.

☐ Don't pack the car the night before — it tells a burglar of your pending departure.

☐ Don't have a cab pick you up at your house. Have them meet you at the nearest corner instead.

☐ Don't board your pets. Have a neighbor come in to feed and care for them.

☐ Don't put your home address on your luggage tags. Use a post office box or your work address.

☐ Don't leave empty trash cans outside.

☐ Don't stop delivery of your mail or newspaper.

that cannot be anticipated or guarded against, the majority of the threats facing travelers can be avoided simply by preparing for them ahead of time. First, check your homeowner's insurance policy to see if it covers your valuables while on a trip — and what proof of ownership is required. If your homeowner's insurance doesn't cover you or is inadequate, you should consider extra travel insurance. Keep separate records of credit card numbers, traveler's checks, passport number and issuance date, and a copy of your plane ticket. Consider purchasing a prepaid hotel package. If your vouchers are stolen, chances are your hotel will still have a record of the purchase and will honor the reservations.

Know something about the language of the country you're going to visit. It may not always be possible to study the language in advance, but at the very least, the traveler should learn some key words and phrases. Knowing how to say "emergency," "police," "danger," "take cover," "doctor," and "help" may be far more important than knowing how to read a menu or ask how much something costs. It's also a good idea to learn something about the culture. You may want to write down a one- or two-page summary of customs and cultural differences in the country you're about to visit. In addition to helping you avoid embarrassing gaffes, it may enable you to understand behavior which you would otherwise take as offensive or respond to inappropriately.

While it's usually a good idea for the traveler to obtain some foreign currency before leaving the U.S. (or immediately upon arrival at a foreign airport), he or she should never carry so much cash that its loss (through pickpocketing or theft of luggage, for instance) would bring the trip to a standstill. Use traveler's checks and eliminate unnecessary credit cards before you leave. It's best to get traveler's checks in dollars rather than local currency. Leave unneeded traveler's checks and valuables in hotel safes or safe deposit boxes. It's also a good idea to leave expensive jewelry and clothing at home. Traveler's checks should be carried in a place other than a wallet or a briefcase so that if a theft occurs, some funds will still be available immediately.

Losing a passport can be extremely upsetting to the traveler and disruptive to the trip. Passports should always be carried separately from a briefcase, handbag, or carry-on luggage. Passports should never be left in hotel rooms or in a coat pocket when the coat isn't being worn. Make photocopies of your visa and the first two pages of your passport, and keep them in your luggage. It is also a good idea to bring along extra passport photos. If your passport is stolen, you will need these to get a new one.

Although most people in America travel everywhere by car, this is not always the case in foreign countries. If you go to London, you should know that the trains there are a convenient and dependable mode of transportation. A map of the city and its subway system (tube) may be helpful, and it's a good idea to know something about the taxi system as well.

Always travel with first-aid supplies. All-night drugstores are not as commonplace in other countries, and many items we take for granted are simply not available elsewhere. Some people travel not only with a basic first-aid kit but with such items as flashlights, smoke detectors, and a few standard tools.

No matter where you journey, you can minimize your chances of being victimized by dressing down, blending in, and not flashing cash. Keep your valuables such as cash, jewelry, and cameras hidden. Keep your purse strap over your shoulder and the bag close to your side, and watch out for purse snatchers, many of whom use mopeds. Wear a money belt. It will protect you from pickpockets, who in many cases are small children. Keep an eye on your luggage. Don't leave luggage unattended at the curb-side waiting for a bellhop or cab driver. Don't carry expensive luggage. The only person you're going to impress is the would-be thief lurking around the airport or hotel.

Anything of value that you're carrying should be protected against theft. It shouldn't be left in the passenger compartment of a car (even if it's locked), in an empty hotel room (even if it's locked), or in a suitcase. All of these locations are burglarized frequently. There are only two reasonably safe places to keep important items while traveling: (1) in the trunk of a car or (2) in the hotel safe.

Airports, domestic and foreign, are known to be frequented by professional groups of pickpockets and bag snatchers who account for up to $400 million in losses in the U.S. each year. A team of skillful airport thieves consists of the "spotter," who watches for the police, selects a victim, and directs the entire operation; the "pick," who relieves the victim of valuables; and the "mule," who transports the bag from the scene. The bag is quickly transferred to the mule, so the pick can't be caught with any evidence and the mule can't be identified as the thief. They work the areas where the crowds are the thickest and busiest: in ticket lines, outside baggage-claim and customs areas, at telephones, and at curbside. Anyone who looks affluent and carries expensive luggage is a potential target.

Distraction is the usual tactic used by thieves. Travelers are frequently victims of self-made distractions like wrestling with too much baggage. If these don't draw a victim's attention, the thieves may ask directions, drop coins or bills, seek to borrow a pen, or stage an incident by starting a loud argument or fight. Be wary of people with empty tote bags or jackets folded over an arm; people facing the wrong way in a ticket line; people casually strolling and observing or signaling each other. If you're jostled, bumped, or crowded, know that it could be a pickpocket at work.

The following steps can help the traveler keep the thieves at bay: (1) Never leave your bags unattended, even briefly. (2) Use pocketbooks with a secure closure, and keep wallets in an inside pocket. (3) Be alert to distractions: money dropped near you; ketchup or mustard soiling your clothing; people persistently asking directions; loud commotions; and people who are too eager to be helpful. (4) Be aware of your own distractions. Greeting relatives, making phone calls, or hailing a taxi. (5) If your pocket is picked or bag snatched, shout for help and say what's missing.

HOTEL SECURITY

Generally speaking, you should stay in a room on one of the lower floors (if it's a high-rise hotel) in case there is a fire, and away from the lobby. As soon as you arrive check out fire escape routes and the location of fire extinguishers, smoke alarms, and emergency lights. A new portable fire escape system called the Exit Traveler from R.A.W. Rescue Products Inc. is on the market and is available in 4-, 7-, and 12-floor models. A 36- floor model will be available soon. The Exit Traveler is designed to lower a person automatically at a constant rate of descent without danger and can handle any weight between 40 and 300 pounds. The 12-floor model has a rate of descent of 89 seconds. Its compact size (9 × 6 × 3 inches) and light weight (under 8 pounds for the 12-floor model) makes it a perfect travel companion. The 12-floor Exit Traveler retails for about $450 and comes with its own carrying case, video instructions, and fire safety booklet from the National Fire Protection Association (NFPA).

Once you're in your room, it should be locked at all times. If the inside door has a security chain or an extra lock, it should be used. Passkeys can be stolen and duplicated without much difficulty. Hide your valuables before you leave the room. This may not deter a good burglar, but if a quick glance shows nothing worth the risk of entering, an impulse thief may pass up your room for another. Use the air conditioner — not an open window or patio door — for ventilation. When you leave your room for dinner, turn on the TV. Noise from inside a room may discourage a thief. If you lose your room key — even for a short time — ask the desk clerk to assign you another room.

Don't open your door in response to a knock until you know who is out there. Use the peephole or open the door with the security chain attached. Ask for ID if the visitor claims to be a hotel security agent or a police officer. If you awake to find someone trying to open your door, don't be quiet. Yell, scream, call the front desk. If this doesn't discourage the burglar, lock yourself in the bathroom. Don't play hero and risk getting hurt. Finally, never invite a stranger into your room, and be cautious about accepting an invitation to visit someone else's room. The person might be trying to set you up for a burglary or robbery.

If your hotel provides room safes or safe deposit boxes use them to secure your valuables. You can also purchase travel locks which you can use to supplement the hotel's door locks. Travel locks are for use when you are occupying the room and don't offer extra protection when you're away. You can also use the new varieties of portable security alarms to give you added protection such as the PIR-40 portable security alarm from Potrans International. The unit is a passive infrared motion detector that is powered by two 1.5V AA batteries and has a 20-foot range. For the traveler who needs more in a security system there is The Protector 502 from Protec Co. Ltd. The system, which is completely portable and comes in a carrying case, includes four battery-powered infrared sensors and four personal alarm transmitters. Both units maintain radio contact with the carrying case base station.

SAFETY FOR THE BUSINESS TRAVELER

Don't advertise. The quickest way to lose something is to let thieves find out you have it. Though most travelers would never think of flashing a roll of money in public, or of wearing expensive jewelry in a dangerous part of town, many unwittingly broadcast the fact that they're carrying valuable material on a business trip. For instance, they carry an expensive portable computer in a fancy case that is tailor-made for it. They register themselves in a hotel by specifying their occupation. Or they talk loudly in a restaurant or a bar about how successful they are or how much money they make.

Business travelers should conceal or disguise those items that they must transport. A sample case that looks expensive shouldn't be left on the front seat of a car while the traveler stops for coffee. And though a camera stuffed under a car seat might be safer than one that's been left in a more visible place, it's no safer than a house key left under the welcome mat. Anyone who breaks into the car is going to find it easily. In most cases, it's better to use a little imagination in concealing or disguising valuable items than it is to draw attention to them by elaborate security measures.

Most experienced business travelers suggest carrying only a small case that can be held at all times. If large items of value must be transported, the following steps can decrease the chances of theft:

- Install an alarm system on your vehicle.

- Keep sample cases, etc., locked in the trunk, where they can't be seen by passersby.

- Don't leave valuable items in a car trunk overnight; ask if the hotel management has a safe area for large items.

- Equip all cases with good strong locks.

- Make sure the vehicle insurance policy covers theft of personal and business property. If it doesn't, add this coverage in a rider to the policy.

- Consider using one large case rather than several small, easily portable ones.

WHAT TO DO IF YOU'RE ARRESTED ABROAD

About 3000 U.S. citizens are arrested abroad each year, and there are probably many more that go unreported. Sometimes the charges are dropped after a day or two. Sometimes a bribe is paid while the detainee is still held by police. In any case, being arrested abroad can be a harrowing experience. In addition to facing a language barrier, you may be denied access to competent legal counsel. In the worst incidents, Americans have been forced into signing false confessions by coercive means — up to and including physical torture.

The most frequent charges on which U.S. travelers are arrested include drug violations, immigration violations, fraud (usually involving contractual or other business issues), customs violations (attempting to bring in or take out of the country currency, antiques, black market purchases, etc.), alcohol violations (particularly in Moslem areas, where liquor is forbidden or restricted), debt violations (bad checks, credit card overcharges), and motor vehicle violations.

There is a great deal that you can do to minimize such problems abroad. Here are some suggestions:

- Don't sign anything.

- Don't talk to anyone, not even to a fellow prisoner. Immediately ask to speak with the nearest American consul.

- Do not threaten, argue, or get physical.

- Comply with any reasonable police demand gracefully and without quibbling. You can always lodge a formal complaint later.

It may be difficult for the American traveling abroad to remember that the local police cannot always be regarded as a source of help. This is especially true in Third World and Communist countries, where the conduct and attitudes of the police may be subject to local politics, the economy, or widespread feelings about American influence. It's important, therefore, to remember that while the police are normally a source of assistance in difficult situations, the visitor should be sensitive to cultural and political differences, and treat the police with some care. It's not a good idea, for example, to demand that the police help you. Ask for their assistance.

PROTECTION AGAINST TERRORISM

American tourists are often the targets of terrorist attacks. The best way to avoid trouble is not to look or act like an American tourist. Because airports have been the site of numerous kidnappings and bombings in recent years, the rule of thumb is to get through the airport as quickly as possible. Seat assignments can be obtained through a travel agent in advance. The sooner you get beyond the security checkpoint, the better. Don't loiter around airport ticket counters, especially in Europe and the Middle East. Go as soon as possible to the relative safety of the departure gate waiting area. Book flights on national airlines (e.g., Lufthansa, Qantas, Air Pacific, etc.) instead of American-owned airlines (e.g., United, Continental, Pan Am, etc.). While abroad, avoid "American"

businesses such as American Express offices, McDonalds, etc. Don't read "English editions" of foreign newspapers while in public places.

Few people are prepared for the physical and emotional shock they are likely to experience when confronted by terrorism. Your response in such a situation affects your chances of survival. Every situation must be judged on its particulars. It used to be widely believed that the best course of action was to do nothing – to comply quickly and silently with any demands made by gunmen. Today, this is no longer always true. Some ill-fated hostages have died just as certainly by doing nothing as they would have by ganging up on their attackers.

If you should someday find yourself held hostage the most important rule to remember is to remain calm. Panic seldom helps the situation. In fact, in some cases the panic of hostages has egged the terrorists on to impulsive acts of violence. Even though total compliance may not be the best course of action overall, it's not a good idea to start off by taking an aggressive stand on a relatively minor issue. Surrender your papers and valuables on demand — they're not worth dying for.

Avoid doing or saying anything that will draw the captors' attention to you. If the terrorists perceive a certain hostage as troublesome, threatening, or aggressive, they may decide to get rid of him or her first. Faking a medical emergency is also unwise, since it draws undue attention to the individual. A hostage who begs, pleads, offers to pay ransom, demands his or her rights, or threatens retaliation is only going to make the situation worse. In responding to terrorists' questions, the best policy is for the hostage to say as little as he or she safely can.

Do not actively resist demands, or even physical mistreatment. A beating is not pleasant, but it's better than a bullet. Remain alert to any reasonable chance for escape. At the first sign of a rescue attempt, get down as low as possible and stay down until official forces say the coast is clear. Even after the shooting stops, a nervous soldier may shoot at the first moving target without asking whether it is friend or foe. If you're shot and survive you should play dead. If a fire breaks out during the rescue attempt, stay low and try to crawl to safety. If you're lucky enough to be released, be careful about what you do and say afterward. If other hostages are still being held, a careless or injudicious remark might prompt the terrorists to take out their anger on the other captives.

Before you go, get the latest government advisories about travel conditions in any country from the U.S. State Department's Citizens Emergency Center. The office is open weekdays from 8:15 A.M. to 5:00 P.M. Eastern time, and can be reached at (202) 647-5225. Another good travel aid is "Smart Travel," an audio cassette and pocket-sized card filled with travel dos and don'ts. Smart Travel retails for about $10 and should be available by mid-1990. Finally, if in doubt — don't go.

9
Apartment Security and Rural Security

Apartment security and rural security are two very different areas, with their own specialized problems. Be sure to read Chapters 1 through 4 carefully first, before going on to the following sections.

SECURITY FOR APARTMENT DWELLERS

Apartments have their own special security problems and needs. Security is limited by the tenant's inability to make substantial changes to the apartment without cooperation from the landlord. The best crime prevention available to apartment dwellers is to get to know your neighbors. People are more likely to look out for someone they know than they are a stranger. If your complex has a neighborhood watch program join. If not you can start one with the help of your local police department. Remember, don't assume since your building has security that you are safe — the best security system can be breached. It is therefore important that you actively practice good security/crime prevention.

The following are some suggestions to make your apartment more secure and you safer. You should always change the lock when you rent a new apartment. Give a duplicate key in a sealed envelope to a friend and let your apartment manager know whom to contact in case of an emergency. Never hide a spare key on the outside of your apartment.

Don't master-key your lock to management locks — the key might fall into the wrong hands. If the management insists that your door be master-keyed consider spending a few dollars to have an auxiliary lock installed. You should also check to see if the locks on the sliding door and windows are adequate. If not, install extra security devices as described in Chapters 2 and 3.

If your complex doesn't have a security system already installed, you should consider installing a wireless security system. You want a wireless system so that you can take it with you when you move. (See Chapter 6 for more information on alarm systems.) A cheaper alternative to an alarm system is portable sliding door/window alarm bars. You place the alarm bar into the track of a sliding door or window and a loud alarm sounds if the bar is tampered with. Honeywell manufactures a bar alarm for both sliding doors and windows that retails for about $30.

Be alert in public areas where an intruder could loiter such as hallways, stairs, laundry rooms, elevators, and garages. Don't ride elevators with strangers or with the roof escape hatch ajar — someone may be hiding on top of the elevator. Don't put your full name or gender identification on mail boxes, posted tenant lists, or your front door. If you live in a high rise be sure to keep your balcony doors secured. Don't assume that just because you live on the twentieth floor that you are safe. Burglars have been known to climb the outside of tall buildings and successfully burglarize apartments where the occupants had left the balcony door open. Likewise don't store valuables or anything that could be used by a burglar to assist him in breaking into your unit on your balcony or patio.

The parking lot is probably more vulnerable to crime then your apartment itself. Thieves like large parking lots because they are less likely to be detected. To protect your vehicle while it is parked, be sure to lock it up and try to park in a well-lighted spot. A vehicle security system is very advisable since you cannot secure your vehicle in a garage. If you are lucky enough to have underground parking make sure that there is some type of system in use that limits access to tenants only.

Fire safety is also an important consideration when living in an apartment. You should practice good fire safety as outlined in Chapter 10. In addition you should report any unsafe fire conditions to the management or the local fire marshal. When you first move in make sure that you establish a fire escape plan for your unit and equip yourself with necessary equipment such as fire extinguishers and fire escape ladders. Apartments should at the very least have smoke detectors in each unit, pull fire alarm stations on each floor, fire escape stairwells and ladders, fire extinguishers, and/or hose reels on each floor. Fire sprinkler systems are the best protection and should be high on your must-have list.

To help you when selecting an apartment complex, follow the checklist on page 89. Fill one out for each complex that you visit. This way you can compare what each complex offers in the way of security. You're better off paying a little more in rent in return for a safer environment. Don't be fooled by outward appearances. The most attractive complex may still have a high crime rate. If you discover problems after moving in talk to other tenants and your landlord to make improvements.

FARM AND RANCH SECURITY

More than eight million crimes occur each year in rural areas and small towns. Many rural residents are easy "marks" for thieves because of the "you don't have to lock your doors" attitude. That used to be true but no longer. Thieves today are very mobile and very willing to "take a drive to the country" to ply their trade. So, no matter how far away from "civilization" you live you still need to practice good crime prevention. This section provides special crime prevention tips for securing livestock, farm products, equipment, and supplies.

Your farm or ranch contains many items attractive to thieves: tools, motors, batteries, tractors and other valuable farm machinery, and supplies such as gasoline are things the rural criminal is eager to steal. Make sure your house, yard, corrals, and gas pumps are lighted. If you're away from home a lot, particularly after dark, use automatic timers or photoelectric eyes on your yard and home lights. Gas pumps, gas tanks, storage bins, milk bulk tanks, and grain elevators should be secured with high security chains, padlocks, and hasps. So should your house and barn. Keep boats, snowmobiles, bikes, fertilizers, tools, and other small equipment in a locked garage or shed, or secured to a stationary object with a strong padlock. Chain and lock drawn implements and irrigation pumps.

It is a good idea to have a security system for your home and outbuildings. You will need to have a centrally monitored system, as there is likely no one close by to call the sheriff's department if all you have is a local alarm. To secure remote buildings or equipment you can utilize mid-range wireless radio transmitters and receivers to connect them to your security system. An alternative to a full-blown security system is the use of door chimes that ring into the house. With door chimes installed on outbuildings, you would have some warning if anyone entered the building. Another product you should consider is Driveway Alert from Alert Systems Inc. This is a passive infrared motion detector that you install outside to cover your driveway. When a vehicle passes through the covered area an alarm is sounded inside the house at the plug-in receiver. This alerts you every time someone drives into your yard. This device would be especially useful for covering access roads that are hidden from view from the house.

CHECKLIST FOR APARTMENT HUNTERS

Location ———————————————————

YES NO Check (✓) the appropriate box

☐ ☐ Does the complex have a high crime rate?

☐ ☐ Is it in a high crime area?

☐ ☐ Is it in a stable neighborhood or is the area full of rundown or vacant buildings?

☐ ☐ Are the streets clean, well-lighted, and regularly patrolled by the police?

☐ ☐ Does the city have a reputation for being well run?

☐ ☐ Does the building itself appear well managed and maintained?

☐ ☐ Is there security at the front entrance — a doorman, guard, closed-circuit TV, intercom, or, at the very least, a strong forced-entry resistant lock?

☐ ☐ Is security equipment kept in good repair?

☐ ☐ Are the building's front and side doors kept locked at all times?

☐ ☐ Are laundry rooms and storage areas kept locked?

☐ ☐ Is the parking area well-lighted and secure?

☐ ☐ Do underground parking garages have remotely operated door opening systems?

☐ ☐ Are elevators attended twenty-four hours a day or equipped with intercoms monitored by security or the doorman?

☐ ☐ Are elevators well-lighted and equipped with interior view mirrors?

☐ ☐ Are there secure locks or other burglarproof devices on ground floor windows, skylights, and windows next to fire escapes?

☐ ☐ Is there adequate lighting in stairwells, parking lots, laundry rooms, and around the exterior of the building?

☐ ☐ Are hallways and stairwells kept clean and are they routinely patrolled/checked?

☐ ☐ Do grilles or grates on ground floor windows and windows adjacent to fire escapes have built in quick release fire escape features?

☐ ☐ Does the apartment's front door meets the specifications for entry doors as outlined in Chapter 3?

☐ ☐ Are the door locks changed each time a tenant moves out?

☐ ☐ Does each unit have its own individual security system?

☐ ☐ Does the building have an intercom to allow you to identify visitors before admitting them to the building?

☐ ☐ Can roof doors only be opened from the inside and are they kept locked at all times?

☐ ☐ Are interior fire escape stairwells and exterior fire escape ladders properly secured?

☐ ☐ Is the building and each unit equipped with smoke detectors?

☐ ☐ Is the building equipped with a fire sprinkler system?

☐ ☐ Are there smoke detectors in each unit and do they work?

☐ ☐ Is the building's owner/manager security conscious?

☐ ☐ Are tenants actively involved in building security/crime prevention?

Never leave tools or guns in an open pickup truck. It's also a good idea to bring your CB radio in at night. It's also not wise to leave major farm equipment in the fields overnight. If you can't bring your equipment in at night, make sure it's locked or left in a lighted area and remove all valuables. Secure power-driven implements with a case-hardened metal tow chain and padlock. Don't let a thief drive away in your vehicle or use it to carry other stolen property. Equip tractors, four-wheel drive vehicles, trucks, and trailers with hidden ignition-kill switches. An alternative is to remove the rotor and distributor cap to prevent hot-wiring.

Livestock theft is now one of the easiest and most profitable crimes. The modern rustler may use a car, light plane, or helicopter to spot a likely target, usually stock in isolated pastures and unlocked corrals. Then thieves move in quickly with campers, vans, or trailers, load up ten or fifteen head of cattle and drive away. In just a few hours the thieves can be in another county or state — easily putting hundreds of miles between victim and buyer. A crime that takes ten minutes can net the rustler several thousand dollars. The risk is low as the theft often goes undetected for several days.

To safeguard your animals use these suggestions:

- Check your stock frequently. If possible, take a daily count.

- Check fences and gates regularly to make sure they are in good repair and locked.

- Lock corrals and loading chutes. Use sturdy chains at least ⅜-inch thick and a good quality padlock with a hardened steel shackle.

- If you're going to be away, arrange to have a neighbor keep track of your animals. Do the same for your neighbors when they're away.

- Report missing stock immediately. Rustlers move fast, so report the loss even if you aren't sure whether the missing animals are stolen or have strayed. Don't wait — delay ensures the rustler a safe getaway.

Mark your animals with a distinctive mark. Mark young stock soon after birth. Be sure to register your marks and brands with your local law enforcement agency. For cattle, the preferred marking methods are freeze or hot iron branding, often in conjunction with lip and ear tattooing or with earmarks or eartags. Brands and tattooing are hard to alter and provide a permanent record. To be safe, do not rely on earmarks or tags alone. Let rustlers know your stock is permanently marked. Thieves are less likely to take property they know can be traced.

Livestock isn't the only target of today's rural thieves. Tobacco, corn, wheat, soybeans, hay, oats, milk, and even timber are being stolen by criminals who have discovered there's big money in this kind of crime. To protect your farm products keep your property where it can be watched. Store grain and tobacco in protected locations. Stack hay where you or your neighbors can see it from the house. Lock your gates and grain elevator at all times. Mark your grain or tobacco with numbered or coded non-toxic confetti. This confetti can be mixed in with the grain, hay, and tobacco for identification at point of sale and can be easily removed by mills. Locate and keep a record of your valuable trees. In your record note the tree's diameter at 4½ feet, the height to the first large branch, and the species. Then mark the tree with a stripe of paint or phosphorescent paint if you're worried about appearance. If a theft does occur, your state Hardwood Lumbermen's Association may be able to help you get a description of the logs. Then see if your state Forestry Division can get this information out to mills and log buyers.

One common scam to be aware of is the "borrowed" battery (or gas) scam. It's done this way: A thief locates a farmer's tractor parked in a field near the road. He removes the battery or siphons off gas and then leaves a note advising the farmer how "his battery went dead" or "he ran out of gas," and he "borrowed" the appropriate item from the tractor. The note goes on to say that he would like to pay the farmer back by leaving him two tickets to a sporting event, concert, or similar event. If the farmer uses the "free" tickets he will come home to find that his house has been cleaned out while he was away.

Farm and heavy equipment is unusual, as it often has no Vehicle Identification Number as your car does. If your equipment does not already have an identification number you need to mark it with your own number. You can get a heavy-duty marking tool from your sheriff's department so that you can engrave your machinery. Or use an arc welder if you own one. On farm machinery you should mark all major components and accessories, plus mark the equipment in a hidden location of your choice. That way, your property can be traced even if thieves find and remove your other markings. Be sure to keep records of what equipment was marked where and with what number. You can use the property inventory form in Chapter 7 to keep track of your heavy equipment.

10
Fire Safety
in the Home

The average fire is far more devastating and life threatening than the average burglary. Each year about 7800 people die in home fires. Monetary damages average well over two billion dollars annually. No one wants to think about the possibility of a fire happening, but we all agree it's much better to be safe than sorry. The good news is that you can protect yourself and your family from fire by taking some simple safety steps today. To help you with the basics of home fire safety I have collected the most up-to-date fire safety information available from the National Fire Prevention Association.

The Fire Safety Checklist included with this chapter is to be completed in the same way as the Home Security Survey from Chapter 2 that you've already completed. In addition to the information contained in this chapter, I suggest that you contact your local fire department's fire prevention unit. They have a wealth of fire prevention information that is available to the public free of charge. Most fire prevention units offer free home fire safety checks in which a trained fire prevention officer inspects your home for fire hazards.

GETTING OUT

Even with an early warning from smoke detectors, escaping a fire can be difficult — or impossible. Fires can spread very rapidly, blocking exits and creating dangerous smoky conditions. It is impor-tant that all family members know what to do when the going gets tough. Try to remain calm and do not panic. Focus all of your attention on how to get out safely. Get out and stay out! Go as quickly as possible leaving all possessions behind. And never go back in — you may not get back out. Don't try to save pets or valuables and don't worry about how you look.

If you hear the detector alarm, smell smoke, or suspect a fire, feel the door. If it is hot, try your other exit; if not, slowly open the door but be pre-pared to close it if smoke or flames rush in. Don't try to go through fire unless you have no other course of action available to you. Smoke is your enemy! Even a few breaths of smoke can choke and kill you. If you become trapped in smoke, crawl low, keeping your head down. Smoke and heat rise, so cleaner air is near the floor.

If smoke, heat, or flames block your escape, stay in the room with the door closed. Stuff sheets, blankets, or towels in cracks around the door and around heating and air conditioning vents to keep out smoke and fumes. Use any available water to dampen the seal. Open a window at the top and bottom as long as no smoke is entering the room. Do not break the window. Keeping low, put a wet cloth over your nose and wait at the window, sig-nalling with a bright sheet or flashlight. If there is a phone in the room, call the fire department and tell them where you are and that you are trapped.

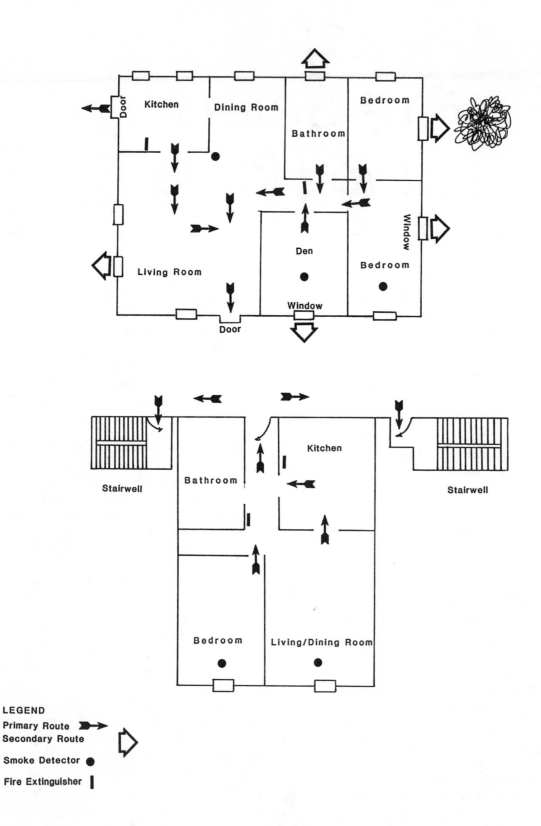

LEGEND

Primary Route

Secondary Route

Smoke Detector ●

Fire Extinguisher ▮

An escape plan map.

If you must jump to safety from the second story or above, climb out the window feet first with your stomach on the sill. Lower yourself as far as possible, then drop, bending your knees when you hit the ground to cushion your fall. If there are children with you, drop them to the ground or to a waiting adult before you jump.

If clothing catches fire, stop where you are, drop to the ground, cover your face with your hands and roll over and over to smother the flames. Running only fans the fire, making it burn more. If you get burned, the best first aid is cool water, which helps prevent further skin damage. Keep running cool water on burns until the pain stops. Salve or butter only traps in the heat. See your doctor right away about any burns that char the skin, blister, look white, or become infected.

EDITH (EXIT DRILLS IN THE HOME) — PLANNING YOUR ESCAPE

If a fire occurs, there's no time for planning. Everyone in the family needs to know in advance the best ways to evacuate the home, so they can move quickly — and without panic — when the alarm sounds. That's why planning and practicing escape plans is so vital. If you move make a new fire escape plan immediately.

The first step is to draw a complete floor plan of your home. Then mark all possible escape routes. Color-code primary exits green; secondary exits yellow; dead ends red. Remember, there should be at least two ways out of every room in case smoke or flames block your primary exit. Make sure you know how to open windows that are designated as escape routes and be sure that they open easily. Decide on a meeting place outside where all family members assemble after exiting the home. This way, you can make sure that everyone is out. Post your fire-escape floor plan in convenient, central areas of the house where guests and baby-sitters can see it.

Once everyone is safely outside at the meeting place, the next step is to call the fire department. Use a neighbor's phone or nearby phone booth. Make sure that all members of the family memorize the fire department's number. It is a good idea when you move into a new home to call the local emergency fire and police departments to find out what number to call in an emergency. Don't assume that 911 is available in your area or that it connects you with the proper jurisdiction.

Consider the special needs of family members. Remember that young, elderly, and disabled persons may need assistance. Locate these individuals as close to an exit as possible, preferably on the ground floor. Train the rest of the family to help them get out in an emergency. Teach your family members to shout "FIRE" to alert the rest of the family. Remind everyone to close doors behind them as they evacuate the home. Closed doors can slow down the spread of fire, smoke, and heat. Assign jobs to family members. Include calling the fire department, circling the house for missing persons, and getting ladders.

Conduct home fire drills often, at least twice a year. When you practice, vary the drill to prepare for different fire situations. Pretend that certain exits are blocked, so that people have to use their second way out. Appoint someone to monitor the drill. This person will sound the alarm and will make the drill more realistic by requiring participants to use their second escape routes or to crawl low in smoke where the air would be cleaner in a real fire. The monitor will also time the drill. Review the drill, discussing any problems in following the escape routes. Correct those problems and practice again.

Before sounding the alarm, the monitor should have everyone go into their bedrooms. This is where most people are when fatal fires occur. Have the monitor sound the alarm. Each person should test the door or knob to see if it's hot. If the door is hot in a real fire you should use your second way out. Everyone should immediately head for the meeting place where the monitor will take a head count. Stop for nothing! In a real fire this is when someone would go to a neighbor's house to call the fire department. If you live in a high-rise building, *never* use the elevator during a fire! Elevators may become trapped between floors or can take you to the fire floor. Use the stairs instead.

By taking the time now to check your home for fire hazards and eliminating them you may never have to put your fire escape plans to the test. Check every room in your house including the basement and garage to identify potential problem areas.

HOME FIRE SAFETY MEASURES

Don't overload electrical outlets or extension cords. Replace broken plugs and all frayed or worn cords. Check regularly for damage. Never yank the cord to unplug an appliance. Grasp the plug and pull it firmly. If appliances aren't working properly, have them repaired. Be sure that all electrical appliances and tools have been listed or labeled by a reputable testing laboratory. Don't block air circulation around TVs, radios, and stereos. Never leave a hot iron unattended.

If a fuse blows in your home, try to determine the cause before turning the power back on. Be sure the new fuse is the correct size and amperage. When using appliances, such as hair dryers, have dry hands and do not stand in water. If the inside of an appliance gets wet, have it serviced. Unplug small appliances when not in use. The outlets in all your bathrooms should be connected to an additional in-line breaker that automatically shuts off power if an appliance is accidentally dropped into the water. If small children are around the house, insert plastic covers into outlets which aren't being used. You can find outlet covers at the hardware store.

Wear tight-fitting sleeves when you cook. Loose garments can catch fire more easily. Do not store things on or over the stove. People have been burned reaching over hot burners. Turn pot handles in so they can't get knocked off the stove or pulled down by small children. Never leave cooking unattended. Fires can start quickly and become serious when no one is watching. Never leave pot holders on the stove. Set the timer so you never forget to turn off the burners or oven when you cook.

Keep your stove and oven clean. Old grease and food particles can catch fire. Be careful when deep-frying or cooking with grease. If a grease fire starts, cover the pan with a lid to smother the flames, and turn off the burner. *Do not* pour water on a grease fire; it only fans the flames. Don't try to thaw frozen pipes with a blowtorch or other open flame. Use hot water or a UL-labeled device for thawing; otherwise a fire could be the result.

Never use a gas range or an oven to heat your kitchen. Any unvented fuel burning appliance is capable of producing deadly levels of carbon monoxide. Don't leave lit oven doors open. Children could burn themselves on the heating elements. Know where the shutoff valve is located and make sure that it is accessible. Also know where the main shutoff valve is located in case you can't turn off the gas at the stove. Have the flexible gas connection (know as a pigtail) checked yearly — old or damaged connections can cause gas leaks.

If a pan catches on fire, do not attempt to carry the pan outside the kitchen. Turn off the heat. Put the pan down on a counter. Put the lid or a cookie sheet completely over the pan to try to smother the flames. Care is needed to avoid burning yourself or catching your clothes on fire while you put the lid on the pan. Cutting off the air supply to the flames should end the fire. Leave the cover on the pan for several minutes and make sure the stove is turned off. If the fire does not go out or if no cover of proper size is available, try pouring baking soda in the pan to put out the flames. You can also use a dry chemical or carbon dioxide fire extinguisher. To use a fire extinguisher you should stand 5 or 6 feet away from the pan to avoid spreading the burning material with the stream from the extinguisher. Remember: Never pour water on a grease fire.

If a fire develops in the oven turn off the heat if it is possible to reach the controls. Try to smother flames by closing – or keeping closed — the oven door. If this does not work, open the oven door a crack and use a dry chemical or carbon dioxide extinguisher, closing the door until the flames are obviously out. When opening the oven door, open it only enough to see any flames or to see that the fire is out.

Use extreme caution with cigarettes! Provide large, deep ashtrays for smokers. Check under couch and chair cushions for smoldering cigarettes and matches before you go to bed (especially after parties). Store lighters and matches up high, where young children can't reach them. Never smoke in bed especially while on medication that might cause drowsiness.

Sleep with your door closed. Consider replacing your bedroom door with either a solid core wood door or a fire resistant door rated for twenty minutes or more. These look like normal interior doors but they could make the difference between life and death if a fire does break out. If your bedroom is located on the second floor or higher have a folding fire escape ladder stored near the window in case your primary escape route is blocked. Have a telephone, flashlight, and fire extinguisher available in your bedroom in case you become trapped. For your kids' rooms you can get window decals that alert rescue personnel to the presence of young children.

Store gasoline and other flammable liquids, such as paint, outside in tight, labelled metal containers. Never use or store flammable liquids near appliances, heat, a pilot light, or while smoking. Do not store gasoline in your home or basement. Never use gasoline on a grill fire. Once the fire has started, use only dry kindling to revive the fire — not charcoal lighter fluid. Move your lawnmower, snowblower, or motorcycle away from gasoline fumes before starting. Cool the motor before you refuel.

Is there a fire hydrant outside of your home? If there should be a fire, firefighters need to be able to hook their hose up to that hydrant. Don't make the firefighters' job more difficult by parking your car in front of the hydrant, blocking access to it. During the winter shovel the snow away from the hydrant. It may save your home, or that of your neighbors.

During the holidays you need to be aware of special fire safety hazards and how to protect yourself. First, choose a fresh Christmas tree. Check the tree by tapping the trunk on the ground a couple of times. A fresh tree won't lose many needles. When you get the tree home, trim the trunk a couple of inches and put it into a non-tip stand. Make sure

it is kept watered and placed away from all exits and sources of heat. All manmade trees should have fire-retardant labels. Make sure all Christmas lights are labeled by a testing laboratory; use only labeled outdoor lights outdoors. Replace any worn sets or those with loose connections. Never put lights on a metal tree and always unplug everything before you leave your home or go to bed. Always put candles in candlesticks before you light them. Never use them in decorations or displays. Keep candles away from curtains or other combustible materials. Never put them in windows or near exits.

HEATING SOURCES

Home heating sources such as fireplaces, wood stoves, portable heaters, and furnaces can be fire hazards if improperly operated and maintained. Listed below are important safeguards for the operation of these common heating sources.

Furnace

Have your furnace checked every year. Be sure all furnace automatic controls and emergency shut-offs are in good condition. Leave furnace work to experts. If the pilot light on a gas furnace goes out, have a qualified specialist relight it. Don't attempt repairs unless you are qualified. Have the repairman check the wall and ceiling near the furniture and flue. If they are hot, additional insulation or clearance may be needed. Check the flue pipes. Are they well supported? Free of holes and clean? Is the chimney solid? No cracks or loose bricks? Uninsulated flue pipes should be at least 18 inches from any combustibles (6 inches for gas furnace). All unused flue openings should be sealed with solid masonry. Keep trash and combustibles away from the heating systems. Don't store hot ashes in the home; take them outside immediately. Keep the basement door closed and make sure the door fits tight.

Wood Stoves

If you have or are considering a wood burning stove, take a few minutes to read this section. It will provide you with some basic information which, combined with your local fire and building codes, can help prevent your family suffering the tragic losses caused by preventable fires.

When selecting a stove, it's best to purchase a new stove from an experienced, reliable dealer. If you purchase a used stove, inspect it thoroughly for cracks and similar defects; also check legs, hinges, door seals, and draft louvers. Although more expensive, plate steel and cast iron stoves last longer and retain heat for longer periods. Check for certification or listings such as Underwriters Laboratory (UL) — it's an indication of successful testing of the stove. Before completing installation, have your local fire department inspect or examine the installation of the stove, clearances, floor and wall protection, and chimney.

When installing your stove be sure to check local fire and building codes. If you're not completely sure of installation requirements or procedures, get a qualified heating contractor experienced with wood-burning stoves to do the job. If you're going to do the job yourself you should start by locating the stove in a place that will be regularly supervised during operation with the stove placed on a fire-resistant base. The stove should be at least 3 feet away from all combustibles, walls, ceilings, and furniture, and there should be a heat-resistant pad under the stove that extends at least 18 inches in all directions. Clearances around the stove and piping are vital considerations because wood burning stoves produce large amounts of radiant heat and most things are capable of absorbing this heat. For example, brick, slate, stone, and cement (less than 8 inches thick) do not offer protection from radiant heat. Clearances to wall can be reduced by using suitable non-combustible material spaced out 1 inch from the wall for ventilation.

The chimney flue should be no more than 25% larger in circumference than the stove pipe, and it should extend at least 3 feet above the highest point where it passes through the roof, and at least 2 feet higher than any portion within 10 feet. A prefabricated metal chimney should be listed as "residential type building heating appliance chimney part" by Underwriters Laboratory or other

recognized laboratory. Stovepipes should run straight and as short as possible — long runs of pipe should be avoided to prevent the formation and fire hazards of creosote. All stovepipe connectors should be of the proper gauge recommended by the National Fire Protection Association (NFPA). Do not pass stovepipe through a combustible wall or floor. Stovepipes may pass through a wall if there is no combustible material within 18 inches of the stovepipe and the opening is closed with a non-combustible material.

Burn only well-seasoned, dry wood to avoid excess creosote buildup. Never use gasoline or kerosene to start a fire — it could cause an explosion. Empty ashes regularly; store them in covered metal containers outside. Inspect and clean the whole system — stove, flue pipes, etc. — each year, at the beginning of the heating season. Check stovepipe and chimney regularly during heating season and clean if necessary.

Fireplaces

Keep a metal screen in front of your fireplace; flying embers can start fires. Use a spark screen or heat resistant glass doors. Clear the area of all combustibles, especially rugs. Store firewood at least 3 feet from the fireplace and burn only dry firewood. Don't use excessive amounts of paper to build roaring fires in fireplaces, and never use flammable liquids to start the fire. It is possible to ignite soot in the chimney by overbuilding the fire.

Never burn charcoal in your fireplace, or in a charcoal broiler or hibachi unit inside. Burning charcoal gives off deadly amounts of carbon monoxide. Don't burn plastic or garbage in the fireplace; plastic can emit toxic fumes and garbage can burn out of control. Never burn painted or pressure-treated wood; the wood can emit toxic fumes. Follow the directions on the package if you use manmade logs. Never break a manmade log apart to quicken the fire.

Be sure no flammable materials hang down from or decorate your mantel. A spark hitting them could ignite these materials and cause a fire. Install a noncombustible hearth. To prevent sparks and burning particles from flying onto nearby rooftops and to keep animals and leaves from entering, install a wire-mesh spark arrester on the top of the chimney. If your house is an older one, the chimney may not be lined with rectangular or spaced fire-clay tiles or round glazed tiles; this can be a fire hazard and should be remedied by a professional.

When you go to bed, be sure your fireplace fire is out. Never leave an open fire unattended. Never close your damper with hot ashes in the fireplace. A closed damper can help hot ashes build up heat to the point where a fire could flare up and ignite the room while you're asleep. Fireplace inserts or stoves in fireplaces will greatly increase chimney temperatures which, in turn, increase the hazard of igniting the wood beams surrounding the chimney in the wall. If your fireplace hasn't been used for some time, have it and the chimney checked and cleaned before using. Check condition of chimney, damper, bricks, etc., at least once a year. Have your chimney cleaned every year, or as often as necessary. (Creosote builds up more quickly if you burn wood or coal.)

Space Heaters

There are two basic types of kerosene heaters, each designed for a particular heating method. Choose the heater that best suits your needs. Convective-type heaters heat the air and circulate it through convective air currents, making these a good choice if the desire is to heat one or more rooms thoroughly. Radiant-type heaters use a reflector to direct heat at people or objects and are useful for specific spot heating.

Heater design should have the fuel tank and fuel feed located below the burner. The heater should have a low center of gravity to minimize the likelihood of accidental tip-over. Check for a safety shut-off device that automatically snuffs out the flame and limits fuel flow if the heater is jarred or tipped. Construction should be of heavy gauge steel with double walls or guards to protect against contact burns. A fuel gauge and siphon pump should be provided to minimize over-filling and fuel spills. Check for a push-button igniter which eliminates the need for matches.

Warnings and cautionary labels relative to hot surfaces, ventilation requirements, fueling, and proximity to combustibles should be prominently posted on the heater. Check the manufacturer's literature for BTU ratings and discuss with the dealer the approximate size unit for the area you wish to heat. Manufacturer's literature should be clear and detailed regarding lighting procedures, fueling, maintenance, and warnings regarding ventilation requirements, potential for burns, and proximity to combustibles. Check for availability of the required 1-K grade of kerosene. Burn only 1-K kerosene. Yellow or colored kerosene may smoke, smell, and interfere with proper wick operation, increasing risk of fire. Use of gasoline, camp-stove fuel, or other fuels may also result in serious fire and health hazards.

Never use fuel-burning appliances without proper vents to the outside. Burning fuel (kerosene, coal, or propane, for example) produces deadly fumes. Be sure your heater is in good working condition. All room heaters need frequent checkups and cleaning. A dirty or neglected heater is a critical fire hazard. Never quicken a fire with kerosene or gasoline. Keep gasoline or other flammable liquids stored outside of the home at all times. Maintain adequate clearance in all directions around space heaters and heating stoves. The surrounding surfaces should not become too hot for your bare hand. Use a screen around stoves or space heaters which have open flames.

If you use an electric heater, be sure your house wiring is adequate. Avoid overloading the circuit and extension cord. Avoid using electric space heaters in bathrooms, and do not touch one when you're wet. Electric space heaters should have an automatic shutoff if the unit is tipped over. When refueling an oil unit, avoid overfilling it. If cold oil is used, it will expand as it warms up inside your home and may cause burner-flooding — this could cause flareups. Don't fill your heater while it is burning or still hot. Keep your children away from space heaters — particularly when they are wearing nightgowns which can ignite if sucked in by a draft created by the heater.

Top: smoke detectors with a built-in escape light provide a lighted escape route in case of fire. Bottom: First Alert®'s Double System smoke and fire detector has a dual ionization sensor for early detection of fast flaming fires and a photoelectronic sensor for early detection of slow smoldering fires. Photos courtesy of BRK Electronics, Div. of the Pittway Corporation.

If you are using an approved, UL-labeled space heater or heating stove in your bedroom, turn off your heater or turn it down low before going to bed. When using a fuel-burning heater in the bedroom, open a window. Ventilation prevents suffocation that can be caused by a heater consuming oxygen. Use only safety listed equipment. If you choose an oil heater, look for the UL label; a gas appliance, the AGA or UL label; or an electric heater, the UL label.

SMOKE DETECTORS

Most fatal residential fires happen between 8 P.M. and 8 A.M., when occupants are more likely to be asleep. Smoke detectors help alert you to a fire before it spreads to you. That way, you've got a chance to get out while there's still time. Smoke detectors are easy to install and maintain. You can purchase one inexpensively at most hardware and department stores.

The National Fire Protection Association has good news and bad news about smoke detectors. The good news is that smoke detector use in the United States rose in 1987 to four-fifths of all homes. The bad news is that in roughly one-third of these homes, the detectors don't work. This means that more than one-fourth of all American homes have non-operational smoke detectors. Power-source problems, especially dead and missing batteries, are the main reason for non-working smoke detectors. Dead batteries probably reflect the lack of regular testing and maintenance, while missing batteries may reflect a wider range of problems, including frustration over nuisance alarms. To combat this problem, the National Fire Protection Association advises that you change the batteries in your smoke detectors each year on the daylight to standard time change.

There are two types of smoke detectors available for residential use: photoelectric and ionization. Photoelectric smoke detectors sense smoldering fires better than the ionization detectors. Photoelectric detectors work by sending a light beam into a sensing chamber. As smoke enters this chamber, light is reflected off the smoke particles. The detector reacts and initiates an alarm when enough particles are present to reflect a predetermined amount of light. Photoelectric detectors react better to smoldering fires because this type of fire produces larger smoke particles which reflect more light.

Fast burning fires are detected more quickly by ionization smoke detectors. They react better than the photoelectric detectors to smaller, less visible smoke particles from rapid burning fires. Ionization detectors use a very small amount of radioactive material to increase the electrical conductivity of air in the detector's chamber. As smoke enters this chamber, the electrical current flowing through the chamber is reduced. A fire alarm is initiated when the reduction drops below a predetermined level. Your safest bet is a combination of photoelectric and ionization detectors, installed where each is needed most.

Both photoelectric and ionization smoke detectors come in battery-powered and house current-powered models. Smoke detectors which operate on batteries tend to take less time and fewer tools to install. Once the battery-powered unit is mounted,

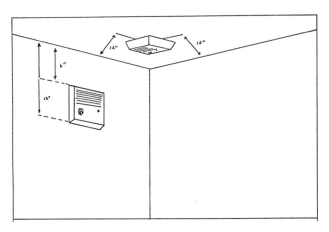   

Place smoke detectors 6 to 12 inches from the ceiling. From left to right: heavy-duty, multi-purpose fire extinguisher, dry chemical fire extinguisher, portable halon fire extinguisher. Photos courtesy of BRK Electronics, Div. of the Pittway Corporation.

the owner simply slips in the battery, tests the unit, and the job is done. In about a year the detector will begin to emit "beeps" every minute or so, and will keep this up for a week or longer, to tell the owner that the battery has begun to fall below a safe minimum of power and should be replaced.

Smoke detectors that operate on household electric current have the power they need to operate as long as there is current in the circuit to which they are connected. However, installation is somewhat more complicated. In the event of a power failure, detectors will become inoperable unless the detector has a battery backup. In most regions this is a rare event, but if power outages are frequent where you live, you might think twice about depending only on this type of smoke detector.

Installing Smoke Detectors

Where and how you install your smoke detectors is very important because an improperly positioned detector may not function properly. You must also be careful to position your detectors so that your entire home is adequately covered. Before you buy a detector make sure that it is UL-listed. Read the instructions enclosed with your smoke detector carefully to find out exactly how and where to install it.

As a rule of thumb you should position a smoke detector on the ceiling just outside each bedroom

and in the escape routes of your home. You should sleep with your bedroom door closed. It limits drafts, holds back toxic gases and slows the spread of a fire. But make sure you can hear the detector in the hall loud and clear. If there is any doubt, or if you smoke, place an additional detector inside your bedroom. If you have a multi-level home, install a detector on every floor. Place a detector at the top of each stairwell. Smoke rises easily through stairwells. Hallways longer than 30 feet should have a detector at each end. In the basement mount the detector on the ceiling at the top of the stairway, not near a furnace exhaust.

Keep detectors away from cooking fumes, fireplaces, wood stoves, and smoking areas. Install the detector at least 3 feet from the nearest air-supply register, window, or door where drafts could prevent smoke from reaching the detector. Smoke detectors should be mounted on the ceiling at least 6 inches from the wall, or on a wall 6 to 12 inches from the ceiling. Don't place detectors on uninsulated exterior walls or ceilings. Temperature extremes can affect batteries. Because cobwebs and dust can impair a detector's sensitivity, vacuum your detectors at least once a year. Never paint a smoke detector.

There is a product on the market from the Eveready Battery Co. called the Eversafe Child Locater. This device combines a smoke detector, which mounts on the ceiling in your child's room, with a flashing red locater light, which is attached to the bedroom window with suction cups. When the smoke detector goes off it sends a signal to the window locator which activates a flashing red light to alert rescue personnel to the presence of children in that room. In addition to children's rooms the light can also be used for the elderly, handicapped, or other family member who might need extra help. The only limitation is that the locater light must be installed within 30 feet of the smoke detector.

HEAT DETECTORS

There are two different types of heat detectors available. The first is the rate-of-rise detector which senses a specific temperature increase over a fixed time period. When the detector senses this change an alarm is initiated. The second type of detector is a fixed temperature detector that has a preset upper temperature limit. An alarm is initiated when the room temperature exceeds the detector's limit. Heat detectors are no substitute for smoke detectors.

FIRE EXTINGUISHERS

A portable fire extinguisher can save lives and property by putting out small fires or containing them until the fire department arrives. Portable extinguishers are not designed to fight a large or spreading fire. Even against small fires, they are useful only under the right conditions: An extinguisher must be large enough for the fire at hand. It must be available and in working order, fully charged. The operator must know how to use the extinguisher quickly, without taking time to read directions during an emergency. The operator must be strong enough to lift and operate the extinguisher. There should be an extinguisher on each floor placed along your escape routes. They should allow for unobstructed access to all family members.

When operating an extinguisher, remember "PASS — Pull, Aim, Squeeze, Sweep." Pull the tab if there is one, aim the extinguisher at the base of the fire, squeeze the nozzle to activate it, and sweep it back and forth. Always keep your back to an exit, so that you can escape quickly if the fire does not go out. Protect yourself at all times! Stay low. Avoid breathing the heated smoke and fumes or the extinguishing agent.

There are four main types of home fire extinguishers: water, dry chemical, carbon dioxide, and halon. For all-around protection, have an ABC rated dry chemical (ammonium phosphate type) extinguisher on every floor of your house. This is the most versatile unit and the least expensive to buy and maintain.

- Water (cools and soaks): For ordinary combustible fires, not flammable liquids or electrical fires.

- Dry chemical multi-purpose type (smothers): For flammable liquids, electrical fires, and ordinary combustibles.

- Carbon dioxide (smothers): For flammable liquids and electrical fires, not for ordinary combustibles.

- Halon (chemical reaction): For ordinary combustibles, flammable liquids, and electrical fires.

Underwriters Laboratories (UL) classifies three kinds of household fires:

- Class A fires involve common solid combustibles: wood, paper, fabric, rubber, and plastics.

- Class B fires are fueled by the vapor-air mixture that forms above flammable liquids such as grease, oil, gasoline, tar, paints, and cleaning solvents.

- Class C fires are sparked by electricity but feed on class A or B materials.

FIRE ESCAPE LADDERS

Homes with bedrooms more than one story off the ground should be equipped with fire escape ladders so that occupants of those rooms can use the window as an escape route in case the stairwell is blocked. The best type of fire escape ladder is the portable type which installs easily, is inexpensive and inconspicuous. Such a ladder should be made of chain or steel cable and fitted with spacers or "standoffs" to keep the rungs away from the wall for toe and handholds. One type of ladder requires no installation. It is kept in a box out of the way, then quickly taken out and hung from the window frame when needed. Other types are anchored permanently near the window.

To use the ladder drop the rungs out of the window and hook the frame over the sill. Climb sideways out the window, straddling the sill so that you can see the ladder beneath you and place your foot on a convenient rung. Have only one person climb down the fire ladder at a time. The first person down should hold the bottom of it steady for the next person. To carry a small child, have him wrap his arms and legs securely around you, then climb down the fire ladder face to face with him. Place an infant in an infant carrier and climb down the fire ladder the same way. Make sure that you practice using your escape ladder so that you can move quickly in case of an emergency.

HOME SPRINKLER SYSTEMS

Sprinkler systems could prevent thousands of fire tragedies, especially in one- and two-family dwellings, where four-fifths of all fire deaths and more than $4 billion in property damage occurred in 1988. With a goal to save more lives, as well as to operate within tightened fire-protection budgets, hundreds of U.S. communities have passed residential fire sprinkler laws. While only about twenty-eight cities and counties in the United States require sprinklers in one- and two-family homes, laws requiring them in multi-family dwellings are much more common. Contributing to the increasing popularity of these ordinances is the fact that modern fire sprinkler systems are more economical than in the past.

Until recently only iron pipe was used to carry water from the main supply to the sprinkler heads. Now less-expensive copper, lightweight steel, and plastic CPVC or polybutylene pipe has been approved for sprinkler systems. Residential sprinklers use water from the household supply, another factor which makes them more economical than

commercial systems, which often require dedicated water supplies. Designed with small water supplies in mind, residential sprinklers are more sensitive to heat than standard sprinklers, and are triggered in the early stages of a fire when the fire can be controlled with less water. When the temperature reaches 165° F., only those sprinkler heads closest to the fire open to spray water on it.

Sprinkler heads designed for residences are smaller and more attractive than commercial heads, also adding to their popularity. Residential sprinklers can be ceiling or wall mounted, and are available in flush and recess-mounted styles. Fire sprinkler systems can be installed in newly constructed buildings or existing homes. A sprinkler system for a typical single-family home with a good municipal water supply costs the homeowner between $1500 and $42,500, according to the National Fire Sprinkler Association. For a home under construction, it usually takes two to three installers a day to a day and a half to put in the sprinkler piping, and another day for the fire inspector to test the system. Whether installed in new or existing homes, sprinklers often mean homeowner's insurance discounts. Carriers reduce premiums 10 to 20% when a home has an automatic fire sprinkler system.

For more information on sprinkler systems contact: National Fire Protection Association, Batterymarch Park, Quincy, MA 02269 (617) 770-3000 and National Fire Sprinkler Association, Inc., Robin Hill Corporate Park, Route 22, P.O. Box 1000, Patterson, NY 12563 (914) 878-4200.

BRUSH FIRE PROTECTION

As more people build beyond the reach of city services in outlying areas they become vulnerable to wildfires. Homeowners in such areas should provide as much of their own defense as they can. If you live in a remote, densely vegetated area — even if you're within reach of city or county services — try taking these steps now to make your home easier to defend and more likely to survive a wildfire.

Clear combustible weeds at least 30 feet away from structures, 10 feet in from roads, and 5 feet from driveways. Stack firewood at least 30 feet from the house or other structures. Nothing that could fuel a wildfire should remain within this close-in belt. Your house should be set back far enough from property lines so that you can maintain a 30-foot wide perimeter that is fuel-free. Drought-resistant and naturally fire-resistant foliage plants spaced well apart will discourage the spread of fire along ground to the house and up to the tree canopy. Plant the yard within 100 feet of the house with ground covers from the chart below. Add shrubs and trees for accent but plant them no closer than 30 feet from the house and no less than 18 feet apart so that a fire cannot jump easily from one to the next and then to the house. The plants listed on the chart all thrive in warm, arid regions where brush fires occur. If you live elsewhere, contact your local garden center or nursery for advice on what plants you should use.

Post your address at the street side of the driveway, using house numbers that contrast with the background and are at least 4 inches high. For fire engine access your driveway should be at least 9 feet wide, with no grades exceeding 16%, and have 13-foot vertical clearance, and 40-foot radius or "T" turnaround. Any bridges should be strong enough to support a fire engine (40,000 pounds).

Your house should have a reservoir of at least 2500 gallons of water for fire fighting (a swimming pool holds about 20,000). You should have a backup electrical generator to power your well or pool water pump in case of power failure so that you can access your water supply to hose down your house. Fire officials don't recommend overhead sprinklers, flooders, and soakers unless they are hooked up to an independent water and power source. The best way to protect your roof is to install fire-retardant roofing material such as tile or composite roofing material.

Using foam concentrate to protect your shake roof is also available. One part foam concentrate mixed with 200 parts water produces "wet water." Ordinary water beads up and runs off quickly. Suspended in a bubble mass, wet water drains from the roof more slowly (1 to 2 hours), greatly extending evaporation time. It also penetrates the wood more deeply, keeping the roof damp for up to 12 hours. The biodegradable foam requires no cleanup and won't damage plants. The Brushfire Hydrant Co. manufactures a residential foam dispensing system. It uses a 3- to 5-horsepower gas-fired pump and requires an independent water supply of at least 800 gallons (a hot tub holds 500 gallons); this is enough for a 2000 square foot roof and adjacent trees. Cost of the system is about $1500. For more information contact Brushfire Hydrant Co., 1818-B Mount Diablo Blvd., Walnut Creek, CA 94596 (415) 932-5080.

Plantings for Wildfire Country

Type of Plant	Plant Name
Ground Covers	Rosea ice plant Jelly beans White clover Trailing gazania Rye grass Trailing African daisy Kentucky bluegrass
Shrubs	Oleander Toyon Elephant bush Common lilac Blue chalksticks
Trees	Gum trees California pepper Carob California laurel Cottonwood

FIRE RATINGS

Common coverings for walls and ceilings are grouped into four classes by "flame-spread ratings." Established by the National Bureau of Standards and national testing laboratories, these ratings are based on a comparison of the materials' burning speeds with those of asbestos (specified as Zero) and dry red oak (100). Class A and B materials are recommended by fire-prevention experts for halls, stairways, kitchens, and utility rooms. Except in these locations, Class C materials may be used to cover small areas, but not an entire room. Class D materials are unsuitable for home use; they do not meet minimum standards of the federal government. Manufacturers of building materials mark many of their products, including acoustical ceiling tiles and wall paneling, with flame-spread ratings.

Fire Ratings for Building Materials

Flame-Spread rating	Wall or Ceiling Material
Class A (0-25) — Excellent	Masonry Glass Plaster Type X gypsum wallboard Flame-resistant acoustical ceiling tile Fire-rated fiberboard Asbestos-cement board
Class B (26-75) — Good	Most gypsum wallboard Pressure-treated wood
Class C (76-200) — Fair	Hardboard Particle board Most plywood Most solid wood, 1 inch thick Most acoustical ceiling tile Fire-rated wall paneling
Class D (over 200) — poor	Unrated fiberboard Unrated wall paneling

FIRE SAFETY CHECKLIST

Date _____

YES NO Check (✓) the appropriate box

Electrical Hazards

☐ ☐ Does every room have enough electrical outlets to avoid the need for multiple attachment plugs?

☐ ☐ Does your home have special circuits for heavy-duty appliances such as ranges and washing machines?

☐ ☐ Do you use fuses no larger than 15 amps for your household lighting circuits?

☐ ☐ If you use extension cords, are they in good condition, and are they out in the open rather than under rugs, over hooks, or through door openings and partitions?

☐ ☐ Is there ample air circulation around your television set and stereo equipment?

☐ ☐ Are all your electrical appliances, small and large, listed by Underwriters Laboratories?

☐ ☐ Do your cooking appliances and electric iron have heat-limit controls?

☐ ☐ Are the motors of your large appliances and power tools cleaned and oiled regularly?

☐ ☐ Do you refrain from wrapping cords around a hot appliance?

☐ ☐ Do you ever use more than one high-wattage appliance on an outlet at a time?

Household Hazards

☐ ☐ Are your kitchen stove, oven, and rotisserie kept clean of grease?

☐ ☐ Do you always place rags covered with oil or paint in metal cans after you use them?

☐ ☐ If you store paints, solvents, waxes, etc., are they in tightly closed cans, away from heat, flames, and sparks?

☐ ☐ Do you use gasoline, benzene, or any other flammable fluid for cleaning clothes, furnishings, or floors?

☐ ☐ Is it a rule in your home never to start a fire in a fireplace, stove, or furnace with a flammable liquid?

☐ ☐ Do you keep ashes from fireplace, stove, or furnace in a metal container away from combustible materials, and dispose of them frequently?

☐ ☐ If you have a woodworking shop, do you clean up scrap wood and sawdust after each job?

Heating Hazards

☐ ☐ Do you have the entire heating system (including burner, flue pipes, chimney, and vents) inspected, cleaned, and repaired by a professional service each year?

☐ ☐ Is your heating system a type listed by Underwriters Laboratories or, if gas-fired, by the American Gas Association Laboratories?

☐ ☐ Is your inside basement door at the head of the stairs well fitted and kept closed at night?

☐ ☐ Have you eliminated all flue pipes and vent connectors passing through closets, floors, ceilings, and attic?

☐ ☐ Are the ceiling, walls, and partitions around all parts of the heating system protected by noncombustible material adequately separated from the heat source?

☐ ☐ Are room heaters located apart from curtains, furniture, and clothing?

☐ ☐ Are all room heaters placed on a steady, level foundation?

☐ ☐ Do room heaters have ample air circulation around them?

Smoking Hazards

☐ ☐ Have you made it a house rule never to smoke in bed or while dozing on the sofa?

☐ ☐ Are there plenty of good-sized noncombustible ashtrays in areas where smoking is permitted?

☐ ☐ Are tobacco ashes disposed of in their own separate containers?

☐ ☐ After having company over, do you check the floor and your furniture for smoldering butts or ashes?

☐ ☐ Do you keep matches and lighters out of reach of small children?

☐ ☐ Has every member of your household been instructed never to use matches or candles to light the way in the attic, closets, or basement?

Smoke Detectors

☐ ☐ Do you have a smoke detector installed outside of each bedroom and at least one on each floor?

☐ ☐ Are your smoke detectors properly installed?

☐ ☐ Do you change the batteries at least once a year?

☐ ☐ Do you frequently test your detectors and clean them at least once a year?

☐ ☐ Do you sleep with your bedroom door closed at night?

☐ ☐ Can you hear the detector with your bedroom door closed?

Fire Extinguishers

☐ ☐ Do you have fire extinguishers in the kitchen and workshop and at least one on each floor?

☐ ☐ Are they accessible to every family member?

☐ ☐ Do you and your family know the proper way to use a fire extinguisher?

☐ ☐ Are your extinguishers fully charged and checked often?

☐ ☐ Do you have the right kind of extinguisher for the type of fire hazards present?

Escape Planning

☐ ☐ Have you drawn a complete floor plan of your home?

☐ ☐ Did you mark all primary and secondary escape routes on the plan?

☐ ☐ Have you specified an outside meeting place?

☐ ☐ Does every family member know at least two ways out of their bedroom, and from each floor?

☐ ☐ Does your family regularly practice your fire escape plan?

☐ ☐ Does every member of your family know how to call the fire department?

11
Security
for Your Car

Each year, more than a million vehicles are stolen in the United States — about one every thirty seconds. During 1988, vehicle theft in the United States increased 11%, 13% in larger cities. The chance of your car being stolen is 1 in 169, and again, that figure is higher for those who live in larger cities. Further, because auto theft is a highly lucrative business, this trend is expected to continue according to the National Automobile Theft Bureau (NATB).

According to the FBI's "Uniform Crime Report, 1988 Crime in the United States" the top ten cities (based on crimes per person) hardest hit by motor vehicle thefts in 1988 were: (1) Newark, NJ (2) Boston (3) Detroit (4) New Haven, CT (5) Bridgeport, CT (6) Pittsburgh (7) Providence, RI (8) Dallas (9) San Diego (10) Jersey City, NJ. The ten cities least touched by vehicle theft in 1988 according to the FBI were: (1) Sandy, UT (2) Watertown, SD (3) Green Bay, WI (4) Aberdeen, SD (5) Pocatello, ID (6) Cheyenne, WY (7) Sioux Falls, SD (8) Bennington, VT (9) Colchester, VT (10) Juneau, AK.

The easiest method of stealing a vehicle is to have its keys. Forty percent of all stolen vehicles had the keys left in the ignition. With a key cutter, key blanks, and the key identification number, obtained from the dealer, manufacturer, or off your spare key, a thief can make his own key. Even without a key thieves can use a common dent puller to remove the ignition lock, and then use a

screwdriver to start the car. A pro can get inside, remove the lock, and start your car in less than a minute.

If you're prone to locking your keys in the car then the Credit Card Key from American Consumer Products, Inc. is for you. The Credit Card Key is a plastic, metal-reinforced emergency key that is slim, flexible, and can fit in the space provided for credit cards. Metal keys are not only bulky and tend to tear up your wallet but are also easily found if you should lose your wallet. The Credit Card Key is not as likely to be found by someone going through your wallet. It is available from most locksmiths and hardware stores.

A new problem, especially for GM cars, is the removal or breaking of the steering column. A thief simply breaks away the steering column housing to expose the vehicle's ignition rods. The car is then started by pushing or pulling on the exposed ignition rods. Towing is another popular auto theft method. Car thieves disguised as legitimate tow truck operators steal vehicles by simply hooking up and towing away desired vehicles. Most people, including the police, don't give a second thought to a tow truck towing a vehicle away.

PREVENTION TIPS

The first and most important prevention measure is always to lock your doors and roll the windows up tight. Don't hide spare keys — they can be found — and never leave your keys in an unattended car, even when running a quick errand. Each year 80% of all stolen vehicles are unlocked, and 40% have the keys left in the ignition. If you must leave your car parked for a prolonged period of time, remove the rotary cap or coil wire or some other necessary part of the engine so that it cannot be driven off.

If you can, keep your car parked safely in the garage. If you don't have a garage, the driveway is the next best parking spot. Always remember to lock the car before you leave it. When away from home, park in well-lighted areas with pedestrian traffic. Thieves don't like working in spots where they are clearly visible. Turn your wheels sharply toward the curb, set the parking brake, and leave manual transmission cars in gear when parking, making it difficult for thieves to tow your car.

Never attach a tag with your name and address to your key ring. If the keys are lost or stolen, the tag will lead the thief directly to your car — and your home. Instead use only your last name and a PO box number or your work address (unless your work keys are on the ring). When parking your car in an attended parking lot leave only your ignition key. Don't leave your house key, which could easily be copied.

Do not leave anything with your name or address inside your car such as vehicle registration papers, vehicle inspection forms, or insurance papers. A thief can use the information contained in these forms to find out where you live. Thieves often steal cars from shopping centers or commuter parking lots. They then obtain your address off the registration or other paperwork, then drive to your home while you're still shopping or at work and burglarize it. You should also hide garage door openers from prying eyes. Thieves look for cars which contain garage openers. They steal the car then drive to the house. Once there they use the opener to open the garage so that they can park inside. This way they don't attract attention while they break into the house unseen.

Don't leave your car running unattended on cold winter mornings. Many car thieves cruise neighborhoods on the lookout for vehicles that are left alone while being "warmed up." To prevent this from happening to you, lock up your car while it's warming up — make sure you have a spare key before doing this. Several auto security systems have remote controlled engine starters available as an option. Remote starters allow you to start your car without ever leaving the house. The vehicle's doors remain locked and the security systems armed until you're ready to go.

Large shopping malls are frequently hangout spots for local teenagers, especially on Friday and Saturday nights. Movie theaters, video arcades, and fast food restaurants are the most frequented areas, avoid them if possible. I recommend that you avoid these areas at night and on the weekends. If you want to go to a movie on a weekend pick an early show that gets out before dark. This way you don't have to fight the crowds and your car will be a lot safer.

Shopping mall and commuter bus parking lots are very attractive targets for auto thieves because of the large number of vehicles to choose from and the fact that they can easily blend in without being noticed. To protect your car always try to park in lighted areas near store entrances or the bus/train stop. Always lock your car and roll up the windows. Lock up all valuables that you're not going to take with you in the trunk. It's also a good idea to turn your car's wheels to the side; this makes it more difficult for your car to be towed away. Don't forget to straighten the wheels out before you leave, otherwise you're likely to hit the car parked next to you.

When returning to your car be on the lookout for people watching or following you. Check around the car and look into the back seat before getting in. If you find that the car has been tampered with (i.e., door ajar, window broken out, etc.) don't approach the car, get security or the police immediately. If you think you're being followed or that someone is watching you, don't go to your car. Instead return to the mall and contact security or the police. Once an officer arrives have him escort you to your car. Make sure to give him a complete description of the person before leaving so that they're aware of the situation.

To protect your motorcycle, park only in well-lighted and well-traveled locations. If possible, chain the bike to a fixed object and/or chain the tires to the frame (this will prevent the tires from being removed and it will also prevent the bike from being operated or pushed away). The Kryptonite Company makes a motorcycle lock specifically designed to lock the tire to the frame. You can also remove the coil wire to disable the bike so that it cannot be started. Don't leave any valuables on the bike or in non-locking saddle bags. Carry your helmet with you or secure it in a locking saddle bag. Engrave all unmarked parts of your bike, especially add-ons that are not standard equipment. You should also take photographs of the bike to help the police if it's ever stolen.

When buying a new car, especially from a private party, make sure that the title papers and Vehicle Identification Number (VIN) match. The VIN is located on a metal plate in the lower left corner of the windshield. If there is any question, contact your local police department. When you're selling your car don't let strangers take the car for a "test drive" unaccompanied. Many such prospective "buyers" never return with the car.

There are several successful auto theft prevention programs operating in the U.S.: C.A.T. — Combat Auto Theft and H.E.A.T. — Help Eliminate Auto Theft. Both programs are essentially the same with the only major difference being the name. Here's the way it works. A vehicle owner voluntarily registers his car with the local police. The owner signs a waiver that if the car is being operated between certain hours, usually midnight and 6 A.M., the police are requested to stop it and question the occupants. Once the car owner is registered, he is given a colored decal to place inside the rear window. The sticker basically says, "We have joined Anytown Police Department Operation HEAT" (or CAT as the case may be). A card with the participant's name, address, phone number, and vehicle information will be kept by the police. The owner will also be given a wallet-size identification card to carry when he drives the car.

The police, seeing the vehicle operated between the target hours, may stop the vehicle and question the occupants. The waiver by the vehicle owner allows them to stop, without any cause. With the publicity being given to these programs it is expected that auto thieves will become more selective with the cars they steal. Vehicle owners who enroll in the program ought to experience a reduction in the rate of auto thefts in their group. The objective is not to catch auto thieves (but, it does), but to prevent the theft.

If your car is ever stolen or broken into, inform the police immediately! Quick action by you may not only aid in the recovery of your vehicle, but prevent its use for illegal purposes. Many stolen cars are often used in the commission of another crime. Keep a copy of your vehicle registration with you at all times. This way you can give the police complete information if your car should be stolen. It doesn't do much good to report your car stolen if you can't provide a complete description and license plate number.

It takes a thief about thirty seconds to steal your car stereo. Smash a window, rip the dash apart, remove the stereo, and they're gone. Why tempt thieves with all that great-looking gear when, with a little extra effort and money, you can hide all your stereo components — cassette deck, CD player, speakers, and equalizers, as well as cellular phones and radar detectors — so they're out of sight. Concealment of car stereos makes a lot of sense. After all, nobody wants his or her car, truck, or van damaged and its contents stolen, regardless of whether the sound system cost $200 or $2000. The trick is to camouflage your components and make it look like you haven't touched a thing. Concealed systems range from the simple — the radio hidden by a piece of black cardboard taped onto the dash — to the sublime — CD players hidden inside flip-down ashtrays, and speakers hidden behind flip panels.

The easiest way to begin building a concealed system is to buy components designed for concealment. Several security-minded auto sound suppliers make in-dash radios with pull-off or fold-up front panels. Pioneer's KEX-M800, which retails for about $600, has a detachable control face. The KEX-M800 is unique in that you can remove the entire face, buttons and all, with just the touch of a button. This leaves a blank space on your dash and the face piece easily fits into your shirt pocket. No longer will you have to pull out the entire tape player to prevent it from being stolen. Stereo components with built-in concealment features are also available from Aiwa and Metrosound.

A product called Lasso Lock which retails for about $40 has been developed to help secure your car stereo equipment. The Lasso Lock consists of a solid brass, stainless steel-jacketed lock that slips into your cassette deck. The cut-resistant PVC-coated braided steel cable is then looped around your steering wheel. Your car stereo cannot be forcibly removed without destroying its resale value. The lock won't harm your stereo, and it is adjustable to fit all side-loading cassette decks.

Never leave your vehicle's sunroof open as it can be easily removed allowing access into your car. To prevent a thief from using a coat hanger to open your doors, install tapered interior door lock buttons. Install locking lug nuts on all your wheels to help prevent them from being stolen. Consider using a locking gas cap to prevent gas siphoning. If your hood can be opened from the outside, you should install a locking hood latch.

To further protect your vehicle you can install a fuel cut-off switch. A fuel cut-off switch is a manual switch which closes the fuel valve. When the valve is closed, the car will run only a short distance before stopping and the vehicle will not restart. Or you can install an ignition kill switch. A manual ignition kill switch prevents electrical current from reaching the coil or distributor. Tech Lock Security Products manufactures a tamper-proof starter interrupt system that can be retrofitted on any foreign or domestic vehicle equipped with a starter motor solenoid. Their interrupt system cannot be bypassed, hot wired, or black boxed.

The Magic-Touch from 4-M Industries is an encoded ignition kill system, which uses a number combination to prevent unauthorized use. You have to enter the proper number combination be-

fore the unit will allow the car to start and a warning siren sounds if the wrong code is entered. The unit can be assigned temporary codes for valet parking, auto mechanics, or others who operate the car in your absence.

A "J-Bar" steering wheel lock bar is used to prevent your vehicle from being driven if a thief manages to get it started. The "J-Bar" steering wheel lock bar locks through the steering wheel and the brake pedal. This prevents the steering wheel from being turned and the brake applied. This device is normally only used in high crime areas or with frequently stolen models. Another option is to remove the steering altogether every time you leave the car. For protection against steering column breaking, a steering column lock has been designed specifically for GM cars. This lock prevents thieves from starting the car by protecting the steering column housing.

Another relatively new auto theft prevention product is window glass etching. Window glass etching allows you to permanently etch your Vehicle Identification Number (VIN) onto each window. Window etching discourages professional car thieves who steal cars for resale, as they would have to replace all the car's windows. A window glass etching kit is available from Security Etch International, Costa Mesa, CA.

VEHICLE SECURITY SYSTEMS

Security systems are the ultimate protection available for your vehicle. They're also the most expensive with basic systems starting at $200 and up. But with average new car prices starting at $10,000 or more and luxury cars selling in the $40-$50,000 range you can justify spending several hundred dollars to protect this kind of investment. Having an alarm system is, of course, no guarantee against theft but without protection the odds are not in your favor, and they're getting worse all the time.

The primary function of any alarm system is to scare off the intruder and summon help. In the case of a car alarm, this is accomplished by triggering a very loud siren. A good alarm system will activate if someone tampers with the doors, windows,

The installer-friendly RF-06 is a basic but unique system from AutoPage. The RF-06 is a passive, true last-door arming system, which can also be remote controlled. It is complete with siren and vehicle control unit and is easily upgraded with plug-in accessory modules. Photo courtesy of AutoPage, Inc.

The RF-09 is AutoPage's most sophisticated security system. RF-09 features a started disabler, programmed automatic re-arming, a pulsating alarm output for light or horn, two positive and two negative trigger inputs for protecting doors as well as all other openings, a 120 decibel siren, three separately adjustable resonant sensor inputs, and remote power door lock actuation. Photo courtesy of AutoPage, Inc.

hood, trunk, or if the car is lifted for towing. The alarm should activate a siren, horn, lights, or all three and be loud enough to be clearly distinguished from other street noises. The alarm should continue to sound even if the thief shuts the door. The alarm should have a timer that will shut it off after a certain number of minutes if the alarm sounds accidentally and you're not around to turn it off. It must also have a rest feature, so that the thief can't simply wait for it to stop blaring, then come back and try again, undisturbed.

The number and types of triggering devices determine how well your car will be protected. The doors, hood, and trunk can be protected by pin switches, the small devices that turn on your car's interior light when you open a door. When connected to your alarm system, pin switches tell the alarm control module whether a door is open or closed. Pin switches are a very effective first line of defense for your alarm system. But they can't stop someone from smashing a window and climbing in your car. You need an audio discriminator which "listens" for the characteristic high-frequency sounds of glass tampering. When it hears the sound of metal on glass or the cracking of glass, the

siren will be triggered. A motion detector will trigger the alarm when someone forcefully bumps your car or attempts to jack it up. Inside the module is a delicately balanced switch that turns the alarm on when it is moved.

If a persistent thief does manage to break through your defenses and attempts to drive off with your car, an ignition cut-off circuit will stop him dead in his tracks. This feature completely disconnects your car's ignition system whenever the alarm is triggered. Other alarm options available to increase your level of protection include relays to flash your lights and sound your car's horn and paging systems that transmit an alert to you via a pocket pager. When your pager goes off, you can immediately call the police.

Another very important consideration is how easy the alarm is to use. Obviously the alarm can only do its job when it's turned on, so passive arming systems are most desirable. As soon as the last door is closed, the alarm system will arm itself automatically. The alternative is to manually turn it on by flipping a switch or turning a key-switch outside your vehicle, usually mounted on the fender. How convenient the system is to disarm is equally important. When armed, many systems have a door-entry delay of two to thirty seconds before the system is triggered. You disarm the system by manually turning it off or by starting your car during the delay interval. More sophisticated systems now use a small remote-control transmitter that lets you disarm the system from outside your car before you open the door.

If you install an ultrasonic alarm in a vehicle, mount the system below the dashboard, then lean the car seat forward when you leave the car. The first thing that a car thief will do is move the seat back to get in the car, and that will set off the alarm. To discourage thieves who manage to bypass your vehicle's perimeter security you can add an electronic shock seat to your auto security system. This device from Skandia Insurance Co., Sweden is connected to the driver's seat and delivers 9000 volts to the thief who ignores the warning signal. You should also install a solar panel on the dashboard. Plug the solar panel into the cigarette lighter so that during the day it trickle-charges the vehicle's battery. That way you know that the battery has enough power to operate the alarm and start the car.

Car owners with cellular telephones can now add a security system interface unit onto their existing auto alarm system which allows the unit to call them anywhere at any time the system is tripped. Users can also call their vehicles from any telephone and control nine different functions, including arming, disarming, panic, and sensor checks. This is a very useful device especially for owners who frequently leave their vehicles parked for extended periods in such places as airports, commuter park-n-rides and downtown. Alpine Electronics of America's 8316 Communicator to my knowledge is the only cellular interface unit currently being manufactured for auto security systems.

There are several portable vehicle security alarms on the market that provide a certain amount of protection for your car. The two that I am aware of are the Security Bear from Rabbit Systems, Inc. and the CarCop from Kansas Microtech. While these alarms do not have all of the features of more expensive installed systems they do have several advantages. First they are portable, you can easily move them from one car to another. They are a little less expensive, from about $80 (for the Security Bear) to $130 (for the CarCop). Your basic installed systems usually start at about $70 (on sale) and up (most systems costing well over $200).

Both of these alarms are battery-powered, self-contained systems with sensor, siren, and controls all together in one package. In the case of the "Security Bear," the package is designed to look like a teddy bear. You anchor him to the seat with his plastic-covered steel restraining cable. Once activated, the bear sits silently waiting for something, such as a door or window opening, to trigger his built-in sensor. Once triggered, the internal 110 decibel siren sounds, emitting an ear-piercing wail. The CarCop hangs from the window of your car. Turn on its power and roll the window up. Ten seconds after you close and lock the door, CarCop activates itself, chirping once to tell you it's armed. Three-way sensitive setting lets you decide the amount of vibration that will trigger the alarm. Even if an intruder shuts off the power switch, the alarm continues to sound. Because it's portable, CarCop can protect all your vehicles by simply removing and remounting.

As with home security systems faux key pads and warning stickers are available and very inexpensive. The imitation key pads are installed on the dashboard or console and are designed to make a thief think the car is protected by a security system. You place the faux alarm warning window stickers on your vehicle in the hopes that a potential thief will think that you have an alarm system.

HOMING DEVICES

Electronic homing devices are a fairly new and promising tactic in auto theft prevention. It works this way. A small electronic homing device connected to your vehicle's electrical system is installed in a hidden location by a professional installer. Not even the owner knows the exact location of the unit. Each unit is programmed with a unique code number which is then given only to the owner. After installation you simply forget about the unit, there is nothing to remember to turn on and off. If the vehicle is ever stolen you call the local police and provide them with your vehicle's code number. The police will broadcast a radio signal of your code number from radio towers situated around the area. Upon receiving this coded radio signal the homing device in your car is automatically activated and it begins to send out a signal. A police vehicle, equipped with a programmable tracking unit that picks up your vehicle's signal is sent to search for your vehicle. The police follow the signal until they find your car, which usually takes only fifteen to thirty minutes. This allows the police to recover the vehicle quicker than ever before and also increases the chances of making an arrest.

Where this system is in operation there has been a drastic reduction in auto thefts. The main drawback is that this system is only in place in Massachusetts and southern Florida with expansion planned in the near future to California, Illinois, and New York. Currently the main manufacturer of electronic homing devices is the LoJack Company. Another alternative is the Intercept security system from Code-Alarm Inc. For this system to work, a vehicle must have a cellular telephone. When an alarm is triggered, the telephone automatically dials a monitoring station operated by Code-Alarm which reports the car's location, which is determined by a receiver installed in the car. Central station operators alert the police only when the car's exact location is pinpointed. Should Code-Alarm sound and the authorities decide it is necessary, the cellular connection allows central station personnel to remotely kill the engine and sound an audible alarm.

TYPICAL VEHICLE SECURITY SYSTEM COMPONENTS AND FEATURES

AUTOMATIC FUEL CUTOFF — A device that stops the flow of fuel to the engine.

AUTOMATIC LAST DOOR ARMING — A system designed to arm the alarm automatically when the last door is closed.

CAR BATTERY ALARM — A stand-alone alarm connected to the vehicle's electrical system, which sounds an alarm if the battery stops functioning or if someone tries to disconnect it.

ELECTRONIC SHOCK SEAT — This device is installed under the driver's seat and delivers 9000 volts to any thief who ignores the warning signals.

GLASS BREAK SENSORS (SOUND DISCRIMINATORS) — Sensors that detect the sounds made by breaking glass and metal prying.

IGNITION KILL — A device which prevents the vehicle from being started until the system has been deactivated. Neither the original key nor hot wiring will start the vehicle.

MOTION/VIBRATION SENSORS (TILT SENSORS) — Sensors that detect attempts at jacking up or towing the vehicle.

MULTIPURPOSE ANTI-THEFT ALARM — Designed for use with car stereos, truck tool chests, boats, and motorcycle access. This compact sensor attaches to any item, triggering a 110 decibel siren if disturbed. The sensor can be located to activate the alarm if a screw is removed, or a panel or rack is pried or pulled.

PASSIVELY ARMED SYSTEM — A system designed to arm themselves automatically whenever the ignition switch is turned off.

POCKET PAGER — This device is a battery-powered pager that alerts you to vehicle tampering when the vehicle's security system is activated.

POWER ANTENNA ACTIVATION — An option which automatically raises any fully automatic vehicle antenna for increased paging range.

PRESSURE SENSORS — Sensors installed under the driver's seat and activated if anyone sits in the seat anytime the alarm is armed.

REMOTE/ARMING/DISARMING — An option that operates when the ignition switch is in the off position, this allows the system to be manually or remotely armed and disarmed.

REMOTE PANIC — A dedicated button on your vehicle pager that, when activated, sounds the vehicle's alarm system. Ideal if you're accosted near your car.

REMOTE STARTER SYSTEM — A device that allows you to start your car and warm it up while the alarm is still armed, good for those cold winter mornings.

SIREN — A weatherproof 110 decibel electronic siren, or a system that sounds the vehicle's horn and flashes the vehicle's headlights.

VALET OVERRIDE SWITCH — The override switch provides convenience in the event of transmitter loss or when circumstances demand that the user vacate the vehicle, i.e., valet parking premises, car wash, or mechanic's garage.

12
Boat and
RV Security

Leisure time activities such as boating and RV camping have become a very important means of escape from the rat race of the workaday world. Because of this increased interest the cost of participating in these types of activities has also increased. It's very easy to invest tens of thousands of dollars in vehicles and equipment with top-of-the-line models going for a hundred thousand dollars or more. This large dollar investment coupled with high demand has made boats and RVs an increasingly favorite target of thieves. In this chapter I will show you how to protect your boat or recreational vehicle before something happens.

SECURING YOUR BOAT

Boating is a popular American pastime with an estimated twelve to fourteen million pleasure boats populating the lakes, oceans, and rivers of the U.S. As the popularity of boating increases so does the threat of theft and vandalism. Each year more than one billion dollars in losses can be attributed to theft and vandalism. Insurance companies further state that 75 to 85% of boating losses are probably not reported. If reported, only 26% of missing boats are recovered, compared to a 63% recovery rate for stolen cars.

Taking the proper precautions to protect your boat and equipment should be top priority. But what should you do? Using good common sense is always the best place to start with any crime pre-

vention program. Often the simple things work best, such as disabling your motor so that it won't start, removing valuables when not in use, and locking down hatches, doors, and windows. Remember, if you can delay the thief, he will likely go on until he finds an easier target.

To protect your motor-powered vessel, remove the distributor's coil wire, this prevents the motor from starting. Or, you can install a keyed master battery switch, which functions like a car's ignition switch. Without the key you can't access the vessel's battery power, and without power to the engine it will not start. Another tactic involves loosening the ground strap from the battery, which also removes power to the engine. The idea is to do anything you can to interrupt the power to the engines; without power the engines will not operate. These tactics work because you know your electrical system better than a would-be thief does. A thief probably won't take the time to trace the system to find the problem.

Sailboats are more vulnerable to theft because if a thief can get the jib up he can sail without relying on the motor for power. You should consider locking down your vessel's sails. To do this, buy several corrosion resistant bicycle chains and locks, or you can use a heavy-duty stainless steel chain and a high security weather-resistant padlock. To secure the main sail to the boom, simply wrap the chain around the sail and the boom, and then secure the chain with the lock. To secure the jib you need to attach a stainless steel chainplate to the deck. Then you wrap the chain around the sail several times and secure it to the bolt with the padlock. In order to raise the sails a would-be thief would have to remove the chains and padlocks. While not an impossible task, how many boat thieves carry bolt cutters with them? You should also remove or disable your sailboat's outboard motor to make it more difficult for a thief to get out of the harbor.

To prevent the theft of boat equipment such as radar, radios, and depth sounders you should remove and securely store the equipment whenever the vessel is docked or in storage. While cruising away from home waters you should always try to leave someone on board to secure the vessel. If you're unable to leave someone on board, you should secure your equipment and valuables inside the cabin and lock the cabin door with a good high security padlock. If you have the room and carry a lot of valuables you should seriously consider installing a wall safe. A good residential style wall safe would give you an extra degree of security without getting in the way. Keep the boat's windows and curtains closed so that you're not advertising your valuables to the whole world.

Maintaining an accurate and up-to-date description and inventory of your boat's contents is another very important aspect of total security. You should keep a copy of the vessel's registration papers and inventory in a secured location away from the boat, so that if your boat is stolen you can make an accurate report to the police. To describe your boat accurately you need to record the make, length, coloring, and type (sail, cruiser, inboard, or outboard). The vessel's inventory should list all valuable equipment, especially electronic equipment. For each item include the following; manufacturer, brand name, model number, serial number, description, and fair market value. For further protection engrave all equipment with your state's two letter abbreviation followed by your social security number. Taking color photographs of the vessel and all listed equipment will increase the chance of recovery in case of theft. See Chapter 7: Property Inventory for more information.

When storing your boat on a trailer it becomes very vulnerable to theft, since a thief can simply hook up the trailer and tow your boat away. To protect your boat while in storage consider implementing the following preventive measures. First, make it difficult for a would-be thief by blocking access to your boat's storage area by parking vehicles in front of the boat or gate. If you can, store your boat inside a fenced area equipped with a locking gate. To secure the gate use a high security padlock and hasp.

For added security set a heavy-duty metal post anchored in cement next to your boat's storage space. Or, install a heavy-duty U-bolt in the pavement. You then secure the trailer to the post or U-bolt with a heavy duty high security chain and padlock. The more barriers a potential thief has to overcome, the more likely he will get discouraged and leave. As always, remove all valuables from your boat and store them in a safe place.

By using specialty alarm sensors with your existing home security system you can further protect your boat while in storage. Magnapull from Sentrol is one such sensor. Magnapull consists of a cable with a switch on one end and a magnet block which is attached to the house. The cable is looped through any part of the item to be protected and the switch end is inserted into the magnet block to complete the circuit. Someone attempting to steal the protected item would have to remove or cut the cable to free the item. This would break the circuit and activate your home's alarm system. This type of sensor can also be used to protect non-stationary items such as trailers, motorcycles, bicycles, and RVs. It's also useful in protecting televisions, stereo equipment, and office equipment.

Another type of sensor is the Loyal Sentry™ SnapSwitch Sensor from Boat Sentry. This sensor protects your boat's canvas cover from being removed. Easy to install, the SnapSwitch Sensor connects to the existing snaps on the canvas cover to complete the alarm circuit. Anyone trying to remove the canvas cover activates the alarm. This sensor can also be used to protect other items stored under canvas such as trucks, cars, motorcycles, machinery, and just about anything you would cover with canvas. To use either sensor described above you will need a dedicated zone on your home's alarm control panel.

Marinas play a very important role in overall boat security and crime prevention. Many stolen boats were taken right from the marina. When looking for a marina you should take security into consideration as well as location and price. The personal integrity of the marina's owners, managers, and employees sets the tone for how secure an operation they run. Interview the owners and managers to find out what security they offer, make sure you're getting what you're paying for. Find out if the marina restricts public access to the boats; the more public access, the more potential there is for problems. Contact local authorities and talk with other boaters to find out what kind of reputation the marina has — is it known for having good security or the lack of it?

Another even more dangerous prospect is being commandeered at gunpoint by drug smugglers. The boats are then used in drug smuggling, often being left adrift after making a delivery. You need to learn to protect yourself while at sea, especially in the Caribbean, which is the main drug route into the United States. First, never go near any vessel in trouble — armed assailants could be hiding, waiting for you to venture close. The best approach is to remain a safe distance away — prepared for a quick escape if something goes wrong — and contact local authorities for help.

Vessels under way after dark without using navigational lights are another indication of trouble. The vessel may be stolen or a drug smuggler making a run. In either case immediately contact the Coast Guard or other local authorities. Never attempt to contact or stop a suspicious vessel — you might be getting in over your head. If you or your boat are ever victimized make sure to make a report with the local police, harbor patrol, or Coast Guard. It's also a good idea to inform the marina about the incident so that they are aware of the situation. Remember, if boaters don't watch out for each other — who will?

Billions of dollars worth of material and equipment that are stored under canvas are vulnerable to theft, vandalism, or mishap. The Loyal Sentry, a rugged, durable snap-switch sensor, fills the need for an all-weather electronic security perimeter. The existing canvas snap becomes the trigger mechanism, so the switch is totally undetectable. Photo courtesy of Boat Sentry.

MARINE SECURITY SYSTEMS

Almost 40% of the boating market is made up of vessels over 35 feet in length and ranging in cost from $100,000 to well over $1,000,000. With this kind of investment at stake you should seriously consider protecting your boat with a marine security system. The equipment and technology used in marine security systems is similar to that found in home security systems. Marine security systems are often sold and installed by home security dealers. These systems can also be easily installed by the average do-it-yourselfer.

A typical marine security system consists of a control panel, sensors, and siren. The control panel should be waterproof, shock resistant, and environmentally sealed. The electronic siren should be self-contained with a weatherproof horn speaker housing. Sensors and any other equipment used need to be suited for marine use. Be sure to choose a system specifically designed for marine use. The Loyal Sentry marine security system from Boat Sentry is one such system. They offer a complete

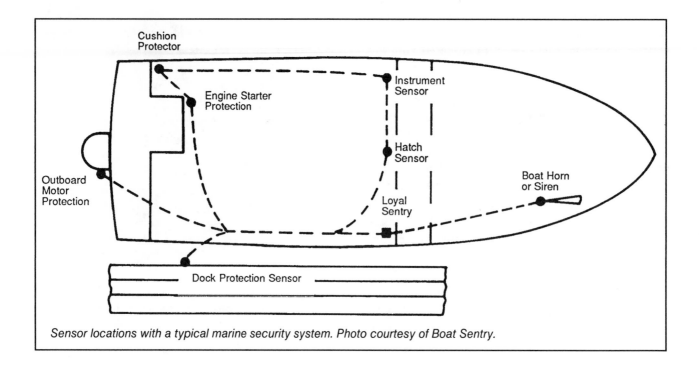

Sensor locations with a typical marine security system. Photo courtesy of Boat Sentry.

security system which has been designed and tested for marine use.

Several different types of sensors are available for use with marine systems. They are: surface mount sensors, flush mount sensors, dock sensors, marine instrument sensors, snap switch sensors and mercury switches. Surface mount marine sensors are used to protect hatches, cuddy cushions, and other areas where a surface-mounted switch is desirable. Flush mount marine sensors are for protecting movable openings where total concealment is desirable, such as doors and windows. Dock protection sensors protect the boat while its moored or stored on a trailer. These can also be used to protect a boat's outboard motor or dinghy. Marine instrument sensors protect radar equipment, depth finders, fish finders, and all other on-board marine instruments.

Snap switch sensors or mercury switches are used for perimeter protection to detect the removal of protective canvas covers. A security key switch is available for installation as an emergency bypass system or for additional remote arming stations.

Another option worth considering is the Solar Guard solar panel from Crimestopper Security Products Inc., Simi Valley, CA. Solar Guard puts out about a 70mA trickle-charge to help ensure that your boat's wet-cell battery has enough power to operate the alarm system, even during prolonged periods when the boat isn't used.

Fire protection is provided by heat sensors and smoke detectors. Heat sensors work by detecting excessive heat and open flames throughout the boat. Smoke detectors detect the smoke and fumes given off by a smoldering fire. Smoke detectors should be installed in the cabin area to protect you when sleeping. Electro Signal Lab manufactures the M-400 series of smoke detectors for marine applications, which can be installed as stand-alone units or as part of a security system connected to a control panel. A complete listing of companies manufacturing devices and controls for the marine industry is located in the Appendix.

When selecting the equipment that you're going to install or have installed the following questions should be considered:

- Is the control unit corrosion resistant? Whether installing in a fresh or salt water environment, corrosion is a problem. The devices used, and especially the control unit, must be corrosion resistant to function properly in a marine environment. Even the hardware you use is important. Steel screws will corrode in the humidity. It's a good idea to use stainless steel fasteners, and when working on fiberglass, use sheet metal screws.

- Is the equipment shockproof? Boats operate on the water and water moves. First, be extremely careful when and if installing motion detectors of any kind. Passive infrareds have proven successful, but only in those cases where placement has been done with all variables considered. Second, because boat hulls will tend to bang on impact in heavy water as well as occasionally be thrown into the dock in bad weather, it is extremely important to make sure that the devices used are shockproof and will withstand the sometimes harsh environment of the marine vessel.

- Is the control unit waterproof? This should go without saying. Any device selected should have been lab tested and preferably U.S. Coast Guard Salt Water Spray tested and approved.

- Does the system provide for engine shutdown? Security systems can provide the best protective loop available, but if the intruder has the ability to start the engine, the system remains ineffective. In addition, make sure the system provides for emergency starting in an armed condition.

- Can the system be monitored by a central station? Without monitoring a marine security system loses most of its effectiveness, as there are no neighbors to be alerted by an audible alarm. There are several options for monitoring including interface with existing radio frequency receiving equipment, and cellular phones.

RV SECURITY

Just as with boating, recreational vehicles, commonly referred to as RVs, have become a very popular recreational pastime. Theft of and from RVs has unfortunately also become increasingly popular. Since most RVs have expensive electronic equipment such as stereos, C.B. radios, microwaves, and televisions, they have become a favorite targets of thieves. Also, RVs are the vehicle of choice for drug dealers to use in smuggling illegal drugs. The fact that most RV owners take few if any added precautions with their vehicle and equipment adds to the problem. If owners would get in the habit of practicing good crime prevention then the likelihood of becoming victimized would be greatly reduced.

First, make sure that all pertinent information regarding the vehicle and its contents has been adequately recorded and stored in a safe location. You'll need to know the vehicle's make, model, type/style, color, Vehicle Identification Number and license plate number. For valuables located inside the vehicle you need to record the make, model, color, and serial number. Engrave the valuables with your social security number or driver's license number and take photos of the items. In addition take photos of the vehicle so that if it's ever stolen the police will know what it looks like. For more information on doing property inventories see Chapter 7.

Most RV break-ins occur while the vehicle is in storage at your home or in a storage lot. To help protect your vehicle when in storage you should, if possible, remove all valuables. Secure the removed items inside your home or other secure location. Make sure that you lock the vehicle's doors, windows, and storage compartments. Use a locking gas cap and store removable propane bottles in a secure location such as a shed or detached garage. You don't want to store propane bottles inside your home — they're a potential fire hazard. If you store the RV at home it's best to build a fenced and lighted parking area with a locking gate. If you have a home security system you can use it to protect your RV by installing an alarm cable as previously described.

If your RV is stored in a storage lot you need to check on what type of security they have, if any. Storage lots are inherently more vulnerable to theft and vandalism because they're often located in isolated areas without twenty-four hour supervision. When checking out storage lots look for the following security measures.

- Is there a resident caretaker? If not, does the lot have security guards or an alarm system?

- Is the site completely surrounded by at least an 8-foot tall chain link fence preferably topped by barbed wire? Does the fence have any blind spots? Is it in good repair?

- Are the gate or gates kept secured during off hours with a high security chain and padlock?

- Are keys to the lot controlled or does everyone have one?

- Is the whole area, especially near the fences, adequately lighted?

- Are good access control measures practiced (do they control who can enter the lot)?

- Does the lot provide insurance coverage in case of theft or vandalism?

Finally, check with the local police or sheriff's department to see if the storage lot has problems with crime.

While on the road you need to take extra precautions because you will be normally carrying more valuables in your RV then when it's in storage. Look for overnight accommodations that provide security such as twenty-four hour or resident attendants, fencing, and lighting. The condition of the park and surrounding area can give you clues as to the probable safety of the area. If the area looks rundown or you're uneasy about the park's employees it's better to look for another park. Secure items stored onto the outside of the vehicle such as propane bottles, bicycles, dirt bikes, and lawn chairs with high security chains and padlocks. Make sure that you always lock your RV when you're away and don't leave valuables unsecured outside the vehicle.

To protect your RV and its contents you might want to consider installing an automobile alarm system. The same type of system that protects your car can be used to protect your RV. You may also want to consider installing a wall safe inside for the storage of small valuables such as jewelry, cash, cameras, and traveler's checks. Electronic equipment security cables are another security product that can help protect your RVs electronic equipment. Security cables are steel cables with one end attached to the rear of televisions, microwaves, or stereo equipment and the other end securely anchored to the vehicle's wall or floor. This product prevents or at least slows down a would-be thief from removing the protected item.

As you can see, most of the precautions outlined in this chapter to help you to secure your recreational vehicle or boat are not expensive at all. Most are simple common sense measures that you can implement today. And, the cost of a security system is reasonable compared to the value of the property protected. Remember, no amount of security will guarantee that you'll never become a victim, but to do nothing almost assures that you will.

STORAGE UNIT SECURITY

If your home is like mine, storage space is often at a premium. Many people store their excess property in commercial storage units. To make sure that your property is safe while in storage take the following precautions. First, look for a storage facility that is concerned about security. At the minimum the entire facility should be protected by a chain link fence at least 8 feet tall. The gates should be kept closed and locked after hours, and during business hours only renters should be allowed in. The gates and individual storage units should be secured with high security chains, hasps, and padlocks. It is best that you use your own lock as long as it is a high security type. The entire area should be kept adequately lighted all night long. If there is not a resident caretaker there should be regular security patrols checking the lot. Avoid storage units in isolated areas or ones that are not fenced or lighted.

Before you put your property in storage, record exactly what you're going to store and keep the list in a safe place. It's a good idea to store only items that have little theft appeal. Valuables should be stored at home or in a bank's safe deposit box. Be sure to check your property regularly to make sure that everything is okay. Report any problems to the management immediately, and if you have had a theft from your unit make a report to the police. Check with your homeowner's insurance company to see if your property is covered while in storage.

13
Preventing
Sexual Assault

Anyone can be a victim of rape. So everyone should think about the kinds of defense she would be willing to use. Now is the time to consider your options — there is little time to think during an attack. Could you really hurt someone who tried to hurt you? Are you willing to scream? Are you able to run? Many rapes and assaults occur in the victim's home, in a garage, or in an apartment building's laundry room. In some cases the attacker may be a burglar who breaks into a house and unexpectedly finds someone home. In others, a rapist purposely looks for women home alone. So one of the best ways to prevent rapes and assaults is to protect your home. Remember, rape is a crime of violence, not sex. You've got to assume that the rapist is willing to use violence. If attacked, your main concern — always — must be your safety.

Here are a few facts about rape. Rape happens to women of all ages, from all walks of life. It's planned! Rapes aren't the result of "uncontrolled passion." The rapist *is not* after sex. Most have normal sexual relations available to them. Instead, the rapist uses sex as a violent way to express his anger. Most people think that rapes occur only in dark alleys. But about one-third occur in the victim's own home. More than half of all victims of rape are between the ages of nineteen and twenty-nine years and 60% are white.

A woman who looks vulnerable, who looks helpless, may be a potential victim of sexual assault. The way a woman walks says a good deal about how confident she feels about herself. The woman whose shoulders are slumped and whose head is down, allowing little eye contact, or who shuffles her feet, looks more vulnerable. Observing a woman behaving in this manner, a potential assailant may choose her over another woman. He is looking for someone who is easily manipulated or intimidated.

Physically, the attacker looks like any other man. He is not the wide-eyed, crazed psychopath that many people envision. He can be a faceless stranger, a friend, a coworker, or a neighbor. He may be aggressive and he may dislike women, but his physical appearance usually will not reveal these characteristics. The attacker has been described as a man who wants to discharge pent-up feelings of anger and rage. He wants to experience feelings of control, power, authority, mastery, strength, and conquest by making the victim feel helpless, controlled, humiliated, and hurt. Stress is dealt with through sexually aggressive acting out. Studies show that the assailant usually was alone when he assaulted the victim. In one-third of the assaults, the assailant was known to the victim as an acquaintance or friend. In 60% of the cases reported, the victim was not aware of the attacker's presence — that is, he ambushed the victim.

Studies indicate that many of the attackers watch their victims before they attack. He watches to discover when the woman is most vulnerable and accessible. A woman's vulnerability, then, is greatly affected by her visibility. Not only can a potential assailant calculate the moment of opportunity, but he can, through observation, evaluate probable responses from the victim. If she appears to be distracted, preoccupied, oblivious of her surroundings as she hurries around, the odds of surprising her are great. If, by her demeanor, he judges her to be careless or overly trusting, passive, or indecisive, and appearing to be less than in control of herself and her belongings, he may determine that she can be easily intimidated and overpowered.

There is a commonly held myth that women who are sexually assaulted put themselves into positions where they can be attacked and that their behavior or attitudes brought on the assaults. In other words, it was the women's fault the assault occurred. While it is true that some women, through a lack of precaution or even common sense, leave themselves vulnerable to sexual assault, it is most important to remember it is still an assault and that the *women* are the victims, not the offenders.

In every rape, the attacker threatens the victim's safety or life. Sometimes a rapist threatens the victim's children or other family members. If you believe you might get hurt by defending yourself or if you are afraid to fight back, don't. Submitting to a rape out of fear for your safety or your family's, does not mean that you consented. It is still a rape, and still a crime, even if you do not have a single cut or bruise. It should still be reported to the police. Victims who do not resist should never feel guilty — it is the rapist who committed the crime.

When attacked or threatened, there are a number of potential responses. Remember, only you can decide the best response, given who you are and the situation in which you are placed. A recent study in Denver revealed that about 55% of reported victims used some type of resistance, ranging from talking to the assailant to physically fighting him. More than two-thirds of the women who

did resist, did so by fighting. Women who did not resist the attacker were much more vulnerable to being raped than those who talked, yelled, or fought back. Nationally, it is estimated that less than 1% of sexual assault victims are murdered each year. information from the Denver study revealed that only one-quarter of the victims were injured and that the injury usually resulted from being kicked, hit, or bitten. Even when assailants had weapons, very few victims were injured with the weapon. The majority of injuries were cuts and bruises, not those which were life threatening.

One response to an attack is to YELL. If you do YELL don't make a helpless, weak yell; make a powerful, blood-curdling YELL! Some suggest that strong, positive words to yell are FIRE, NO, and STOP. One reason to YELL is to get your adrenalin going. It helps you hit harder, move faster, jump higher. The yell also has the potential benefit of startling your attacker. When he hears you yell, he may fear that it will bring you assistance, he may be startled into loosening his grip for a moment, long enough for you to escape. The third possible benefit is that someone may hear you yell and call the police.

The instant the attack begins, yell. It is a visible display of resistance and may give you the time you need to escape. Once you have gotten away, RUN! Do not look back to see where he is, continue moving quickly to a lighted area: a store, gas station, or residence. At this point yell, "Fire" or "Call the police." If you must, break a window to attract attention, but do so as a last resort. Remember, the best time to escape is at the first moment of the confrontation — yell and then run. Don't be embarrassed if you yell and the attack does not materialize. People will understand. Your safety is the most important issue.

Another response is to fight. Hit to hurt and then run. There are areas of the body which are more vulnerable than others, which can be the target of your physical resistance. They are the eyes, nose, throat, groin, knees, shins, and insteps. Focus your energy and attack the sensitive body points. Don't become involved in a blind struggle with the attacker. Think of the attacker as a series of targets, not as a person. Strike these targets with the same determination you would use in slamming a door, or slamming down a book. Some of your weapons are your fists, elbows, knees, feet, teeth, and the back of your head. Never feel sorry for your attacker.

The body has various areas that are sensitive to pain. In the head area poking the eye, hitting the nose upward, or striking the adam's apple can create severe pain. Most women believe that just kicking or striking the groin will stop an attacker. The important area of pain in the groin is the testicles. Aim between the legs behind the penis at the testicles. Your attack must hit the testicles to inflict the most pain. The leg of an attacker has several areas where pain can be inflicted. Start with the knee if possible. The kneecap is very sensitive and if kicked with enough force can be hyperextended. If the knee is missed, you can then firmly scrape the side of your shoe down the shin and stomp hard on the top of the attacker's instep.

Fighting with an attacker may not stop an assault, but it can give you more time to think and react during the assault. The more time it takes during an initial attack, the better your chances are that someone may observe the attack and summon help, or the attacker may get scared and break off the attack. An important element in being able to hurt your assailant is that you have decided, ahead of time, that you are willing to injure someone who is hurting you. This is a decision only you can make. Think about it. Think about the fact that he is willing to injure, possibly kill you. Recognize, too, that you have the right to protect yourself and to injure/kill someone who is attempting to injure/kill you. You are defending yourself.

Sometimes a victim may want to resist but is afraid to scream or fight back. In these cases, a more passive type of resistance may help to "defuse" the violence of the attacker. Try to calm the attacker. Talk to him and try to persuade him not to carry out the attack. If you win his confidence, you may be able to escape. Claim to be sick or pregnant. Tell him you have VD or AIDS — this may intimidate the attacker. Try to discourage the rapist. Some women pretend to faint, some cry hysterically, oth-

ers act insane or mentally incapacitated. If you're at home, tell the attacker that a boyfriend is coming over, or that your husband or roommate will be home soon.

Nobody can tell you whether active resistance — screaming, struggling, fighting back — will be the "right" thing to do. In some cases, it can frighten off or discourage the attacker. But resistance may also lead the rapist to become more violent, or increase his desire to subdue the victim. A scream can surprise or frighten an attacker away if he fears that people will come to help. But screaming won't help in isolated areas. A forceful struggle also may discourage the rapist. If you are not afraid to hurt someone, and can land a strong kick or hit, fighting back may give you the opportunity to escape.

There are many self defense devices available that can be carried and used in an attack situation. These devices include tear gas, shrill alarms, keys, books, lit cigarettes, and the purse. Any device you carry must be available to you immediately. It does no good to carry a protective device in your purse or a coat pocket. Some women carry weapons such as guns, knives, or mace to ward off attackers. Unless you are trained — and not afraid — to use these weapons, they can be very dangerous. The attacker might be able to turn them against you. In many states, it is illegal to carry some weapons. So check with local law enforcement authorities before you select a weapon. Remember, protective devices such as mace or shrill alarms must be tested periodically to make sure they work properly.

It is advisable to take a basic course in self-defense in order to learn some simple, effective techniques. In choosing a basic self-defense class, there are some things to look for. Choose a class designed specifically for women. Women are different from men both physically and psychologically. Issues which should be addressed in a women's class include: a woman's center of gravity as opposed to a man's; using balance and leverage against strength; how to motivate your strength and power; learning how to hit and that it is all right to hurt someone who is trying to hurt you; home, car, and street security; relaxation and body awareness; discussion of the criminal justice system; and discussion of the issues of sexual assault, why it happens, and how it affects the victim and society as a whole. For information on classes, call your local police department, rape crisis center, or women's resource center or look in the phone book.

Victims of sexual assault usually don't know where to turn for help or what to do after being assaulted. Many victims are afraid or ashamed to seek help. If you have been sexually assaulted please get help quickly. Go to the emergency room of a hospital, call your doctor, call the police, or seek help from a crisis center but get help! If you have been raped, it is very important to remember to resist the impulse to take a bath or shower, or to wash or douche after the attack when you are seeking help. Don't touch anything and don't change your clothes. Physical evidence is essential for the police investigation and subsequent prosecution, if the attacker is caught. Don't be embarrassed by having to give any of your clothing to the police for their investigation.

Seeking help immediately is important because the effects of the sexual assault may not be felt immediately. It may be some time after the assault before the emotional and psychological effects are felt. Women who have been assaulted usually experience a stress called Rape Trauma Syndrome, which may consist of feelings such as shock, disbelief, anxiety, humiliation, degradation, shame, guilt, embarrassment, and self-blame. Fears of injury and death may be strong and long lasting, especially if the assault occurred at a place considered safe, such as at home or at work.

Because so many women today say that they feel threatened by men when they're out in public unescorted, it is a good idea for men to obey the following rules. Don't sit too close to an unescorted woman when using public transportation. Don't walk behind a woman who is walking alone on the street. Cross over to the other side of the street so that she can be assured you're not following her. Remember that a woman out on her own may feel nervous and apprehensive, and what you consider innocent flirting may be very threatening

to the woman. Treat them like you would want your wife, girlfriend, sister, or mother treated.

SAFETY IN THE HOME

About one-third of sexual assaults take place in the victim's home. About 70% of these attacks followed an illegal entry, usually taking place at night. In a large proportion of the cases, the assailant did not use force to enter the home. He merely entered by way of an unlocked or open door or window. So practice good home security at all times. Make sure all doors, windows, screen doors and window screens have good locks and are secure — and keep them locked!

While at home don't admit an unidentified stranger without determining who he is before you open the door. Demand identification from any stranger at the door. If you have any doubts about the identification, try to verify it. Don't let anyone at the door know you are at home alone. Make the person at the door think there is someone with you. If someone needs help, offer to call for assistance for him while he waits outside. Likewise, don't let anyone inside for a drink of water; they may be casing your home or are distracting you while an unseen accomplice sneaks into your house to burglarize it.

If you live alone, don't advertise it. Use only your last name and initials on your mail box and phone listing without listing your address. Don't reveal your phone number to wrong number callers. Ask them what number they wanted. If you have an answering machine don't use your name in the greeting — say "you have reached 555-4567 (your phone number)." Women should get a male friend or relative to record the greeting so that no one will know that you live alone. Do not give out personal information to anyone over the phone such as your credit card number, income, where you work, or what you look like. A random telephone survey may be legitimate, or may be a setup for a burglary.

Don't be lured away from your home. Verify all unusual calls asking you to leave your house, such as an unknown school official calling to advise that one of your kids is ill and needs to be picked up, or a call from a hospital advising that a family member has been injured. Verify with the office before admitting an unknown salesman or repairman. If you live in an apartment, avoid being in the laundry room or garage by yourself, especially at night. Tell your landlord if security improvements are needed. Better lighting, stronger locks, night security guards — all are ways to make a building safer. If you come home and find a door or window open or signs of forced entry, don't go in or call out. Go to the nearest phone and call police.

SAFETY ON THE STREET

About 20% of reported assaults take place on a public street, in a parking lot, or in a park. More than 90% of these assaults involved the victim being ambushed or jumped. Ninety percent of the victims also reported that their assailants were strangers. Most of the street assaults occurred at night. The way a woman carries herself when walking down the street indicates to an observer what she thinks of herself. Awareness of what is going on around her, of who is on the street, and of areas that may be potential hiding places for someone, are very much a part of a positive approach to preventing sexual assault.

Walk with confidence — project an image of being sure of yourself. An attacker looks for someone who appears vulnerable. Avoid walking alone at night. If you have to do so, do not walk near parked cars or close to doorways or shrubbery. Sometimes it is even safer to walk in the street rather than on the sidewalk. Remember that there is safety in numbers. Avoid dimly lit streets and stay out of alleys. Stay in well-lighted areas as much as possible and never use little traveled shortcuts. Walk facing traffic carrying your purse or briefcase on the side farthest from the curb. Be careful when people stop you for directions. Always reply from a distance, and never get too close to the car. If someone drops you off near your home, have them wait until you are safely in the house before they leave. Have your car or house key in hand as you approach your vehicle or home.

If you're being followed, speed up, slow down, or change direction then go into an occupied store for help. Don't run home unless help is there. If you are in trouble, attract help any way you can. Scream, yell for help, yell "FIRE," "NO," "STOP," or break a window in a house where you think someone is home. Women should carry a shriek alarm, whistle, or other noisemaker and should sound it loudly if you feel you're in danger. Remember, don't drop your guard because you are walking in an area that is familiar to you. Exercise care at all times. Walk away from crime rather than into it!

When jogging, don't run alone, try to go with a group of two or more. Stay out of known high-crime areas and places where muggers are likely to congregate, such as public parks. Choose routes in advance that are safe and well populated and vary your route and schedule. Avoid jogging and biking at night. Know businesses that are open and locations of police and fire stations. Consider not wearing your stereo headphones — they block out too much sound and it's safer to be alert. Don't wear expensive jewelry or watches that will attract a mugger's attention. Carry your identification but not your wallet. Make sure you carry enough change so that you can use a pay phone if you run into trouble.

Be alert. Watch for any unusual or suspicious persons or activity around you when you run. Be wary of strange joggers who suddenly show up during your runs. Just because they may be wearing jogging clothes doesn't mean they're automatically okay. Always run facing oncoming traffic. If confronted don't try fighting — run away as fast as you can and don't stop until you've reached a safe place. If unable to escape don't argue with a mugger — just give him what he wants. Your life is worth more than a watch or some cash. If you become a victim or see a suspicious person always call the police and make a report.

SAFETY IN A VEHICLE

About one-fourth of sexual assaults are committed in a vehicle — usually the assailant's car. There is a higher probability of being sexually assaulted at night in a car than there is in being assaulted in a home. Injuries are also more likely to occur in a vehicle than in any other location. In half the assaults occurring in cars, the woman willingly entered the car with the assailant, but in one-third of the assaults she was attacked without warning. In a small number of cases, the assailant pretended to have car trouble to make contact with the victim and then assaulted her.

Keep your car in good running condition to avoid breakdowns. Plan your route in advance, particularly on long or unfamiliar trips and have enough gas and money to get there and back. Always drive with all car doors locked and keep windows rolled up whenever possible. If your car breaks down, raise the hood, use flares, tie a white cloth to the door handle, or use the "Need help, please call police" side of your auto-shade. Stay in the car with the doors locked. Do not accept unsolicited offers of assistance, ask them to phone for help instead. Don't stop to help a motorist in trouble. Tell the motorist that you will get help, then drive to the nearest phone and call for help. Don't be fooled if the motorist is a woman. She may have a hidden accomplice or it may be a man disguised as a woman.

Park in well-lighted areas that will still be well-lighted when you return. If you leave after dark, always try to leave in a group or with someone you know. Avoid parking on dark, deserted streets. Choose parking spots near lights, other cars, or homes that look occupied, even if it means you have to walk a bit farther. Be particularly alert and careful when using underground and enclosed parking garages. Always lock your car doors and keep all valuables and your pocketbook out of sight. Check all four sides of your car and look in the back seat before getting in.

Don't get out of your car at night or if you are in an isolated area, even if you have been involved in an accident. Wait until the police arrive. Men have been known to deliberately stage minor accidents to get women to stop their cars. If it appears the accident was deliberate, get the other vehicle's license number, description and, if possible, a description of the driver of the other car. If your car

can be driven, go to the nearest police station and report the accident.

Never pick up strangers or hitchhikers and never hitchhike by yourself or accept a ride from a stranger. Never hitchhike alone or in deserted places. If you must accept a ride, accept rides from older couples or women, never from men or from rowdy groups of men. If you must take a ride with a strange man, refuse the ride if the door locks can be controlled from the driver's side. Always watch the driver's behavior. Hold your keys, a lighted cigarette, or something else in your hands that can be used as a weapon to defend yourself if you must. Always sit next to the door. If the driver does not let you off where you want, try to get him to stop for something to eat or drink and then run from the car or yell for help. If you can't get out of the car, do something to draw attention to the car such as honking the horn or yelling. If the car stops for some reason, such as a traffic light, leave the car and run to an area where there are people.

If you are being followed while driving do not go home, drive to the nearest police or fire station, open gas station or other business, or well-lighted residence where you can safely call police. Try to get the car's license number and description. If menaced while in your car repeatedly sound your horn, yell, turn on your emergency flashers, or flash your high beams on and off.

When taking public transportation avoid sitting next to the exits. Sit with a companion or by the bus driver if you are alone. Stay alert at all times and don't fall asleep. If you must use a bus, look for a frequently used, well-lit bus stop. Have someone you know wait with you if a well-used bus stop cannot be located. While waiting for the bus, stand behind the bus stop bench, away from the street. In the subway, stand back from the platform edge. Avoid sitting near the exit door as an attacker could reach in and grab your purse or jewelry as the train is pulling away. Take a seat in the subway car near the conductor. Try to use only well-lighted and frequently used stops. While waiting, stand with other people or near the token or information booth. If you are verbally or physically harassed, attract attention by talking loudly or screaming. Be alert to who gets off the bus or subway with you. If you feel uncomfortable, walk directly to a place where there are other people.

SAFETY IN SOCIAL SITUATIONS

Approximately 34% of the women sexually assaulted were acquainted with the men who attacked them. The large majority of these relationships (about 80%) were categorized as casual at best. Women attacked by acquaintances frequently had been involved in some social activity with the assailants. Most of these assaults took place in his car (70%) or at his home (24%). About one-fourth of the victims had been using alcohol or drugs before the assault, with most of these women being drunk at the time of the assault.

When meeting new people trust your instincts. Pay attention to what the person is saying and how he is acting. Don't leave with anyone you have just met. Don't give out personal information such as your phone number or address. Take his number and contact him. When going out, watch the amount of alcohol you use, especially when casually acquainted with the man. Remember that drugs and alcohol can alter the personality of the person you are with. The unthinking acceptance of rides or assistance from strangers or casual acquaintances increases the potential for sexual assault. Meeting new people at bars and other social night spots is a popular pastime. These places offer expanded opportunities to establish relationships with men. In establishing a relationship, a woman may be expected to ride home with the new acquaintance. She may not refuse the ride for fear of terminating a potential relationship. Saying no, however, may be considerably safer.

Let someone know where and with whom you are going when you go out, especially when you are only casually acquainted with the man. Also, let someone know when you will return. Agree to meet a new acquaintance at a public place where other people are present. Plan ahead and always be prepared to find your own means home. Don't remain passive if anyone touches you when you don't want to be touched. Attract attention. Let

him and other people know that you object to being touched.

SAFETY AT WORK

Many women feel secure at their places of work. However, areas such as stairwells, rest rooms, and elevators are potential sites for attacks. Too frequently, the security around the workplace is taken for granted. Five percent of sexual assault victims said they were working when attacked. The majority of these attacks took place during the day. To protect yourself while on the job, all you need to do is to take a few simple precautions. First, you should have access to a phone and know the emergency numbers for security and the police department. Don't hesitate to call security or the police if a stranger looks out of place or is hanging around.

Let people, such as the security guard, fellow employees, family members, or friends, know when you are working early or late alone in the building. Don't advertise your schedule for coming to or leaving work, especially when you are going to work late. Don't leave the building alone at night. Ask the security guard to accompany you or walk with other employees, if possible. If you are going to leave work late at night, park in a lighted area as close to the building as possible. Don't leave valuables in sight. Purses and other items of value left out may attract not only the thief but also someone who may sexually assault a woman. Keep them locked in a desk or a locker and keep the office door locked if possible. Don't wear clothing such as tight skirts which will restrict your ability to physically resist or run from an attack, especially when you are working after hours. Avoid wearing shoes that limit your movement.

If your building has elevators, be sure to look in before getting in to be sure no one is hiding, especially after hours. Check to make sure that the emergency hatch is in place, if it's ajar — DON'T go in — someone could be hiding on top of the elevator. Get in the habit of always standing near the controls and watch who gets on with you. If someone suspicious enters, especially if you're alone — get off. If you're worried about someone who is waiting for the elevator with you, pretend you forgot something and don't get on. Be sure to report any suspicious persons or activity to building security or the police. If you're attacked while in the elevator, hit the emergency alarm and as many floor buttons as possible.

If you observe problems with a building's security, bring it to someone's attention. Notify the building's security director, the building manager or owner, and your boss. If major changes need to be made it is a good idea to get together with the other tenants and approach the building's owner to work on solutions. If necessary remind the owner that it's his responsibility to provide a safe building and he could be held liable for not doing so. If your employers own the building, they are likewise responsible for providing a safe working environment.

14
Protecting Your Children

Wanting to protect your children comes naturally to most parents; it is part of loving them. But most parents are not aware of the dangers that are lurking for the unsuspecting, the unprepared. Abduction, molestation, abuse, and running away can and do happen to nice kids from good families, like yours. These facts are very disturbing and many parents are asking "What can we do?" You can increase the odds in your favor by taking the time now to prepare yourself and your children. Begin today! Don't put it off until tomorrow, or you may find yourself someday saying "If I'd only known, I would have done something different." This chapter contains some hints to help you prevent such crimes from occurring to your family.

Start by teaching your children their full names; complete address including city, state, and zip code; home telephone number; parents' work numbers, including area code; and both parents' full names. They should know how to use the telephone, including how to find and use a public pay phone. Teach them how to dial "911", or other emergency numbers used in your area. You should keep a list of emergency phone numbers — the fire and police departments and a close relative's or friend's number — posted near each of the phones in your home.

Of the between 5000 and 50,000 children abducted by strangers each year, many are never found. Most of these abductions occur in public places such as shopping malls, rest rooms, or places of public entertainment. Keep your children close to you when in a crowded place and never leave your child alone in the car or let them go into a public rest room alone. Teach your children to SCREAM "This is not my father (or mother)" if someone they don't know tries to take them. They should also know who to go to if they are lost — a police officer, security guard, "Block Parent" safe house, or a clerk in a busy store. Teach your children that there is safety in numbers and that they should stick together and watch out for one another.

Always know where your child is and what your child is wearing; or, for older children, always know where your child is going, with whom, and when he will return. Know all of your children's friends and where they live. Don't personalize your children's clothing or property and never dress them like rich kids. Your children should know NEVER to take shortcuts or accept rides, candy, gifts, money, or medicine from a stranger. They should be taught not to get close to a car if a stranger calls out to them for directions or anything else. Teach your children NEVER to leave your home or yard or to go off with anyone, including your divorced spouse or a friend, without your permission. Children six and under should never be outside unsupervised. Children should NEVER walk, play, or loiter in public areas such as washrooms and elevators or in deserted areas such as the woods, a parking lot, an alley, deserted buildings, new construction, or be outside alone at night.

Your children should know to stay away from strangers, usually out of reach (approximately 8-10 feet) and explain to them what a stranger is: "A stranger is any person that you don't know even if they say they know your parents or know your name." Explain to your children that most people they do know are nice people, but that you cannot tell the difference by looking at them whether they are good or bad, so all strangers must be treated the same way — stay away from them! Teach your children to trust their instincts if something doesn't feel right and to tell you if anything happens. Establish a "Code Word" between you and your children, something that they can remember but one that can't be easily guessed by a stranger. Teach them not to go with any stranger who does not know the code word.

When your children are home alone they should keep the doors locked and be taught never to let a stranger inside the house. When answering the phone they should never tell a stranger that they're home alone. They should tell the stranger that their parents are busy or can't come to the phone. Latchkey children should never wear the house key on a chain or string around their neck, where it can be seen. Teach your children never to volunteer family vacation plans or other information about your home.

Select one or two neighbors who are willing to provide sanctuary for your children should any threat or emergency arise while you are away from them. Provide these neighbors with phone numbers where you can usually be reached. Locate and point out to your children "Block Parent," "Helping Hand," "McGruff Safe Home," or similar safe homes in your neighborhood and along your child's route to and from school and explain the meaning of such refuges. Give the school instructions only to release your children to the people you have designated in writing in case of emergency. Make sure you have an understanding with your child's school that you'll call to report when he or she won't be in class, for example, if he's at

home sick. That way, if your child isn't there and you haven't called, the school will call you.

Finally, spend time with your child talking about potential dangerous situations that they may encounter and play a game of "what if" or "let's pretend." To play a game of "what if," you set up various situations to your child and then ask him what he would do in that situation. For example, you say to your child "You're walking home from school and a stranger in a car stops by you and tells you that I sent him to pick you up. What do you do?" These games will help your child to prepare for problem situations and it will allow you to see how your child thinks and reacts when you might not be there. Let your child know that you are always willing to listen and encourage him to come to you whenever something is bothering him. Be prepared to assist a child who appears lost or in trouble. Do not hesitate to notify the police if you think a child needs assistance. Report suspicious individuals or vehicles lurking in areas where children play to the police. Obtain license numbers and descriptions whenever possible.

CHILD MOLESTATION

Each year an estimated 100,000 U.S. children suffer some form of sexual abuse. The average age of the child victim is ten. Teaching "stranger rules" is smart, but not enough. In the majority of cases, the child sexual molester is known to the child and the child's family. The abuser is often a parent, relative, baby-sitter, or close family friend. Children may give in to adults' sexual advances because they fear losing their love, or fear their punishment. Children are trusting and defenseless. Therefore, they are especially vulnerable to sexual abuse by someone they know, such as people who care for them regularly.

A child may not recognize sexual abuse when it happens, or even know it's wrong, especially if the abuser is someone the child knows. Children must learn what appropriate "touching" is. Discuss it with your child. Many children instinctively know what "proper distance" should be kept between them and other persons. Sometimes a child may be uncertain about the intentions of another person.

In this situation, children should know it's okay to respond in away that makes them feel safe and more comfortable. Children usually know that genuine and gentle affection is different from someone who tries to touch their genitals or fondle them in any way that makes them feel unsafe. They should pull away immediately if someone suggests such actions, even if they're offered a present as a bribe.

Children often make up stories, but they rarely lie about being victims of sexual assault. If a child tells you about being touched or assaulted, take it seriously. Your response is very important and will influence how the child will react and recover from the abuse. Stay calm. In a reassuring tone, find out as much as you can about the incident. Explain to your child that you are concerned about what happened. Don't be angry. Many children feel guilty, as if they had provoked the assault. Children need to be reassured that they are not to blame, and that they are right to tell what happened.

Sometimes, a child may be too frightened or confused to talk directly about the abuse. Parents should be alert to the indicators of sexual abuse:

- Changes in behavior, extreme mood swings, withdrawal, fearfulness, and excessive crying.

- Bed-wetting, nightmares, fear of going to bed, or other sleep disturbances.

- Acting out inappropriate sexual activity or showing an unusual interest in sexual matters.

- A sudden acting out of feelings or aggressive or rebellious behavior.

- Regression to infantile behavior.

- A fear of certain places, people, or activities, especially being alone with certain people.

Children should not be forced to give affection to an adult or teenager if they do not want to. A desire to avoid this may indicate a problem. Some physical signs of sexual molestation are: pain, itching, bleeding, fluid, or rawness in the private areas.

Children should be taught that no one should ask them to keep a special secret. If someone does, they should tell you or their teacher. Your child should know that if someone wants to take their picture, that they should tell him or her "NO" and then tell you or their teacher. Teach them that their body is special and private and no one should touch them in the parts of their body covered by the bathing suit, nor should they touch anyone else in those areas. It's important that parents tell their children that they can be assertive, and have the right to say "NO" to anyone who tries to take them somewhere, touches them, or makes them feel uncomfortable in any way.

If your child is unsure about a person's intentions he can: Say "NO." Give your child the right to say no to any person who wants to touch or hurt them or anyone who wants to give them a gift or take them someplace. GET AWAY. Your children should walk or run away from anyone who frightens them, but they should always remember to stay away in the first place. Teach them that if someone ever does grab them, they should yell, scream, kick, scratch, bite, or do whatever it takes to get loose, then run away to a crowded place or safe house. TELL SOMEONE. It's very important that your child tell you, a teacher, a policeman, or any trustworthy adult when something has happened or seemed as though it was about to happen to them. Let your child know that these adults will help them and protect them.

If your child becomes a victim of molestation don't panic or overreact to the information disclosed by the child. Don't criticize the child and respect the child's privacy. Support the child and his decision to tell the story. Explain to the child that he has done no wrong. Seek out appropriate medical attention and alert the child protection, youth services, child abuse, or other appropriate social services organization. The police, sheriff's office, or other law enforcement agency must also be notified. You should also consider the need for counseling or therapy for your child if he or she is ever victimized.

RUNAWAYS

Running away can be a frightening experience — for both the child and the parents. Your child becomes vulnerable as soon as he or she leaves home

— potentially falling victim to drugs, drinking, crime, sexual exploitation, child pornography, or child prostitution. It is important for parents to remain calm and rational when they discover that their child has run away. The first forty-eight hours following the runaway are the most important in locating the child. The chances that one of your children will be abducted by a stranger are very remote, but as we all know it is better to be safe than sorry.

To help locate your runaway child, follow these steps immediately. Check with your child's friends, school, neighbors, relatives, or anyone else who may know of your child's whereabouts. Ask them to notify you if they hear from the child. Completely search your home and yard to make sure that the child is not hiding. If you can't locate your child within thirty minutes after discovering that he is missing call the local police or sheriff's department to make a runaway report. With preschool age children you should call the police immediately before you begin the search. Don't wait several hours hoping that your child will "turn up" on his or her own, you will be wasting precious time if there has been a kidnapping. You should also call or check several local spots that your child may frequent, and check with area hospitals and treatment centers. If your child was employed, call the employer or coworkers. You need to be ready to provide the police with a complete description of your child including a recent photo. If you have fingerprints and dental records of your child make them available to the police.

In addition to the aforementioned steps there are several national organizations in existence to help the families of missing or runaway children. The National Center for Missing and Exploited Children at (800) 843-5678 is the primary governmental agency for coordinating information on missing children. They also have child protection literature available to parents. (See the Appendix for a complete listing of available material and ordering information.) You can also call your local runaway hotline (if there is one) as well as the National Runaway Switchboard at (800) 621-4000. Ask if your child has left a message, and leave a message for him or her. Contact local runaway

shelters and those in adjoining states. There are over 500 runaway shelters throughout the country, and they will be able to give you assistance and advice.

If your child is still missing after contacting the police and child protection agencies you can then take the next step, which is the production and distribution of posters. Using the missing child poster format, have posters or fliers made, then distribute them to truck stops, youth-oriented businesses, hospitals, treatment centers, and law enforcement agencies. Place them in store windows, hand them out on street corners, and put them on car windows at local shopping malls. The idea is to get out the word to as many people as possible that your child is missing. Someone somewhere may have seen your child or have information that may help the investigation.

If your finances permit, you should consider hiring a private investigator. A private investigator has more time to devote to the search for your child then does the police department. Look for a private investigator who is experienced in locating missing children, and be sure to check out his credentials to your satisfaction before hiring. A private investigator will be very expensive, but what price can you put on your child's future? Another good resource is the local news media, especially television stations. The media is always willing to help in missing children cases by getting the word out to the viewing public. In larger metropolitan areas local television stations often have news helicopters which they use to assist in the search, especially in wooded or remote areas.

BABY-SITTERS

You entrust your baby-sitter with your most precious possession, your children. Many people don't give a second thought to leaving their child with someone who might be a complete stranger. Unfortunately, there are people who pose as baby-sitters to kidnap children. Imagine coming home to find that your child and the baby-sitter are gone without a trace. But you can take a few simple precautions to safeguard your children when selecting a baby-sitter or day-care provider.

Have You Seen This Child?

WANTED:
Arrest Warrant Issued

MISSING CHILD

OPTIONAL

PHOTO
OF ABDUCTOR
(if warrant issued
for arrest)

CHILD'S PHOTO

CHILD'S PHOTO,
DIFFERENT ANGLE

(Date of Photo)

(Date of Photo)

(Date of Photo)

NAME OF ABDUCTOR

Date of Birth:

Ht.:   Wt.:

Hair: Eyes:

Complexion:

Scars, etc.:

Occupation:

Race:

NAME OF CHILD

Date of Birth: Age: Race:

Grade in School:

Ht.:   Wt.:   Hair: Eyes:

Complexion:

Scars, etc.:

Hobbies, sports, etc.:

Details of Abduction—Date, Place:

Indicate violation of court order, warrant on file.

Indicate if abuse has occurred.

IF YOU HAVE ANY INFORMATION, PLEASE CONTACT:

Officer's Name, Police Department:

Phone Number:

Case Number:

Warrant Number (if secured):

National Center for Missing and Exploited Children
1-800-843-5678

This material is reprinted from Patricia M. Hoff, Parental Kidnapping: How to Prevent an Abduction and What to Do if Your Child is Abducted. *(3rd edition, 1988, by Janet Kosid Uthe and Patricia M. Hoff, National Center for Missing and Exploited Children.) Single copies are available free of charge from the National Center for Missing and Exploited Children, 2101 Wilson Blvd., Suite 550, Arlington, VA 22201.*

First, don't leave your children with anyone who you don't know. Be sure that you carefully check the references of baby-sitters, day-care centers, and recreational leaders. Start by interviewing the sitter, on the phone or in person. Check references. Call at least one family and ask questions about how the sitter worked out. If the sitter is in your home, watch how he or she interacts with your children. Trust your intuition. If, after speaking to the sitter and checking references, you still feel uneasy, move on to another candidate.

Make sure that he or she is a mature, experienced, and capable individual who truly cares about the welfare of children. Write down his or her name, home address, and telephone number and, if an adult, driver's license number. This information will be important if something should happen and you need to file a report with the police. If you are considering a day-care provider make sure that they are state licensed and have a qualified staff. Go to the licensing agency and check to see if there have been any problems with the person or facility you're considering. Once you've selected a sitter, help him or her succeed by providing the right information. Studies have shown that baby-sitters can become frustrated and even abusive when they are unprepared or ill-informed.

When the baby-sitter, arrives carefully go over any family rules and daily routines, paying special attention to eating or sleeping arrangements. Provide information about the children's habits, dislikes, and medical conditions. Take the sitter on a tour of the house, showing him or her where the first-aid and cleaning supplies are and how to operate important appliances. You should be sure to familiarize the sitter with your fire evacuation plans and point out fire extinguishers and all doors and other possible exits. It is a good idea to discuss the family rules regarding television, snacks, and bedtime with both the baby-sitter and the children present. It is the parents' responsibility to let the children know what rules are to be obeyed when the parents are out of the house. It's also the parents' responsibility to let the baby-sitter know whom the children may play with or visit.

The baby-sitter should be given specific written instructions along with a list of local emergency phone numbers and where you can be reached. You should instruct the sitter to lock all doors as soon as you leave and keep them locked during your absence, and not to open the door to anyone unless you have given prior permission. The children should be watched carefully while they're awake and kept away from dangerous objects or chemicals and protected from household accidents. When the children go to sleep, they should be checked regularly. The sitter should stay awake during his or her stay in the house and should not be permitted visitors or guests, nor should the sitter leave the children alone in the house at any time. If the telephone rings, the sitter should not tell the caller that the children are alone or with a baby-sitter. She should ask the caller to leave a message. If the children are taken outside to the yard, they must be watched carefully. If the children are with the baby-sitter in a public place, they must be watched carefully and not permitted to wander.

You should suggest to your regular sitter that she attend CPR and first-aid classes. Super Sitters, an in-home training program for baby-sitters and parents is available from Super Sitters, P.O. Box 218, Mequon, WI 53092 (800) 558-2001, ext. 118. Finally, ask your children whether they like and trust the baby-sitter and what activities took place during your time away. It's also a good idea to have a trusted neighbor watch your house while the baby-sitter is there.

KEEPING RECORDS

There are several ways that parents can be prepared in the event that their child runs away or is abducted. While some of these measures may be more appropriate for a younger child, they all provide valuable information to aid in the quick recovery of a runaway or missing child. Start by having your child carry identification in the form of a card, bracelet, or necklace with them at all times. Keep an up-to-date portfolio on each of your children in a readily accessible location. Your records should include: your child's date of birth, height, weight, hair color, eye color, and a recent photo. Keep the records updated as these features change.

Color photographs should be taken four times a year (especially for preschoolers), and they should show your child's face and profile. Note any birthmarks and other distinguishing features. In addition, the description should contain any identifiers such as eyeglasses or contact lenses, braces on teeth, pierced ears, and other unique physical attributes.

It is also a very good idea to have your children fingerprinted. Have fingerprint cards taken every two to three years starting at about three years of age. (Most police and sheriff's departments will do this free of charge.) Know where your child's medical records are located and how you can obtain them if the need arises. Make sure that your dentist maintains accurate, up-to-date dental charts and x-rays on your child as a routine part of his or her office procedure.

Missing Persons Report
for Abducted Child

Complete this worksheet and make a copy. Bring the copy to the police station when you go to report your child as missing. This will speed up the process of entering a missing persons report on your child into the NCIC computer. If you cannot make a copy, bring this book with you and ask the police officer to have a copy made of this worksheet.

Child's name_____

Sex_____

Race _____

Date of birth_____

Mother's maiden name_____

Date of abduction_____

Place of abduction (home, school, etc.)_____

Age at time of abduction_____

Height_____

Weight_____

Hair color_____

Eye color_____

Glasses?_____

Birthmarks_____

Unique characteristics (scars, limp, stutter, tattoo, jewelry, etc.)_____

_____

Grade in school_____

Medical or dental problems_____

Circumstances of abduction_____

_____

(Attach photo of child here.)

Key Contacts in Parental Kidnapping Cases

Police Department (Sheriff) in your community

Name of officer assigned to case_____

_____

Badge number_____

Telephone number_____

Address_____

_____

Police report/case number_____

Prosecutor (District Attorney, State Attorney, Commonwealth Attorney, Assistant Attorney General, Solicitor)

Name_____

Telephone number_____

Address_____

_____

Assistant Prosecutor assigned to your case

Name_____

Telephone number_____

Address_____

_____

Your Lawyer

Name_____

Telephone number_____

Address_____

FBI

Agent(s) spoken to_____

_____

Telephone number_____

Address_____

_____

U.S. Attorney for your district

Name_____

Telephone number_____

Address_____

_____

Assistant U.S. Attorney assigned to your case

Name_____

Telephone number_____

Address_____

_____

Support Groups

Name_____

Telephone number_____

Address_____

_____

Name_____

Telephone number_____

Address_____

_____

SAMPLE

REQUEST FOR FERPA RECORDS

(Name)
(Principal, or other title)
(School)
(Street address)
(City, state, zip)

(Date)

Dear _____ :
　　　　　(Name)

I am the (Mother/Father) of _____.
　　　　　　　　　　　　　　　(Child's first, middle, and last names)

My child attended your school from _____ to _____ (or is currently attending your school). My child was abducted by (his/her) other parent on _____. (*Optional:* I have/share custody of _____.)
　　　　　　　　　　　　　(Child's name)

Please review your records for _____ and send me
　　　　　　　　　　　　　　　　(Child's name)

the most recent address you have for (him/her). If my child no longer attends your school and you have received a request to transfer (his/her) records to a new school, please send me the name, address, and telephone number of the school requesting the records. Because I am a parent, the federal Family Educational Rights and Privacy Act (20 U.S.C. Section 1232g) entitles me to this information about my child.

I would also appreciate it if you would "flag" the school records of my child and notify me in the event you receive any information that would assist me in finding my child.

You can reach me at _____
　　　　　　　　　　　(Your name)

_____
(Your street address)

_____
(Your city, state, zip)

_____
(Your telephone number)

Please keep this inquiry confidential.

Thank you for your assistance in this matter.

Sincerely,

(Your signature)

Note: If possible, attach a copy of your custody order, your child's birth certificate, and a copy of the Family Educational Rights and Privacy Act.

15
Avoiding Consumer Fraud and Con Games

Most people tend to be more aware of street crimes: burglary, auto theft, robbery, and assaults than they are of frauds and con games. But the dollar loss from white collar crime is an estimated $40 billion a year to con artists and swindlers. Some of the most popular frauds involve offers of:

- Prizes (to get unwary consumers to buy water purifiers or vitamins)

- Penny stocks

- Office supplies

- Credit repair (services that promise to give you a good credit record regardless of past problems)

- Precious metals

- Travel deals

- Works of art

- Phony insurance claims, some related to health insurance

- Magazine subscription contracts

- Land sales, home sites, retirement estates, and condominium schemes

- Worthless stocks, bonds, oil and gas leases

- Business franchise or distributorship promotions

- Work-at-home plans

Smooth-talking con artists make their living by convincing you to hand over your hard-earned cash for products or services they'll never deliver. They may be young or old, men or women — "nice" people, the kind you run into every day. The first rule in fraud prevention is that you don't get something for nothing. It has been said before, but people still seem to forget this very simple and important rule. You have to remind yourself that you never, ever get something for nothing. That's sometimes hard to do, since most of us are natural optimists. It's easy to go from wishful thinking to the belief that someday, somehow we're going to strike it rich through some get-rich-quick scheme. After all, that's really the only way we could ever get rich! That's when people get into trouble. No one ever got rich from a con game — and no one ever will.

Senior citizens are especially vulnerable, as con men prey on their natural truthfulness, loneliness, and isolation. A large number of senior citizens are victimized each year, many more than once. Con artists move fast and most victims don't realize that they've been had until it's too late. To protect yourself, never trust strangers or casual acquaintances who tell you how you can "get rich quick" or who ask you to give them large sums of money, even for what seem to be good reasons. Don't be taken in by their warmth or friendliness — you may never see your money again. Senior citizens should protect their financial lifelines by using direct deposit for their social security or retirement checks. That way you won't be as easily tempted to give money to a con man on impulse. If you have to go to the bank to get your money you will have time to think things over before committing yourself.

Always get several written estimates for home repair work and check out each company with the Better Business Bureau before signing anything. Don't let yourself be pressured into making a quick decision on the spot. High pressure sales tactics are a common ingredient in frauds and con games. The con men want to get your money and run before you have a chance to think it through. It's a good idea to have someone you know and trust, a family member or friend, to help you make important money decisions. The more people you get advice from before spending your money, the less likely you're going to be victimized by a con artist.

Most frauds and con games are based on several commonly used tactics, which if you learn to recognize will help you avoid becoming a victim. Be extra cautious when dealing with anyone who uses any of the following scenarios or buzz words in their sales pitch. Watch out! Here are some typical tricks: They offer you "something for nothing," you can bet you're getting nothing for something. If the deal is "too good to be true," the merchandise is incredibly cheap, or the offer is an "amazing investment opportunity" or is a "deal" on home repair, it is usually no bargain. They want "good faith" money or insist on cash payment before delivering your purchase. Don't be fooled. If you hand over your cash, that's the last you'll see of it — and the swindlers.

Lots of pressure to sign a contract? They might not want you to notice something. Wait a while and read it over carefully. Take it to a lawyer, or ask your Better Business Bureau if the seller is on the level. If you sign a contract but later you have second thoughts, don't be afraid to call it off! In most states the law gives you three days to change your mind. Never give your money or power of attorney to anyone you don't know well and trust implicitly or haven't thoroughly investigated.

Don't make loans to anyone who offers as collateral unregistered stock, deeds to property you haven't title-searched, untitled motor vehicles, or unauthenticated items, including negotiable securities, artwork, and antiques.

Don't buy expensive merchandise, particularly jewelry, precious gems, paintings, or other forms of art from people you don't know, especially if they offer them at "discount" prices. Have an expert appraise any merchandise you are considering buying, but there is still the possibility that the merchandise is stolen. Finally, keep an eye on the local news for reports on new con games being run in your area, and if anyone approaches you with a proposition that sounds suspicious, call the police.

TYPICAL SCAMS

The "pigeon drop" is a common con game in which the swindlers claim they've found a large sum of money and offer to share it with you. They ask you to put up some "good faith" money before you get in on the deal. If you give them your money that's the last you'll see of them and your cash. You're left with nothing but phony instructions on how to collect your share of the "found" cash. Another popular scam is the bank examiner scam. A phony "bank examiner" calls and asks you to help catch a dishonest bank employee. You're asked to withdraw some cash from your account and turn it over to the bank examiner, who will check the serial numbers and catch the embezzler. After you turn over your money, you'll never see it or the "bank examiner" again.

Home repair fraud is one of the most common of all frauds with senior citizens the primary target, especially elderly women living alone. This type of scam is perpetrated by clans of rip-off artists called "travelers" or "gypsies." They travel from town to town looking for victims. They usually find their targets by simply cruising neighborhoods looking for seniors doing yard work or sitting on their porch. They contact the unsuspecting victim with an opening line something like, "We just happened to be in the neighborhood and noticed your home needs repairs." They offer to do the work at a bargain price because there is "material left over from another job."

They usually offer such services as fireproof spray coatings for the roof, aluminum siding coatings, and driveway coatings. Their workmanship and the quality of materials are often very inferior and overpriced, if they finish the work at all. They often require cash up front and have been known to start work even when told by the homeowner not to. They then intimidate the elderly victim into paying or they simply walk into the house and take any cash they can find before leaving. These con artists are rarely arrested because the elderly often don't report the crime, and when they do they often can't make a positive identification of the suspects.

Home repair con artists are usually white males and work alone or in pairs. "Travelers" are clans of English, Scottish, or Irish descent and operate out of South Carolina. They frequently drive new pickups with camper shells and ladders on the top. One unusual feature that distinguishes their vehicles is the use of locking handles, the type commonly used on camper rear windows, on the side windows of their camper shells. "Gypsies" often travel around the country in RVs and trailers, staying in local overnight trailer parks while working an area. Both groups are very clannish and keep to themselves, often intermarrying and many within the clan have the same last name. To protect yourself you should: avoid keeping large sums of money in your home, get written estimates from three contractors before having repair work done, check out all contractors with the Better Business Bureau, don't be afraid to call the police immediately if approached or victimized by one of these con artists.

Another typical con game is called "The Fence." An individual approaches a victim with a "good deal," usually a television, stereo, etc. He may advise that the merchandise is "hot," but cannot be traced. The suspect requires cash so he can pick up the merchandise. The individual goes away with your money and is never seen again. Another scheme is for a "salesman" to appear at the home of a recently bereaved victim with a Bible or piece of jewelry in hand, claiming that the deceased person made a down payment on the item and that the victim owes him for the rest of the purchase price. The swindler can be very convincing by displaying knowledge of the victim and the deceased, gleaned from the obituary column, and by taking advantage of a very emotional situation.

To protect yourself from mail-order fraud you should consider looking for a better deal at a local store. If you do order by mail, remember that the Federal Trade Commission requires that most mail-order companies fill your order within thirty days unless the order states otherwise. You can cancel the order if it's not filled within the thirty days and the company must return your money in seven days. If you receive an item in the mail that you didn't order, you do not have to pay for it or return it. Beware of "winning" a contest you never entered or a "free" vacation — a technique to dupe you into buying something you don't want.

Watch out for look-alike envelopes marked "open immediately" or "important notice" that appear to be from government agencies such as the FBI or the Internal Revenue Service. When opened, however, they contain sales promotion material and a toll-free phone number from the "Federal Bureau of Information" or the "Internal Review Service." Another common fraud perpetrated through the mail is the sale of governmental services by fake "official services" companies. They have official sounding names and forms to defraud consumers into buying free government forms and services such as social security cards, name changes, etc. Don't be taken in, these services and forms are available free from the Social Security Administration.

Don't fall for bogus health care promotions for phony arthritis and baldness remedies, sexual aids, and weight-loss plans. Check with your doctor or local health clinic before you buy. Don't take anyone else's word. Be wary of "mail order" labs or clinics that offer to diagnose and cure diseases through the mail. Only go to medical laboratories and clinics recommended by your doctor or hospital. A lot of senior citizens worry about getting sick and being unable to pay for medical expenses that Medicare doesn't cover. There is health insurance that is supposed to pick up where Medicare leaves off. However, many such policies offer inadequate coverage, or the type of coverage provided by the policy may not be right for you. Before you buy a "medigap" policy, check with the State Insurance Commission.

Are you in debt, the bills piling up, can't get a loan, getting desperate? BEWARE. There are many so-called "credit repair" consultants who claim that they can repair your bad credit for a fee of $50 to $1000. The federal Fair Credit Reporting Act specifies exactly what can be written into your credit report and how long it must stay there. So unless your credit record contains outright errors, which you can fix yourself by writing to the credit bureau, there is often little that consultants can do. For real help, call the National Foundation for Consumer Credit at (800) 388-2227, a nonprofit organization with almost 500 counseling centers in the U.S. and Canada. Its counselors can help you design a budget and negotiate with your creditors a program to repay your debts, usually in two to four years. Their fee is about $10. Credit is available from many different sources, so it's wise to shop around. Be wary of "low monthly payments." Find out the total amount of interest you'll pay over the life of the loan. The Truth-In-Lending Act requires that creditors tell you the annual interest rate and the total cost of the credit.

Watch for the phony mortgage company scheme. In this scheme you'll get a letter stating that your home's mortgage has been bought by a new mortgage company. They advise you to mail your next payment to them instead of to your old mortgage company. You comply only to find out later that you've been taken, when you receive a late payment notice from your original mortgage company. To avoid this scheme don't send any money until you've verified the sale with your current mortgage company. A variation on this scheme is the mortgage acceleration. Scalpers promise to "help" homeowners save money by paying off their loan obligations early, but actually wind up costing them much more.

Be suspicious if someone calls to "check the address" for delivery of a "gift" ordered by a "friend." Often the victim unwittingly supplies the name of the "friend" when asked to guess who could have sent the gift. The caller then casually mentions the fact that he represents an out-of-town warehouse which is going out of business and offers to take an order for goods to be delivered at a later date when the "gift" is delivered. A cash payment for the "goods" is, of course, required. If the victim sends cash he'll never receive either the original "gift" or the "goods" he ordered. He will also find that the con artists have moved on leaving him without recourse.

Beware of door-to-door salesmen. At the least they are an annoyance, and at the worst they are con artists or burglars checking to see if you're home. When sales people call, wait. Don't buy today. If it's legitimate, they'll come back tomorrow. In the meantime, check out the company with your local Consumer Affairs Office or Better Business Bureau. Remember that whenever you make a purchase in your home totaling $25 or more, the salesperson must give you a written contract and two Notice of Cancellation Forms. You have three days to change your mind and use one of those forms to cancel your contract. Don't sign anything until you get another opinion and other estimates. Before you sign a contract or agreement, make sure you understand and agree with everything it says. Don't skip the small print and never sign a blank contract or one with blanks to be filled in later.

Be wary of door-to-door sellers of home insulation, roofing, painting, termite inspection, or other energy-saving devices. Other popular door-to-door frauds involve: cleaning products that the seller claims are the best invention since toilet paper, when in reality it is just a common household cleaner in their bottle and at a higher price; magazine subscriptions peddled by supposedly underprivileged youth who are trying to win a trip or a college scholarship. These youth are recruited out-of-town and shipped around the country and forced to spend hours walking door-to-door selling these supposed magazine subscriptions.

Consumers are most frequently targeted by schemes to sell property ostensibly located in resort areas or urban developments which in reality is undesirable or unsuitable for reasonable use. Land fraud con artist usually employ high-pressure sales tactics. Their printed literature, usually sent through the mail, and their verbal sales pitches, often delivered by phone, may contain glittering generalities about the benefits of owning property in the bustling inner city or land in sunny resort locales. More specific, informative details are much more difficult to come by. Bogus offers that "guarantee," for a hefty fee, help in selling that vacation timeshare unit you got stuck with in the 1980s has also become a popular fraud.

Fraudulent firms specializing in invention marketing may advertise in the same scientific and business journals, magazines, and news publications as their legitimate counterparts. The illegal operations may charge various "up front" fees for nonexistent services. They may promise to research the uniqueness of an invention, survey its marketability, obtain a patent, and produce and market the product. Con artists have been known to swindle inventors out of thousands of dollars by claiming they are developing a prototype or arranging for the mass production of an invention. But what these firms do best is swindle their unsuspecting victims by preying on vanity, emotions, hopes, and inexperience.

Securities and commodity futures investment schemes involve the sale of fraudulently represented properties. Examples include the sale of counterfeit or stolen securities, schemes that rely on the deceitful practices of traders or employees "inside" stock or bond clearinghouses, and international schemes involving sales of securities in nonexistent companies. The swindlers generally are smooth-talking, persuasive individuals who try to overwhelm their targets. Telephone solicitors contact hundreds of prospects a day in search of the few who seem receptive; then the real "professional" comes on the line and attempts to close the sale. A messenger may be dispatched to pick up money immediately, before the victim has a chance to investigate or reconsider the offer. Fraudulent commodity sales operations may use glossy brochures touting trading "successes." They may adopt a legitimate-sounding name and impressive mailing address — which in reality may be nothing more than a mail-drop or rented back office. Most of these questionable operations are not registered with any regulatory agency, even though, in most instances, registration is mandatory.

Watch out for these warning signs of fraudulent investment activity:

- Unsolicited, high-pressure phone calls

- Claims of inside information

- "You must act at once!" warnings

- Forecasts of large, quick profits

- Claims of virtually no risk

- Contracts with names such as "deferred delivery," "fixed maturity," or "cash forward," which are not traded through regulated commodities exchanges. These contracts may be legal, but unlike those traded through regulated exchanges they do not carry many customer protection features.

BUSINESS OPPORTUNITY SCHEMES

The opportunity to "be your own boss," "work your own hours," and earn "unlimited amounts of money" are very attractive inducements. Unfortunately many of these opportunities are fraudulent schemes run by con men intent on parting you from your hard-earned cash. Victims lose an average of $20,000 on business-opportunity schemes. Most fraudulent business-opportunity schemes are found advertised in the "business opportunity" listings of daily newspapers, business journals, weekly newspapers, or magazines.

While the majority of franchisors are legitimate, a growing number operate under false pretenses. In these cases, the victim may be subjected to a fast-paced, high-pressure sales pitch — complete with fictitious sales projections, testimonials, slick promotional brochures — in which he is urged to "act immediately" to take advantage of a "ground floor" or "exclusive territory" opportunity. After a sale has been completed and money collected, any of a number of possible scenarios may ensue. The sales representative and the company represented disappear with the investment. The franchisor goes out of business.

Products or services turn out to be inferior, overpriced, or unmarketable. The franchise location has very low traffic. The specialized training promised by the franchisor is insufficient or nonexistent. Field support from the franchisor is inadequate. Advertising or promotions promised by the franchisor are inadequate or nonexistent. Whatever the reason, the investor duped into purchasing a business franchise under false pretenses sees plans for success fall to pieces.

Like franchising frauds, vending machine frauds are aimed at investors hoping to tap a time-tested, nationally recognized consumer market. The victim of this type of scheme usually relies on the vending company to select the product, equipment, and optimum location. Often, the outcome is similar to the franchising schemes already discussed. Additional factors in the failure of vending machine business include: machines placed in arcades or other location where numerous other machines offer similar or better products; machines that do not work properly; vending supplies that cannot be sold at a reasonable profit, and machines that require servicing and refilling far more often and in a more time-consuming manner than anticipated.

Mail-order business opportunities commonly are offered through advertisements in newspapers, magazines, and business journals. The ads may promise would-be entrepreneurs the chance to supplement their income by selling products through the mail. Huge returns, with virtually no expense or labor, are promised. But in reality, the products offered by the promoter, either directly or through unnamed suppliers, are shoddy, stale, and of dubious sales appeal. Of equally dubious value are the instructions, catalogs, mailing lists, and advice some promoters provide.

Multi-level marketing, a legitimate form of retailing, is a system in which independent business people, often known as distributors, sell the products or services of a multi-level marketing company to small business or consumers. Most sales are made in customers' homes, and distributors set their own hours, with earning levels dependent upon the extent of their efforts and sales ability. Legitimate multi-level marketing companies stress that there is no easy path to riches — that success can come only through consistent dedication and hard work.

Pyramid schemes, also known as "chain letter" schemes, are illegal variations of the multi-level marketing system. The emphasis in a pyramid scheme is on the quick profits to be earned by recruiting others, who in turn will recruit others, and so on – with each new recruit paying a specified sum which goes to those higher up in the chain. Although promotional literature or sales pitches may present this as a business opportunity, the merchandise or service to be sold is largely ignored. In some pyramid schemes, there is no product or service, or the product exists only in token form to show others that the individual is a member of the "sales team." These members are then paid commissions or bonuses for recruiting other investors, who also receive token products. Scant mention is made of the fact that the ever-increasing number of participants, all attempting to recoup their investments by recruiting from the ever-decreasing ranks of potential investors in a given area, will quickly result in market saturation.

Consider the results if one person recruited six distributors, each of whom in turn recruited six others, and carry the process through nine steps. At more than ten million people for every nine steps in the distribution program, the distributors soon would be recruiting one another. In order for everyone to profit in a pyramid scheme, there would have to be a never-ending supply of potential (and willing) participants. Obviously, there isn't. When the supply runs out, the pyramid collapses and most participants lose their investment.

Victims of work-at-home schemes usually are "hooked" through newspaper advertisements. A typical ad might offer to show the respondent how to "earn $100 a week by addressing envelopes in your spare time at home." Unsuspecting victims who mail their $19.95 for details are sent instructions on how to write and place similar ads in their own local newspapers. Other more complex, costlier schemes might offer to set up the respondent in a full-fledged business enterprise. If you were to respond, you might be trained to produce, for example, a certain mechanical or electronic device which supposedly is part of a larger mechanism to be assembled by the mail-order company. The company guarantees it will purchase your products, and after investing several thousand dollars in training, equipment, and supplies, you begin turning out the devices and shipping them to the company. The devices are returned with a letter explaining that their quality is inferior and below standards. The small print in your signed contract explains that the mail-order firm has the option of rejecting products it considers unacceptable — and what it considers acceptable turns out to be beyond your reach.

HOW TO PROTECT YOURSELF

Caution is your best line of defense. Before you enter into a business arrangement, find out as much as possible about the reliability of the firm offering the business opportunity and make certain you fully understand the responsibilities of all parties. To avoid becoming a victim of a business opportunity scheme use the following methods to "check out" all business and investment opportunities.

Ask for financial statements for the past three years and verify that they have been audited by a reputable firm. Financial statements should include full details on operating revenues and source of revenues, as well as a profit and loss statement. Ask for evidence or research to support claims of growth potential and profitability, and have an accountant look it over.

Find out how long the firm has been in business, and ask for information on its litigation record. Look for lawsuits, bankruptcy proceedings, and charges of embezzlement, fraud, and unfair or deceptive practices. Ask for and check business, bank, and credit references. Be wary if references seem to respond too quickly and eagerly; they may be accomplices waiting for such calls. Never sign

anything until you have thoroughly documented the deal beyond reasonable doubt and have more than satisfied yourself that it's safe and solid. Remember that firms offering legitimate business opportunities are interested in answering your questions fully. If a firm cannot or will not answer key questions, you would be wise to avoid further involvement.

In the case of business opportunities that appear to guarantee "territorial rights," insist on a written explanation of the restrictions to be imposed upon you or potential competitors who also may buy into the business. Be wary of sales agents who emphasize the profitability of recruiting others into the business, rather than making sales and providing exceptional service. Be wary of sales agents who offer you "free" merchandise as an inducement to buy.

Check the qualifications of sales agents or dealers. Often the easiest way to do this is by contacting the associations that license agents in their area of specialty. For example, agents selling land or property must possess a real estate license issued by the state's real estate commission. Be wary of business opportunities that promise quick or unusually high returns on "once in a lifetime" investments. Be skeptical of "private sales" or offerings, particularly those in which substantial discounts are offered on so-called list prices. Don't be taken in by impressive-sounding company names or addresses.

If you are asked to pay an initial fee far greater than the combined worth of the kits, training, and equipment the company offers you, stay away. Be particularly cautious about doing business with firms located outside the U.S. It may become difficult or even impossible to trace and recover your money. Look closely at the quality of printed documents. Deeds, securities, guarantees, or other supposedly official documents may be counterfeits, and an unprofessional printing job could be a tip-off.

Don't be fooled by initial easily obtained returns on your investment. A smooth con artist may use your investment to pay these returns, in order to entice you to invest even more heavily. Before buying or investing in an enterprise, product, or property, check with others in similar businesses to see if the price quoted is reasonable. If the business opportunity involves door-to-door sales, find out if the firm is a member of the Direct Selling Association.

Before buying into a sales or mail-order business, look carefully at the quality of the product or service, its potential market, your profit margin, and the reliability and background of the mail-order company. Find out if the mail-order business is a member of the Direct Marketing Association.

The Alliance Against Fraud in Telemarketing — composed of consumer groups, trade associations, consumer protection offices, labor unions, industry, and government agencies — points out that legitimate telemarketers (and there are many) do not use high-pressure tactics and that consumers are frequently able to be duped because they don't fully understand the offer being made. Franchises are governed by FTC regulations. Distributorships are not. If you're looking at a franchise offer, be sure to ask for the franchisor's offering circular or disclosure document. Check with the FTC. The commission has lots of useful information available for free about franchise and business-opportunity investment. Before doing business with a firm, contact your local Better Business Bureau for a company reliability report.

IF YOU ARE VICTIMIZED

If you are victimized by a con artist, fraudulent business opportunity, or investment you should:

- Stop payment on checks in transit

- Notify your local police department

- Contact the state or federal agencies that oversee activities in your area of concern and provide them with full details, in writing, of the fraud

- Call your local Better Business Bureau and send the bureau copies of the material going to the federal or state agency

Appendix

SECURITY PRODUCT MANUFACTURERS

To assist you in locating specific home security products I have compiled the following list of manufacturers. I have grouped the manufacturers according to product, with the products listed in alphabetical order. Most of these companies will be happy to send you product information and direct you to their dealer nearest you. No endorsement of the listed companies or their products is made or implied by the author or publisher.

COMPUTERS

Security Hardware

Mac Products (Mac Lock)
20231 San Gabriel Valley Dr.
Walnut, CA 91789
(714) 595-4838

Secure-It Inc.
10 Center Square
East Longmeadow, MA 01028
(800) 451-7592

Inventory Software for IBM and IBM-compatibles

Dynacomp, Inc. (Home Insurance Inventory & Home Insurance Protector)
Dynacomp Office Bldg.
178 Phillips Rd.
Webster, NY 14580
(716) 265-4040

HomeCraft Computer Products (Home Insurance)
P.O. Box 974
Tualatin, OR 97062
(503) 692-3732

Zephyr Services (Home Inventory)
1900 Murray
Pittsburgh, PA 15217
(412) 422-6600

Inventory Systems for Macintosh

Software Excitement (Home Inventory)
6475 Crater Lake Hwy.
Central Point, OR 97502
(800) 444-5457

DOORS

Residential Metal and Fire Doors

Residential Metal & Fire Doors
American-Standard (Steelcraft)
9017 Blue Ash Rd.
Cincinnati, OH 45242
(513) 745-6400

Amweld Building Products, Inc.
1500 Amweld Dr.
Industrial Park
Garrettsville, OH 44231
(800) 248-6116

Ceco Door Division
One Tower Lane
Oakbrook Terrace, IL 60181
(312) 242-2000

General Products Co., Inc. (Benchmark)
P.O. Box 7387
Fredericksburg, VA 22404
(703) 898-5700

Johnson Metal Products
305 Industrial Parkway
P.O. Box 667
Richmond, IN 47374
(317) 962-8515

Minton Co.
100 View St., Suite 100
Mountain View, CA 94041-1342
(415) 961-9800

Pease Industries, Inc.
(Ever-Strait Door Systems)
7100 Dixie Hwy.
P.O. Box 14-8001
Fairfield, OH 45014-8001
(800) 543-1180

Sun-Dor-Co
P.O. Box 13
Wichita, KS 67201
(800) 835-0190

The Maiman Co.
505 East Trafficway
Springfield, MO 65802
(800) 641-4320

Steel Security Doors

Weatherguard Ornamental Iron (Sears)
6890 S. Emporia
Englewood, CO 80112
(800) 525-0329

FIRE PROTECTION

Fire Escape Ladders

All-Safe, Inc.
Box 2417
Newport Beach, CA 92663
(714) 646-7988

M & G Products Inc.
284 Seigel St.
Brooklyn, NY 11206
(718) 497-7316

R.A.W. Rescue Products, Inc. (Exit Traveler)
P.O. Box 314
Ambler, PA 19002-0314
(215) 643-1007

Fire Extinguishers

Ansul Fire Protection, Wormald U.S., Inc.
One Stanton St.
Marinette, WI 54143
(715) 735-7411
All types

Badger Powhatan, A Figgie International Co.
Box 7146
Charlottesville, VA 22906
(804) 973-4361
Carbon dioxide, dry chemical, halon.

Black & Decker
P.O. Box 5259
Clifton, NJ 07012
(800) KEEPOUT
Carbon dioxide.

Cato, Inc.
345 W. Fullerton Pkwy., Suite 701
Chicago, IL 60614
(312) 477-8811
Halon.

Falcon Safety Products, Inc.
25 Chubb Way
Box 1299
Somerville, NJ 08876-1299
(201) 707-4900
Halon.

General Fire Extinguisher Co.
1685 Shermer Rd.
Northbrook, IL 60062
(312) 272-7500
Carbon dioxide, dry chemical, water.

Great Lakes Chemical
Box 2200
West Lafayette, IN 47906
(317) 497-6234
Halon.

ICI Americas, Inc.
Box 819
Valley Forge, PA 19482
(800) 458-8342
Halon.

J L Industries
4450 W. 78th St. Circle
Bloomington, MN 55435
(612) 835-6850
Carbon dioxide, dry chemical, foam, halon.

Kidde, Walter
Walter Kidde Dr.
Wake Forest, NC 27587
(919) 556-6811
Carbon dioxide, dry chemical, foam, halon.

Pittway (First Alert)
780 McClure Rd.
Aurora, IL 60504-2495
(312) 851-7330
Carbon dioxide.

Porta-Matic Corp.
156 Railroad Ave.
Box 353
Closter, NJ 07624
(201) 768-8196
Dry chemical.

Potter-Roemer, Inc.
16833 Edwards Rd.
Cerritos, CA 90701
(213) 404-3753
All types.

R.C. Industries (Fyr Fyter)
Linden, NJ 07036
Carbon dioxide.

Foam Dispensing Systems

Brushfire Hydrant Co.
1818-B Mount Diablo Blvd.
Walnut Creek, CA 94596
(415) 932-5080

Smoke Detectors

Black & Decker (Long-Life)
701 E. Joppa Rd.
Towson, MD 21204
(301) 828-3900

BRK Electronics (First Alert)
780 McClure Rd.
Aurora, IL 60504-2495
(312) 851-7330

Eveready Battery Co. Inc. (Eversafe)
39 Old Ridebury Rd.
Danbury, CT 06817-0001
(203) 794-2000

Family Gard Inc.
P.O. Box 68
Aurora, IL 60507-0068
(312) 851-7330

Fyrnetics Inc. (Lifesaver & Fire Sentry)
1021 Davis Rd.
Elgin, IL 60123
(800) 654-7665

Jameson Home Products (Code One 200)
2820 Thatcher Rd.
Downers Grove, IL 60515
(312) 963-9850

Sprinkler Systems

Automatic Sprinkler Corp.
19668 Progress Dr.
Strongsville, OH 41136
(216) 238-9330

Globe Fire Sprinkler Corp.
P.O. Box 796
4077 Airpark Dr.
Standish, MI 48648
(517) 846-4583

Central Sprinkler Corp.
451 N. Cannon Ave.
Lansdale, PA 19446
(215) 362-0700

Firematic Sprinkler Devices Inc.
900 Boston Tpke.
Shrewsbury, MA 01545
(508) 845-2121

Grinnell Corp
3 Tyco Park
Exeter, NH 03833
(603) 778-9200

Reliable Automatic Sprinkler Co.
525 N. MacQuesten Pkwy.
Mount Vernon, NY 10552
(914) 668-3470

Star Sprinkler Corp.
307 W. Layton Ave.
Milwaukee, WI 53207
(414) 769-5500

The Viking Corp.
210 N. Industrial Dr.
Hastings, MI 49058
(616) 945-9501

LIGHTING

General Lighting Hardware

General Electric Corporation
Nela Park, Unit 4338
Cleveland, OH 44112
(216) 266-8502

Halo Lighting
400 Busse Road
Elk Grove Village, IL 60007
(312) 956-8400

Home Equipment Mfg Co. (Hemco)
P.O. Box 878
Westminster, CA 92684
(714) 892-6681

Honeywell Inc.– Residential Division
1985 Douglas Drive N.
Golden Valley, MN 55422
(612) 542-3339

Hubbell Lighting
2000 Electric Way
Christiansburg, VA 24073
(800) 521-2737

Intermatic Inc.
Intermatic Plaza
Spring Grove, IL 60081
(815) 675-2321

L.E.Mason Co.
98 Business St.
Boston, MA 02136
(617) 361-1710

Lights of America Inc.
611 Reyes Dr.
Walnut, CA 91789
(714) 594-7883

Regent Lighting Corporation
P.O. Box 2658
Burlington, NC 27216
(919) 226-2411

Stanley
41700 Gardenbrook Rd.
Novi, MI 48050
(313) 344-0070

Toro Home Improvement Div.
5300 Shoreline Blvd.
Mound, MN 55364
(612) 472-8300

Motion Detectors

Consumer Group (Electripak)
P.O. Box 30489
Memphis, TN 38130-0489

Intelectron
21021 Corsair Blvd.
Hayward, CA 94545
(415) 732-6790

TestRite Products Corporation (Dusk to Dawn)
395 Allwood Rd.
Clifton, NJ 07012
(201) 773-9109

Solar Lighting Hardware

Chronar Corporation, Sunergy Inc.
P.O. Box 177
Princeton, NJ 08542
(800) CHR-ONAR

Potrans International Inc.
500 E. Pacific Coast Hwy., No. 210
Seal Beach, CA 90740
(213) 596-4456

Timers

Cable Electric Products Inc. (Power Command)
P.O. Box 6767
Providence, RI 02940
(401) 781-5400

Hunter Fan Company
2500 Frisco Ave.
Memphis, TN 38114
(901) 743-1360

Leviton Mfg. Co., Inc.
59-25 Little Neck Pkwy.
Little Neck, NY 11362

Paragon Electric Co. Inc. (Time Command)
606 Parkway Blvd.
P.O. Box 28
Two Rivers, WI 54241
(414) 793-1161

Toastmaster Inc. (Ingraham)
1801 N. Stadium Blvd.
Columbia, MO 65201
(314) 445-8666

X-10 (USA), Inc.
185A Legrand Ave.
Northvale, NJ 07647
(201) 784-9700

LOCKS
Automotive Locks and Accessories

Alba Security
5420 Netherland Ave.
Bronx, NY 10471
(212) 543-8559

Anes Electronics
4112 Del Rey Ave.
Marina Del Rey, CA 90292
(213)306-8115

Argus Security International, Ltd.
94-28 Northern Blvd.
Jackson Heights, NY 11372
(800) 882-7487

Auto-Matic Products Co.
1918 S. Michigan Ave.
Chicago, IL 60616
(312) 842-1600

Automotive Security Systems, Inc.
9715 Miller, Suite 35,
Dallas, TX 75238
(214) 348-4497

C & A Control Systems, Inc.
7117 Commercial Park Dr.
Knoxville, TN 37918
(615) 922-2148

Chapman Products, Inc.
2638 United Ln.
Elk Grove Village, IL 60007
(800) 242-7626

Colorado Carsafe Co.
1944 S. Kearney Way
Denver, CO 80224
(303) 692-8044

Covr-Larm
7841 Alabama Ave., No. 12
Canoga Park, CA 91304
(818) 704-5552

ETIP, Inc.
P.O. Box 571
Addison, IL 60101
(312) 530-8393

Excalibur of America
8757 S. Flatrock Rd.
Douglasville, GA 30134
(404) 942-9876

Great Bend Marketing Systems, Inc.
1117 Washington
Box 1349
Great Bend, KS 67530
(316) 793-5018

Levy, David, Co. Inc.
6825 Whitehall Way
Paramount, CA 90723
(213) 408-6717

Lok-Itt Co., Inc.
27000 Richmond Rd.
Solon, OH 44139
(216) 349-0110

MaxiGuard of America
2700 Touhy Ave.
Elk Grove Village, IL 60007
(800) 323-6601

Ped-Al-Loc Mfg., Inc.
Box 17107
Pittsburgh, PA 15235
(412) 795-8700

Ranger Vehicle Security
One Naclerio Plaza
Bronx, NY 10466
(800) 223-1451

Scosche Industries, Inc.
5160 Gabbert Rd.
Box 8099
Moorpark, CA 93020-8099
(800) 621-3695

Seco-Larm U.S.A., Inc.
17811 Sky Park Circle, D & E
Irvine, CA 92714
(800) 662-0800

Speco
Box 624
Lindenhurst, NY 11757
(800) 645-5516

Steal Stopper Div., Directed Electronics, Inc.
1413 Linda Vista Dr.
San Marcos, CA 92069
(619) 471-1714

Tourek, J.J.
1800 Touhy Ave.
Elk Grove Village, IL 60007
(800) 323-8172

Vehicle Security Electronics, Inc.
21540-F Prairie St.
Chatsworth, CA 91311
(818) 700-7900

Locks — Bicycle Locks

Kryptonite Corp.
95 Freeport St.
Dorchester, MA 02122
(617) 265-4800

Master Lock Co.
2600 N. 32nd St.
Box 10367
Milwaukee, WI 53210
(414) 444-2800

U.S. Lock Corporation
77 Rodeo Dr.
Brentwood, NY 11717
(800) 525-5000

Locks — Door and Window Security Hardware

Belwith International Ltd.
18071 Arenth Ave.
City of Industry, CA 91748
(213) 965-5533

Brainerd Mfg. Co.
115 N. Washington St.
E. Rochester, NY 14445
(716) 586-0028

Don-Jo Manufacturing
45 Granite St.
P.O. Box 62
Leominster, MA 01453
(508) 534-1115

M.A.G. Engineering & Mfg. Co. Inc.
15261 Transistor Lane
Huntington Beach, CA 92649
(714) 891-5100

National Mfg. Inc.
P.O. Box 577
Sterling, IL 61081
(815) 625-1320

Slide-Co Mfg. Inc.
P.O. Box 725
Mira Loma, CA 91752-0725
(714) 681-6862

U.S. Lock Corporation
77 Rodeo Dr.
Brentwood, NY 11717
(800) 525-5000

VSI Hardware Industries (Fortress Hardware)
P.O. Box 4445
Sylmar, CA 91342
(818) 367-2131

Locks — Door Locks and Hardware

Abloy Security Locks, Div. of Wartsila, Inc.
6200 Denton Dr.
Box 35406
Dallas, TX 75235
(214) 358-4762

Best Lock Corporation
6161 E. 75th St.
Indianapolis, IN 46250
(317) 849-2250

Corbin, Hardware Div.
225 Episcopal Rd.
Berlin, CT 06037
(203) 225-7411

Dexter Lock
300 Webster Road
Auburn, AL 36830
(205) 887-3300

Kwikset Corporation
516 E. Santa Ana St.
Anaheim, CA 92803
(714) 535-8111

Lori Lock Corp.
9 Old Turnpike Rd.
P.O. Box 490
Southington, CT 06489
(203) 621-3601

Medeco Security Locks Inc.
P.O. Box 3075
Salem, VA 24153
(703) 380-5000

National Lock Corporation
104 Keystone Dr.
Sikeston, MO 63801
(314) 472-0220

Preso-Matic Lock Co., Inc.
3048 Industrial 33rd St.
Fort Pierce, FL 34946
(407) 465-7400

Schlage Lock Co.
2401 Bay Shore Blvd.
San Francisco, CA 92803
(415) 467-1100

Ultra Hardware Products Inc.
9246 Commerce Hwy.
Box 679
Pennsauken, NJ 08110

U.S. Lock Corporation
77 Rodeo Dr.
Brentwood, NY 11717
(800) 525-5000

Weiser Lock
555 McFadden Ave.
Huntington Beach, CA 92649
(714) 898-0811

Weslock
13344 S. Main
Los Angeles, CA 90061
(213) 327-2770

Willock
8086 S. Yale, Suite 170
Tulsa, OK 74136
(918) 481-0467

Yale Security Inc.
P.O. Box 25288
Charlotte, NC 28229-8010
(704) 283-2101

Locks — Gun Locks

Master Lock Co.
2600 N. 32nd St.
Box 10367
Milwaukee, WI 53210
(414) 444-2800

U.S. Lock Corporation
77 Rodeo Dr.
Brentwood, NY 11717
(800) 525-5000

Locks — Padlocks

Abloy Security Locks, Div. of Wartsila, Inc.
6200 Denton Dr.
Box 35406
Dallas, TX 75235
(214) 358-4762

Abus Lock Co.
Box 2367
Woburn, MA 01888
(617) 935-8370

American Lock Co.
3400 W. Exchange Rd.
Crete, IL 60417
(312) 534-2000

Best Lock Corporation
6161 E.75th St.
Indianapolis, IN 46250
(317) 849-2250

Chicago Lock Corp.
4311 W. Belmont Ave.
Chicago, IL 60641
(312) 282-8199

Fort Lock Corp.
3000 N. River Rd.
River Grove, IL 60171
(312) 456-1100

Illinois Lock Co., Div. of The Eastman Co.
301 W. Hintz Rd.
Wheeling, IL 60090
(312) 537-1800

Master Lock Co.
2600 N. 32nd St.
Box 10367
Milwaukee, WI 53210
(414) 444-2800

Medeco Security Locks Inc.
P.O. Box 3075
Salem, VA 24153
(703) 380-5000

Sargent & Greenleaf, Inc.
1 Security Dr.
Nicholasville, KY 40356
(606) 885-9411

U.S. Lock Corporation
77 Rodeo Dr.
Brentwood, NY 11717
(800) 525-5000

VSI Hardware Industries (Fortress Hardware)
P.O. Box 4445
Sylmar, CA 91342
(818) 367-2131

PERSONAL PROTECTION DEVICES

Non-lethal Weapons

Accuracy Systems, Inc.
15205 N. Cave Creek Rd.
Phoenix, AZ 85032
(602) 971-1991

Aero Chem Corp.
11520 N. Port Washington Rd.
Mequon, WI 53092
(414) 241-8833

Bestex Co.
3421 San Fernando Rd., Unit B
Los Angeles, CA 90065
(213) 255-4477

Everquest, Inc.
875 S. 72nd St.
Omaha, NE 68114
(402) 554-0383

Gripton International Corp.
10850 Wilshire Blvd., Suite 1025
Los Angeles, CA 90024
(800) 999-4442

Law Enforcement Assoc., Inc.
Box 1117
Medford, NJ 08055
(201) 864-0001

Luckey Police Products
Box 23339
Oakland Park, FL 33307
(305) 564-3321

Peterzell Co., The
Box 521357
Longwood, FL 32752-1357
(407) 830-1171

Price, G.T., Products, Inc.
2223 E. 37th St.
Los Angeles, CA 90058
(213) 583-1281

RBS Industries Corp.
1312 Washington Ave.
St. Louis, MO 63103
(314) 241-8464

Security Equipment Corp.
2120 Miami St.
St. Louis, MO 63118
(800) 325-9568

Shamash International
249 N. Brand Blvd., Suite 425
Glendale, CA 91203
(818) 243-8469

Personal Alarms

Korex Industries (The Screamer)
51 El Pueblo
Scotts Valley, CA 95066

Sportsman Athletic Truss
   (Body Guard Personal Alarm)
11875 Caminito Ronaldo #104
San Diego, CA 92128

SECURITY SYSTEMS

Automotive

Accele Electronics
1860 Obispo
Long Beach, CA 90804
(800) 822-2353

Ademco
165 Eileen Way
Syosset, NY 11791
(516) 921-6700

Alba Security
5420 Netherland Ave.
Bronx, NY 10471
(212) 543-8559

Alpine Electronics of America,
   Mobile Electronics Div.
19145 Gramercy Pl.
Torrance, CA 90501
(213) 326-8000

American Security Equipment Co.
236 E. Star of India Ln.
Carson, CA 90746
(213) 538-4670

Anes Electronics
4112 Del Rey Ave.
Marina Del Rey, CA 90292
(213)306-8115

Argus Security International, Ltd.
94-28 Northern Blvd.
Jackson Heights, NY 11372
(800) 882-7487

Arthur Fulmer, Inc.
2nd & Gayoso
P.O. Box 117
Memphis, TN 38101

Audiovox Security (Prestige)
150 Marcus Blvd.
Hauppauge, NY 11788
(516) 231-7750

Auto Alarm Supply Corp.
1814 Woodson Rd.
St. Louis, MO 63114
(314) 428-7500

Auto Security, Inc.
6136 S. Dixie Hwy.
South Miami, FL 33143
(800) 334-7814

Autoguard, Inc.
3885 Convoy St.
San Diego, CA 92111
(619) 279-4551

Auto-Matic Products Co.
1918 S. Michigan Ave.
Chicago, IL 60616
(312) 842-1600

Automotive Security Products
550 S. Columbus Ave.
Mount Vernon, NY 10550
(914) 668-3887

Automotive Security Systems, Inc.
9715 Miller, Suite 35
Dallas, TX 75238
(214) 348-4497

AutoPage, Inc.
1815 West 205th St., Suite 101
Torrance, CA 90501-1525
(800) 262-2527

Autosafe Electronics, Inc.
201 E. Campbell Ave.
Campbell, CA 95008
(408) 378-3423

Baretta
4645 Van Nuys Blvd.
Sherman Oaks, CA 91403

Bathurst, Inc.
Box 27
Tyrone, PA 16686
(814) 684-2603

Blue Grass Electronics, Inc.
602 W. Jefferson St.
LaGrange, KY 40031
(502) 222-7174

C & A Control Systems, Inc.
7117 Commercial Park Dr.
Knoxville, TN 37918
(615) 922-2148

Calrad Electronics
819 N. Highland Ave.
Los Angeles, CA 90038
(213) 465-2131

Campbell Co.
6036 Muldrow Rd.
Carmichael, CA 95608
(916) 961-9594

Chapman Products, Inc.
2638 United Ln.
Elk Grove Village, IL 60007
(800) 242-7626

Clifford Electronics, Inc.
20750 Lassen St.
Chatsworth, CA 91311
(800) 824-3208

Close Associates, Inc.
1 Diamond Rd.
Danbury, CT 06810
(203) 792-4797

Code-Alarm Vehicle Security Systems
950 E. Whitcomb St.
Madison Heights, MI 48071
(800) 421-3209

Covr-Larm
7841 Alabama Ave., No. 12
Canoga Park, CA 91304
(818) 704-5552

Crimestopper Security Products Inc.
1770 S. Tapo St.
Simi Valley, CA 93063
(800) 662-5276

Dalme, Inc.
7234 Eton Ave.
Canoga Park, CA 91303
(818) 712-0422

David Levy Co. (Truster, Black Widow)
6825 Walthall Way
Paramount, CA 90723
(213) 408-6717

Directed Electronics, Inc.
1413 Linda Vista Dr.
San Marcos, CA 92069
(619) 471-1714

Electrolert, Inc.
4949 S. 25A
Tipp City, OH 45371
(513) 667-2461

Electronic Security Products of California
21200 Van Owen St.
Canoga Park, CA 91303
(818) 999-0990

Electronics of North America, Inc.
6725 Mesa Ridge Rd.
San Diego, CA 92121
(619) 458-1744

Enerco
9615 W. Marginal Way S.
Seattle, WA 98108
(206) 762-1422

Excalibur of America
8757 S. Flatrock Rd.
Douglasville, GA 30134
(404) 942-9876

Fox Technology
4518 Taylorville Rd.
Dayton, OH 45424

Gard-A-Car, Inc.
8143 Macomb
Grosse Isle, MI 48138

Granada Electronics, Inc.
485 Kent Ave.
Brooklyn, NY 11211
(718) 387-1157

Great Bend Marketing Systems, Inc.
1117 Washington
Box 1349
Great Bend, KS 67530
(316) 793-5018

Harrison Electronics
51 Gravel St.
Wilkes Barre, PA 18705

Hi-Pro-Tech, Inc.
Box 1357
Lansdale, PA 19446
(215) 822-2114

Highland Mobile Electronics
8280 A. Castleton Corner Dr.
Indianapolis, IN 46250
(317) 849-5870

Intrusion Components, Inc.
277 Elm St.
Bridgewater, MA 02324
(508) 697-3355

Kenwood Electronics
2201 E. Dominquez
Long Beach, CA 90810
(213) 639-9000

KSP America Corp.
259 Wattis Way
South San Francisco, CA 94080
(415) 952-5347

KTK Engineering Co., Inc.
820 S. Palm Ave., Suite 21
Alhambra, CA 91803
(818) 308-9871

Kolin Industries, Inc.
Box 300
Pound Ridge, NY 10576
(914) 764-5775

Landia, Inc.
450 3rd St.
Excelsior, MN 55331
(612) 474-4116

Logitran Security System
11052 Washington Blvd.
Culver City, CA 90232
(213) 837-3562

Lo-Jack Corp.
72 River Park
Needham, MA 02194
(617) 444-4900

Magnadyne Corporation (Carbine Auto
    Alarm & Stereo Camouflage Kits)
P.O. Box 5365
Carson, CA 90749-5365
(800) 421-1928

Magnum Auto Security Systems
21822 Lassen St., Bldg. K
Chatsworth, CA 91311
(818) 700-2728

Majestic Electronics, Inc.
14614 Lanark St.
Panorama City, CA 91402
(800) 423-2961

MaxiGuard of America
2700 Touhy Ave.
Elk Grove Village, IL 60007
(800) 323-6601

McDermott, Julian A., Corp.
1639 Stephen St.
Ridgewood, NY 11385
(718) 456-3606

Minatronics Corp.
3046 Penn Ave.
Pittsburgh, PA 15201
(800) 344-5952

Mindreader
1923 Bomar St.
Fort Worth, TX 76103

Monroe Timer Co., Inc.
264 East 3rd St.
Mount Vernon, NY 10550
(914) 699-6612

Optex (USA), Inc.
363 Vanness Way, Suite 402
Torrance, CA 90501
(800) 556-7839

Paragon Security Corp.
10 Taylor St.
Freeport, NY 11520
(516) 546-0855

Pentron Products, Inc.
1560 Montague Expy.
San Jose, CA 95131
(800) 654-4454

Pioneer Electronics
2265 East 220th St.,
Long Beach, CA 90810
(213) 746-6337

Rabbit Systems, Inc.
100 Wilshire Blvd.
Santa Monica, CA 90401
(213) 393-9830

Radio Shack/Tandy
1300 One Tandy Center
Fort Worth, TX 76102
(817) 390-3011

Ranger Vehicle Security
One Naclerio Plaza
Bronx, NY 10466
(800) 223-1451

Sansui Electronics Corp.
1250 Valley Brook Ave.
Lyndhurst, NJ 07071
(201) 460-9710

Seco-Larm U.S.A., Inc. (Enforcer)
17811 Sky Park Circle, D & E
Irvine, CA 92714
(800) 662-0800

Serpico
3885 Convoy St.
San Diego, CA 92111
(412) 854-1300

Speco
Box 624
Lindenhurst, NY 11757
(800) 645-5516

Steal Stopper Div., Directed Electronics, Inc.
1413 Linda Vista Dr.
San Marcos, CA 92069
(619) 471-1714

Tech Lock, Inc.
16461 Sherman Way
Van Nuys, CA 91406

Techguard Industries, Inc.
53A Otis St.
West Babylon, NY 11704
(800) 247-3287

Techne Electronics Ltd.
916 Commercial St.
Palo Alto, CA 94303
(800) 227-8875

Thug Bug Corp.
205 Nutmeg Rd. S.
South Windsor, CT 06074
(203) 282-9220

Triple G, Inc.
2101 Corvus Dr.
San Jose, CA 95124
(408) 559-7720

Ultrason Int'l, Inc.
11601 Wilshire Blvd.
Los Angeles, CA 90025
(213) 852-9827

Ultratech
4A Keith Way
Hingham, MA 02043

Ungo/Techne Electronics Ltd.
916 Commercial St.
Palo Alto, CA 94303
(415) 856-8646

United Sound Systems
5005 W. Century Blvd., Suite. 108
Inglewood, CA 90304

Vandal Alert
3555 Harbor Gateway So., Suite C
Costa Mesa, CA 92626
(714) 549-2218

Vehicle Security Electronics, Inc.
21540-F Prairie St.
Chatsworth, CA 91331
(818) 700-7900

Vocalarm Security Products
6860 Canby Ave., Suite 120
Reseda, CA 91335

Watchdog Car Alarms, Inc.
61-35 Freash Meadow Ln.
Flushing, NY 11365
(718) 358-2771

Wolo Mfg. Corp.
1 Saxwood St.
Deer Park, NY 11729
(800) 645-5808

U.S. Lock Corporation
77 Rodeo Dr.
Brentwood, NY 11717
(800) 525-5000

Home

Ademco, a Div. of Pittway Corp.
165 Eileen Way
Syosset, NY 11791
(516) 921-6704

ADT Security Systems Inc.
300 Interpace Pkwy.
Parsippany, NJ 07054
(800) 238-4636

Aritech-Moose Security Products
1510 Tate Blvd S.E.
P.O. Box 2904
Hickory, NC 28603
(800) 438-8118

AT&T Consumer Products
5 Wood Hollow Rd., Rm. 1145
Parsippany, NJ 07054
(800) 523-0055

Audiovox Security, Div. of Audiovox Corp.
150 Marcus Blvd.
Hauppauge, NY 11788
(516) 231-7750

Automotive Security Systems, Inc.
9715 Miller, Suite 35
Dallas, TX 75238
(214) 348-4497

Black & Decker, U.S. Household Products Group
6 Armstrong Rd.
Shelton, CT 06484
(800) 533-7688

Brink's Home Security
1628 Valwood Pkwy.
Carrollton, TX 75006
(214) 484-1755

Capricorn Electronics Inc.
P.O. Box 66
48 Capricorn Drive
Maiden, NC 28650
(800) 438-3750

Dicon Systems Inc.
631 Executive Dr.
Willowbrook, IL 60521
(800) 387-2868

Eversafe, Eveready Battery Co. Inc.
Checkerboard Sq.
St. Louis, MO 63164
(314) 821-3777

Heath Zenith Consumer Products Group
Hilltop Rd.
St. Joseph, MI 49085
(616) 982-5642

Homes/Dictograph Security Systems
26 Columbia Tpk.
Florham Park, NJ 07932
(201) 822-1400

Honeywell Protection Services
Opus Center
9900 Bren Rd. E.
Minnetonka, MN 55345
(612) 931-7200

Hyundai Electronics of North America
6724 Mesa Ridge Rd.
San Diego, CA 92121
(800) 272-1800

ITI "Interactive Technologies, Inc."
2266 North Second Street
North St. Paul, MN 55109
(800) 777-5484

International Consumer Brands Inc.
   (Security Force)
126 Monroe Tpke.
Trumbull, CT 06611
(203) 268-0200

Linear Corp., A Nortek Co.
2055 Corte Del Nogal
Carlsbad, CA 92009
(800) 421-1845

Mitsubishi Electic Sales America Inc.
Box 6007
Cypress, CA 90630
(714) 220-2500

Napco Security Systems, Inc.
333 Bayview Ave.
Amityville, NY 11701
(800) 645-9445

NuTone
Madison and Red Bank Rds.
Cincinnati, OH 45227-1599
(513) 527-5100

Radio Shack, Tandy Corp.
300 One Tandy Center
Fort Worth, TX 76102
(817) 390-3011

Schlage Lock Co. (Keepsafer)
2401 Bay Shore Blvd.
San Francisco, CA 92803
(415) 467-1100

Seco-Larm U.S.A., Inc.
17811 Sky Park Circle, D & E
Irvine, CA 92714
(800) 662-0800

Security Electronic Sales Ltd. (Call For Help)
9 E. 45th St.
New York, NY 10017
(212) 309-6949

Sentrol, Inc.
10831 S.W. Cascade Blvd.
Portland, OR 97223
(800) 547-2556

Sescoa (Body Guard I)
6535 E. Osborn Rd.
Scottsdale, AZ 85251
(800) 528-4455

Silent Knight Security Systems
1700 Freeway Blvd. N.
Minneapolis, MN 55430
(800) 328-0103

Sonitrol Corporation
424 N. Washington St.
Alexandria, VA 22314
(703) 549-3900

Transcience
179 Ludlow
Stamford, CT 06902
(800) 243-3494

United Security Products, Inc.
2171 Research Dr.
Livermore, CA 94550
(415) 455-8866

Unity Systems Inc. (Home Manager)
2606 Spring Street
Redwood City, CA 94063
(800) 55-UNITY

Universal Security Instruments
10324 S. Dolfield Rd.
Owings Mills, MD 21117
(301) 363-3000

VSI Hardware Industries
   (Fortress Home Security System)
P.O. Box 4445
Sylmar, CA 91342
(818) 367-2131

Marine

Aqualarm
1151 D Bay Blvd.
Chula Vista, CA 92011
(619) 575-4011

Audiovox Security
150 Marcus Blvd.
Hauppage, NY 11788
(516) 231-7750

Auto-Matic Products
1918 S. Michigan Ave.
Chicago, IL 60616
(312) 842-1600

AutoPage, Inc.
1815 West 205th St., Suite 101
Torrance, CA 90501-1525
(213) 618-2002

Automotive Security Systems, Inc.
9715 Miller, Suite 35
Dallas, TX 75238
(214) 348-4497

Boat Sentry
271 Rte. 46 W., Suite A-104
Fairfield, NJ 07006
(201) 989-1904

Brisson Development, Inc.
13845 Nine Mile Rd.
Warren, MI 48089
(313) 778-3038

CAM Co., Inc.
400 Rhodes
Big Rock, IL 60511
(708) 556-3110

Close Associates, Inc.
1 Diamond Rd.
Danbury, CT 06810
(203) 792-4797

Cord Marine Industries Inc.
8800 N. Bayshore Dr.
Miami, FL 33138
(305) 756-0666

Covr-Larm
7841 Alabama Ave., No. 12
Canoga Park, CA 91304
(818) 704-5552

Crimestopper Security Products Inc.
1770 S. Tapo St.
Simi Valley, CA 93063
(800) 662-5276

Enerco
9615 W. Marginal Way S.
Seattle, WA 98108
(206) 762-1422

Falcon Safety Products,Inc.
25 Chubb Way
Box 1299
Somerville, NJ 08876-1299
(201) 707-4900

Intrusion Components, Inc.
277 Elm St.
Bridgewater, MA 02324
(508) 697-3355

Marine Technologies
1001 Brentwood Lane
Mt. Prospect, IL 60056
(312) 577-3717

Marinetics
P.O. Box 2676
Newport Beach, CA 92663
(714) 646-8889

MaxiGuard of America
2700 Touhy Ave.
Elk Grove Village, IL 60007
(800) 323-6601

Metro Auto Marine Accessories
P.O. Box 3629
Annapolis, MD 21403
(301) 263-7608

Minatronics Corp.
3046 Penn Ave.
Pittsburgh, PA 15201
(800) 344-5952

Northstar Systems, Inc.
2476 Co. Rd. 137N.
Brainerd, MN 56401
(218) 963-4275

Paragon Security Corporation
10 Taylor St.
Freeport, NY 11520
(516) 546-0855

Pentron Products, Inc.
1560 Montague Expy.
San Jose, CA 95131
(800) 654-4454

Seco-Larm U.S.A., Inc.
17811 Sky Park Circle, D & E
Irvine, CA 92714
(800) 662-0800

Steal Stopper Div., Directed Electronics, Inc.
1413 Linda Vista Dr.
San Marcos, CA 92069
(619) 471-1714

Tele Comm Communications
P.O. Box 3232
Margate, NJ 08402
(609) 822-8588

Triple G, Inc.
2101 Corvus Dr.
San Jose, CA 95124
(408) 559-7720

Watch Products Ltd.
Link House, Works Rd.
Letchworth, Hert. SG6 1LR, England
0462 678131

Wolsk Safeguard
P.O. Box 1006
Bethesda, MD 20817-0321
(301) 229-2786

Medical Alert

AES Corp.
285 Newbury St.
Peabody, MA 01960
(508) 535-7310

B.E.R.S. Corp.
P.O. Box 251
Gwynedd, PA 19436
(215) 699-5766

Cable Call Corp.
10324 S. Dolifield Rd.
Owings Mills, MD 21117
(301) 363-3000

Charter Security Alarm Corp.
1038-B Village Walk
Mt. Pleasant, SC 29464
(803) 884-9684

Companion Products International
134 Farnham Ct.
San Jose, CA 95139
(408) 281-0702

Crimeguard, Inc.
Box 746
Old NC 42
Apex, NC 27502
(800) 647-6444

Med Call Corp.
1038-B Village Walk
Mt. Pleasant, SC 29464
(803) 884-9622

Microlert Systems, Inc.
Box 401
Narberth, PA 19072
(215) 527-0883

Sendex Security Systems
501 W. Commercial St., E.
Rochester, NY 14445
(716) 385-6870

Sentry Products, Inc.
2225 Martin Ave.
Santa Clara, CA 95050
(408) 727-1866

Transcience
179 Ludlow
Stamford, CT 06902
(800) 243-3494

SPECIAL PURPOSE PROTECTION

Alarm Screens

Imperial Screen Co. Inc.
5336 W. 145th St.
Lawndale, CA 90260
(213) 772-7465

Maxwell Alarm Screen Mfg. of Ca. Inc.
2326 Sawtelle Blvd.
West Los Angeles, CA 90064
(800) 4-SCREEN

Security Screens, Inc.
2576 Stirling Rd.
Hollywood, FL 33020
(305) 921-7454

Trico Alarm Screens Inc.
8130 W. 26th Ave.
Hialeah, FL 33016
(800) 237-8277

Faux Alarms

Dynatec International, Inc. (Security Guard)
3594 West 1820 South
Salt Lake City, UT 84104
(800) 722-7425

Home Automation Systems

Mitsubishi Electronic Sales America, Inc.
P.O. Box 6007
Cypress, CA 90630
(714) 220-2500

Unity Systems Inc.
2606 Spring Street
Redwood City, CA 94063
(415) 369-3233
(800) 55-UNITY
In California: (800) 85-UNITY

Intercoms

Aiphone Intercom Systems
1700 130th Ave., N.E.
Bellevue, WA 98005
(206) 455-0510

Alpha Communications Inc.
89-D Cabot Ct.
Hauppauge, NY 11788-3717
(800) 666-4800

Broan Manufacturing
Box 140
Hartford, WI 53027

Fasco Industries
Box 140
Fayetteville, NC 28302

Fisher-Price
East Aurora, NY 14052

Lee Dan Communications Inc.
155 Adams Ave.
Hauppage, NY 11788
(800) 533-3261

Linsay Manufacturing, Valet Div.
Box 1708
Ponca City, OK 74602

M & S Systems Inc. (System 2000 Intercom)
2861 Congressman Lane
Dallas, TX 75220
(214) 358-3196

NuTone
Madison and Red Bank Roads
Cincinnati, OH 45227
(513) 527-5100

Talk-A-Phone Co.
5013 N. Kedzie Ave.
Chicago, IL 60625
(312) 539-1100

Tandy Radio Shack
1700 One Tandy Center
Fort Worth, TX 76102
(817) 390-3011

TekTone Sound and Signal Mfg. Inc.
1331 S. Killian Dr.
Box 12427
Lake Park, FL 33403-0427
(407) 844-2383

Siedle Intercom USA
780 Parkway
Broomall, PA 19008
(215) 353-9595

Ultrak Inc.
660 Compton St.
Broomfield, CO 80020
(800) 535-5567

Windsor Industries
131 Executive Blvd.
Farmingdale, NY 11735

Metal Security Fencing

Jerith MFG. Co., Inc.
2716 Salmon St.
Philadelphia, PA 19134

Leslie-Locke, Inc.
Box 723727
Atlanta, GA 30339
(404) 953-6366

Pool Alarms

Electromatic Control Corporation
2495 Pembroke Ave.
Hoffman Estates, IL 60195
(312) 882-5757

Optex (USA), Inc.
363 Van Ness Way, Suite 402
Torrance, CA 90501
(800) 556-7839

Remington Products, Inc.
60 Main St.
Bridgeport, CT 06602
(203) 367-4400

Pool Covers — Automatic

Poolsaver
679 W. Terrace
San Dimas, CA 91773
(800) 22COVER
In CA: (714) 592-4355

Safes

Adesco Safe Co.
16720 S. Garfield Ave.
Paramount, CA 90723
(213) 630-1503

Armor Safe Corp.
Box 1719
San Marcos, CA 92069-0580
(800) 345-1207

Defiant Safe
3218 Beltline Rd.
Dallas, TX 75234
(214) 243-3711

Empire Safe Co.
433 Canal St.
New York, NY 10013
(800) 543-5412

Fire-Fyter Safe Co.
540 Goodrich Rd.
Bellevue, OH 44811
(419) 483-5107

Majestic
1000 E. Market St.
Huntington, IN 46750
(219) 356-8000

Major Safe Co.
11925 Pacific Ave.
Fontana, CA 92335
(714) 685-9680

Schwab Safe Co., Inc.
3000 Main St.
Box 5088
Lafayette, IN 47903
(800) 428-7678

Sentry Group
900 Linden Ave.
Rochester, NY 14625
(800) 828-1438

U.S. Lock Corporation
77 Rodeo Dr.
Brentwood, NY 11717
(800) 525-5000

Yard Signs and Window Decals

The Leading Group
2450-H Marilouise Way
San Diego, CA 92103-1050
(619) 295-8273

WINDOWS
Attack-Resistant Glass & Glazing Products

Globe-Amerada Glass Co. (Secur-Lite)
2001 Greenleaf Ave.
Elk Grove Village, IL 60007
(800) 323-8776

Security Glass Systems of California, Inc.
    (ArmorCoat)
1032 Serpentine Ln., Suite 102
Pleasanton, CA 94566
(415) 484-4730

Monsanto (Saflex)
800 N. Lindbergh Blvd.
St. Louis, MO 63167
(314) 694-1000

3M Energy Control Products (Scotchshield)
3M Center
St. Paul, MN 55144-1000
(612) 733-1110

Security Screens

Kane Manufacturing Corporation
P.O. Box 777
Kane, PA 16735
(814) 837-6464

Security Shutters — Roll-down

Environmental Seal and Security Co. Inc.
    (Enviroblind)
2621 East Katella Ave.
Anaheim, CA 92806
(714) 635-5775

European Rolling Shutters
150 Martinvale Ln.
San Jose, CA 95119
(408) 629-3740

Rollag Manufacturing Corporation (Herol)
7401 Pacific Circle
Mississauga, Ontario Canada L5T 2A1
(416) 670-1014

Roll-A-Way Insulating Security Shutters
Eastern Office:
10601 Oak St. NE
St. Petersburg, FL 33716
(800) 245-9505
Western Office:
5635 E.Washington Blvd.
City of Commerce, CA 90040
(800) 237-0996
In California: (800) 821-9922

Solaroll Shade & Shutter Corporation
915 S. Dixie Hwy. E.
Pompano Beach, FL 33060
(305) 782-7211

Security Shutters — Folding and Traditional

Folding Shutter Corporation
7089 Hemstreet Place
West Palm Beach, FL 33416
(407) 683-4811

Willard Shutter Co., Inc.
,4420 NW 35th Ct.
Miami, FL 33142
(800) 826-4530

Steel Window Guards

Bar Safe, Inc.
129 Weston St.
Hartford, CT 06120
(203) 247-1804

John Sterling Corporation (Burglar Bars)
11600 Sterling Parkway
Richmond, IL 60071
(815) 678-2031

U.S. Lock Corporation
77 Rodeo Dr.
Brentwood, NY 11717
(800) 525-5000

Weatherguard Ornamental Iron
6890 S. Emporia
Englewood, CO 80112
(800) 525-0329

Miscellaneous

American Consumer Products Inc.
    (CreditCard Keys)
5777 Grant Ave.
Cleveland, OH 44105
(216) 271-4000

Armour Products, Inc. (Series 1050 &
    1060 Garage Door Locking Systems)
2554 Lincoln Blvd., Suite 405
Marina Del Rey, CA 90291
(213) 823-6041

Consumer Engineering, Inc. (911 Flash-lite)
1240-A Clearmont Street, N.E.
Palm Bay, FL 32905
(407) 984-8550

Daisy Mfg. Co. (Portaguard —
    Solar Powered Portable PIR Alarm)
P.O. Box 220
Rogers, AR 72757
(800) 643-3458

Security Etch International
    (Auto Window Glass Etching)
3303 Harbor Blvd., Suite B-12
Costa Mesa, CA 92626
(714) 557-8311

Leigh Products Inc.
    (Mailguard)-Locking Mailbox
411 64th Ave.
Coopersville, MI 49404
(616) 837-8141

Kalglo Electronics Co. Inc.
    (Watchdog)-Doorknob Alarm
6584 Ruch Rd.
Bethlehem, PA 18017
(215) 837-0700

Honeywell Protection Services (Sliding Door
    Electronic Alarm & Lock Bar)
Honeywell Plaza
Minneapolis, MN 55408
(800) 328-5111 Ext. 2030

Timtronics Technology (KNIGHT STICK)-
 Sliding Door & Window Alarm
P.O. Box 34136
Granada Hills, CA 91344

Heath Zenith Consumer Products Group
 (Barking Dog Security Alarm)
Hilltop Rd.
St. Joseph, MI 49085
(616) 982-5642

Alert Systems Inc. (Driveway Alert)
P.O. Box 2268
Westport, CT 06880

T.I.M. Manufacturing, Inc. (SECO-LOC-BAR)
 -Sliding Door Lock Bar
7519 Mentor Ave.
Mentor, OH 44060
(216) 951-1890

Churchill Mills, Ltd. (Churchill Mills
 Burglar Bar-Sliding Doors)
Suffolk Place
25 Suffolk Street East
Guelph, Ontario N1H 2H7 Canada

Trimark Venture Development Corp. (Portabolt)
P.O. Box 3587
Vancouver, B.C. V6B 3Y6 Canada

RETAIL SOURCES FOR SECURITY PRODUCTS AND SERVICES

Unfortunately there is no one retail outlet that you can go to for all of your security needs. To find locks you have to go to one store, for lighting another, and home security systems still another. To make your search more effective and less time consuming use your local Yellow Pages to locate the products and services that you're looking for before you drive all over town. To assist you in using the Yellow Pages to their fullest I have created the Yellow Pages Reference Guide (Table 7). This guide lists the major security product or services groups and the corresponding Yellow Pages headings for the retail outlet that offers the product or service.

To use the Reference Guide you first look under the Product or Service heading for the product or service that you are looking for. Then look under the Retail Source Listed Under heading for the corresponding Yellow Pages heading that your local businesses are listed under. Then go to your Yellow Pages and look up the businesses nearest you.

For example, if you're looking for a home security system, you first find "Home Alarms" under Product or Services, then look under Retail Source Listed Under to find the Yellow Pages headings for home security systems, which in this case are: Burglar Alarm Systems, Security Control Equipment & Systems, and Locks & Locksmiths. You then turn to the above listed sections in your local Yellow Pages to find a complete listing of companies in your area that sell residential security systems. You can then contact the companies by phone to see if they're offering the type of service or product that you're looking for.

TABLE 7: YELLOW PAGES REFERENCE GUIDE

Product or Service	Retail Source
Bicycle Locks	Bicycle Racks & Security Systems, Bicycles — Dealers, Locks, & Locksmiths
Car Alarms	Burglar Alarm Systems, Locks, & Locksmiths
Crime Prevention	Crime Prevention Programs
Door/Window Hardware	Building Materials — Retail, Hardware
Doors	Building Materials — Retail, Doors
Fire Extinguishers	Fire Extinguisher
Home Alarms	Burglar Alarm Systems, Security Control Equipment & Systems, Locks & Locksmiths
Locks	Building Materials — Retail, Hardware, Locks, Locksmiths, Locks — Wholesale & Retail, Locksmiths' Equipment & Supplies
Locksmiths	Locks & Locksmiths
Security Doors	Doors, Guards — Door & Window, Building Materials — Retail
Security Glass	Glass — Auto, Plate, Windows
Security Lighting	Building Materials — Retail, Lighting Fixtures
Self-Defense Devices	Protection Devices — Self Defense, Police Equipment
Smoke Detectors	Building Materials — Retail, Hardware
Video Inventory	Video Production Services, Inventory Services
Windows	Windows

SECURITY PRODUCT CATALOGS

Listed below are catalogs that carry unique and hard to find security-related products. Some products are exclusive to specific catalogs and are not available at retail outlets.

B N Genius
The Sporting Edge Companies
22121 Crystal Creek Blvd. S.E.
Bothell, WA 98021
(800) 468-4410
Unique and hard to find electronic security devices and security products

Galls Inc.
2470 Palumbo Dr.
P.O. Box 55268
Lexington, KY 40555-5268
(800) 524-4255
Security books and videos

Hammacher Schlemmer
(800) 543-3366

Icon Review
101 Reighard Ave.
Williamsport, PA 17701
(800) 228-8910
Computer security equipment

The NFPA Catalog
National Fire Protection Association
Batterymarch Park
Quincy, MA 02269
(800) 344-3555
Everything you ever wanted to know about fire safety: books, brochures, and videos.

The Sharper Image
(800) 344-4444

Special Interest Video
475 Oberlin Ave. South
Lakewood, NJ 08701-1062
(800) 522-0502
Child safety videos

U.S. Cavalry
2855 Centennial Ave.
Radcliff, KY 40160-9000
(800) 626-6171
Personal protection devices, covert safes, reference book safes

ADDITIONAL READING

CHILD ABUSE AND NEGLECT

The National Center for Missing and
    Exploited Children (NCMEC)
2101 Wilson Blvd., Suite 550
Arlington, VA 22201
(703) 235-3900

To report information about missing or exploited
children (800) 843-5678

TDD hotline (800) 634-9821

To order publications (800) 843-5678

Ordering information: Single copies of all books
and up to fifty copies of all brochures are available
free of charge by writing to Publications Department at the above address or by calling the toll-free
number above.

Books

Child Molesters: A Behavioral Analysis — A
    handbook for law-enforcement officers inves-
    tigating cases of child sexual exploitation and
    abuse.

*Child Pornography and Prostitution: Background
    and Legal Analysis* – For specialists only.

Children Traumatized in Sex Rings — For health
    professionals treating child victims of sexual
    abuse and exploitation.

Interviewing Child Victims of Sexual Exploitation
    — For social service, law-enforcement, and le-
    gal professionals.

Investigator's Guide to Missing Child Cases — A
    handbook for law-enforcement officers locat-
    ing missing children.

Parental Kidnapping — A handbook for parents
    and other persons seeking an overview of legal
    remedies in parental kidnapping cases.

Selected State Legislation — State laws in effect to
    protect children.

Summary of Selected State Legislation — A sum-
    mary of the above.

Youth at Risk — Understanding runaways and ex-
    ploited youth.

Brochures

Child Protection — Safety and precaution tips.
    (Also available in Spanish.)

Child Protection Priorities in State Legislation —
    Seven legislative priorities to prevent child
    victimization.

For Camp Counselors — Detecting child sexual
    abuse and exploitation.

Informational Brochure

*Just in Case . . . You Are Considering Family
    Separation*

*Just in Case . . . You Are Dealing with Grief Fol-
    lowing the Loss of a Child*

*Just in Case . . . You Are Using the Federal Parent
    Locator Service*

Just in Case . . . You Need a Babysitter (Also avail-
    able in Braille.)

Just in Case . . . Your Child Is a Runaway

Just in Case . . . Your Child Is Missing

Just in Case . . . Your Child Is Testifying in Court

Just in Case . . . Your Child Is the Victim of Sexual Abuse or Exploitation

National Committee for Prevention of Child Abuse (NCPCA)
332 S. Michigan Ave., Suite 1600
Chicago, IL 60604-4357
(312) 663-3520

Ordering Information: No telephone orders are accepted. All orders must be prepaid including shipping and handling charges. NCPCA publishes new materials on an ongoing basis. To receive notices as new titles are published, write to NCPCA, P.O. Box 94283, Chicago, IL 60690 and ask to be placed on the catalog mailing list.

Child Abuse Prevention

A Look at Child Sexual Abuse — This booklet reviews and summarizes current understanding of the painful subject of child sexual abuse.

An Approach to Preventing Child Abuse — A model for community action to prevent child abuse; for professionals, volunteers, and civic leaders.

Basic Facts about Child Sexual Abuse — Answers twenty-seven basic questions about the incidence, nature, and legal aspects of child sexual abuse.

Emotional Maltreatment of Children — Describes emotional maltreatment and prescribes actions for prevention.

Guidelines for Child Sexual Abuse Prevention Programs — Contains recommendations for the selection, effective use, and evaluation of child sexual abuse prevention programs.

Guidelines for Establishing Family Resource Programs — The professional or layperson interested in establishing such a program will find this booklet a helpful and thorough guide.

It Shouldn't Hurt to Be a Child — Basic information about child abuse and an outline of NCPCA's approach to preventing child abuse.

Maltreatment of Adolescents — Discusses the complex family and societal issues involved in adolescent maltreatment and proposes preventive and rehabilitative measures.

Physical Child Abuse — Causes and effects of physical child abuse.

Physical Child Neglect — Describes the characteristics of both severe and moderate neglect; for professionals, volunteers, teachers, and students.

Selected Child Abuse Information and Resources Directory — Lists national resources and gives information on locating facts and services in the child abuse field and related areas.

Talking about Child Sexual Abuse — Lists signs and behavior that may indicate abuse, provides instructions for screening baby-sitters and child-care centers and for reporting suspected abuse.

Think You Know Something about Child Abuse? — This brochure answers twenty-two basic and important questions that many people ask about child abuse. (Also available in Spanish.)

You Don't Have to Molest That Child — A plan on how the offender can break out of the vicious cycle of child molestation; for the offender and the family.

Materials for Parents

Annie Overcomes Isolation — This upbeat, clearly illustrated, and easy-to-read pamphlet suggests the best tools and techniques for overcoming isolation.

Caring for Your Children — Full of helpful hints on ways to provide the right kind of attention, food, and sleep.

Child Discipline: Guidelines for Parents — This booklet looks at discipline as a positive experience for children and clarifies the differences among discipline, punishment, and abuse by investigating the purposes and probable results of each. (Also available in Spanish.)

Emotional Abuse: Words CAN Hurt — Helpful tips for readers who might contribute to this problem and for aiding children who might be experiencing it.

Foster Parenting Abused Children — Reviews the common forms and causes of child abuse, and notes the range of reactions that children may have to foster care.

Getting New Parents Off to a Good Start — Provides insight into the prenatal period and offers specific measures of support for new parents from pregnancy through the first month of the baby's life.

Growth and Development through Parenting — Explains the types of behavior characteristic of each of the four stages of childhood (infancy, toddlerhood, school age, and adolescence) and suggests effective techniques for dealing with the child at each stage.

I Hear You — Teaches parents how to observe, understand, and respond to their own needs and problems as well as to their child's.

Making the World Safe for Jeffery — Helpful ideas for preventing stress, handling it, and making it work for an individual.

My Brother Got Here Early — What families can expect when they have a premature baby and where they can get help.

Parent-Child Bonding: The Development of Intimacy — Discusses what "bonding" is, when it occurs, who is capable of it, factors that hinder it, and ways in which parents can assess and encourage the process. (Also available in Spanish.)

Stress and the Single Parent — Suggests ways to reduce stress and the likelihood of child abuse.

What Every Parent Should Know — Provides practical suggestions on how to cope with kids, explains concepts of discipline and suggest techniques for the successful resolution of conflicts.

Who Stole Mrs. Wick's Self-Esteem? — This pamphlet explores the causes of low self-esteem and indicates what can be done about it.

Materials for Children

Amazing Spider-Man™ and Power Pack™ on Sexual Abuse — Full-color comic book includes two stories that teach children how to protect themselves from sexual abuse.

Amazing Spider-Man™ on Emotional Abuse — Full-color comic book includes two stories that teach children how to deal with emotional child abuse.

You're Not Alone — Relates the sure signs of alcoholism and explains how each member of the family is affected. (Also available in Spanish.)

Special Subjects

Catapulting Abusive Alcoholics to Successful Recovery — Defines alcoholism and co-alcoholism; discusses confrontation techniques; stresses the importance of treatment for the entire family; and outlines preparatory steps for appropriate intervention.

Child Abuse and the Law (A Legal Primer for Social Workers) — Takes the mystery out of the judicial system by giving some clear, basic information on legal procedures as they relate to child abuse.

Child Care and the Family — Guides the reader through the often confusing child care options available.

Educators, Schools, and Child Abuse — Educators can make the most difference in child abuse prevention; this book tells how.

Evaluating Child Abuse Prevention Programs — Presents specific strategies for evaluating a wide variety of primary prevention programs.

Self-Help and the Treatment of Child Abuse — Acquaints the reader with the wide range of available self-help groups and describes self-help groups in general.

Strengthening Families through the Workplace — This booklet examines issues such as the need for adequate child care and the effect of unemployment on the family.

Teacher's Guide to Spider-Man™ on Emotional Abuse — This guide helps the teacher discuss emotional abuse in an open, protective, and nonthreatening way.

Teacher's Guide: Amazing Spider-Man™ and Power Pack™ on Sexual Abuse — Helps teachers present in a comfortable, effective way the stories in the comic book *Amazing Spider-Man™ and Power Pack™ on Sexual Abuse.*

The Disabled Child and Child Abuse — Discusses reasons why the disabled child may be at high risk for abuse and presents evidence that abuse can cause handicapping conditions.

When School's Out and Nobody's Home — Gives parents, policymakers, and employers a comprehensive look at the problem and discusses the risks and benefits of self-care.

Clearinghouse on Child Abuse
  and Neglect Information
U.S. Department of Health and Human Services
P.O. Box 1182
Washington, DC 20013
(703) 821-2086

The clearinghouse was established primarily as a major resource center for professionals concerned with child maltreatment issues. The clearinghouse maintains a database of documents, audiovisual materials, service programs, excerpts of state statutes, and ongoing research projects concerning child abuse and neglect. Available material is too numerous to list here. To obtain a current catalog contact the clearinghouse at the above address.

Corporation For Public Broadcasting
1111 16th St., NW
Washington, DC 20036
(202) 955-5100

Ordering Information: Send check for $1 to Corp. for Public Broadcasting, Dept. P, P.O. Box 33039-LK, Washington, DC 20033

Booklet

What If I'm Home Alone? — A very good resource for latchkey children and their parents.

FIRE SAFETY

National Fire Protection Association
Batterymarch Park
Quincy, MA 02269
(800) 344-3555

Ordering Information: Call toll-free line to order brochures and free catalog. Brochures may also be available from your local fire department free of charge.

Brochures for Children

E.D.I.T.H. — Exit Drills in the Home — Shows youngsters how to draw up an escape plan for their apartment or house. (Also available in Spanish.)

Let's Be Fire Smart — Shows children ways to prevent and escape fires at home.

Sparky and Smokey Team Up for Outdoor Firesafety — Safety tips for camping, cooking out, boating, and more.

Sparky's Activity Book — Kids learn fire safety as they play. Games and puzzles such as crosswords, connect the dots, and mazes each have their own important fire safety message.

Sparky's Firesafety Coloring Book — Each picture shows Sparky the Fire Dog performing specific fire safety behaviors. Kids learn vital fire safety lessons while they color.

Sparky's Inspection Checklist — Home fire safety checklist for children.

Sparky's Second Chance — Fire safety comic book full of important information for kids.

Sparky's Team: Fire Prevention for Everyone Comic Book — Captain Sparky leads his team of kids in an adventurous fight against home fires.

The School Fire Drill: A Life Saving Lesson — Tips for students on what to do during fire drills — or if a real fire occurs.

Brochures for Adults

10 Tips for Firesafety — Covers the ten most vital fire safety procedures.

10 Tips for Hotel/Motel Firesafety — Vital facts about how to prevent fire and escape should a fire break out in a hotel or motel.

Be a Firesafe Neighbor — Fire prevention information focusing on apartments and condominiums.

Don't Go Up in Smoke — Fire prevention information for smokers.

Fire in Your Home — Fact-filled fire safety guide gives residents the knowledge they need to protect their homes against fire.

Fire Prevention All Over Your Home — Discusses specific hazards and provide fire safety guidelines to follow in all areas of the home: kitchen, living, and family rooms, bedrooms, storage areas, and outdoors.

Firesafety for People with Disabilities — Safety tips and planning for persons with physical disabilities.

Firesafety in High-Rise Office Buildings — Fire safety and escape information for people who work in high-rises.

Firesafety in the City — Directed towards people who live in inner cities.

Firesafety on the Job — Encourages employees to watch out for and eliminate fire hazards in the workplace.

Firesafety Tips for Babysitters — How to prevent fire accidents and how to act properly if an emergency does occur.

Fireworks: Spectacular Danger — Facts about fireworks and ways to prevent accidents.

Have a Firesafe Holiday — Firesafety tips for the special fire hazards present during the holidays.

Heat . . . Without Getting Burned — Shows homeowners how to select reliable equipment, recognize and correct common heating hazards, and what to do if fire strikes.

Keeping Current on Electrical Firesafety — How to recognize the danger signs and prevent electrical hazards throughout the home.

Play it Safe Plan Your Escape — Guidelines describe how to install and maintain smoke detectors, how to make and practice a home escape plan, what to do if escaping a fire is difficult or impossible, and how to select and operate fire extinguishers.

Recipe for Firesafety — Details fire hazards in the kitchen, explaining how to prevent fires from starting and what to do if fire strikes.

Senior Citizens Firesafety Tips — Focuses on the special needs of senior citizens.

Smoke Detectors: A Firesafety Basic — Helpful facts about selecting detectors, where to install them, and how to maintain them.

Teaching Little Ones to be Firesafe: Fire Information for Preschoolers — Children under five are twice as likely to die in fires as the rest of the population. These brochures offer creative suggestions for teachers and day-care employees about how to incorporate fire safety lessons into regular activities.

MISCELLANEOUS

Books

Sunset's, Making Your Home Child-Safe. Menlo Park, CA: Lane Publishing Company, 1988.

Fix-It-Yourself, Home Emergencies. Alexandria, VA: Time-Life Books, Inc., 1988.

Videos

Here is a partial listing of instructional and how-to video tapes that are available for rent or sale. Many of the larger video rental chains carry some of the titles listed below; others are only sold through video and specialty catalogs. The production company and retail sources are listed if known.

Complete Guide to Home Security — Learn how a reformed master thief protects his own home. Do-it-yourself secrets show you step-by-step how to secure your home against burglary. Includes features on timers, exterior lighting, sliding glass doors, alarms, and more. Available from Gall's Inc. "Gift Catalog" (see Security Product Catalogs for more address).

Self-Defense & Awareness for Children — Instructs children on how to quickly stun and disable an attacker with one of eight easy moves. Teaches children to be alert and to protect themselves should the need arise. Available from Gall's Inc. "Gift Catalog" (see Security Product Catalogs for more address).

How To Save Your Child When Every Second Counts — Teaches you CPR, the Heimlich maneuver and instructions for handling choking for newborns to eight years. Prepared under the American Heart Association guidelines. Available from Special Interest Video (see Security Product Catalogs for address).

Super Sitters — Shows you how to find and train sitters who can cope. Video comes with first aid manual, phone directory, emergency phone stickers, sitter's guide on how to handle the kids, parents' guide on how to handle the sitter. Available from Special Interest Video (see Security Product Catalogs for address).

Be Smart — Stay Safe — An excellent video that teaches your children about crime prevention. Available free (you make a copy of the tape and return the master) from Child Find of America, P.O. Box 277, New Paltz, NY 12561-9277 (914) 255-1848

The Baby-Safe Home (McGraw Hill) — Host David Horowitz takes you through the typical home pointing out potentially unsafe situations and how to correct them.

Dr. Heimlich's Home First-Aid Video (MCA Home Video) — First aid for the whole family. Includes CPR, Heimlich maneuver, and more.

How to: Save Your Child's Life (Xenon Video Inc) — First aid training for parents with small children, covers CPR, Heimlich maneuver, and more.

Consumer Reports . . . Home Safe Home (Karl Lorimar) — Covers home safety and security issues with sections on child safety proofing your home, basic security measures, kitchen safety, and more.

Protect Yourself with Simon Rhee (USA Sports Video) — Instructional martial arts self protection training suitable for the whole family.

First Aid For The Family (Paramount) — Host Henry Winkler and familiar cartoon characters teach first aid skills to children.

Home Security (Hometime) — Step-by-step video instruction on how to make an assessment of your home security needs, install a deadbolt lock in an exterior door, secure your windows against forced entry, install exterior and interior security lighting, install an automated home security system, and how to set up a Neighborhood Watch Program.

GLOSSARY

ACCESSIBLE WINDOW — Any window located within 12 feet of grade or a building projection such as roof, covered patio, etc.

ACCORDION GATE — An assembly of metal bars, jointed so that it can be moved to and locked in position across a window or other opening, in order to prevent unauthorized entry through the opening.

ALARM CONDITION — A threatening condition, such as an intrusion, fire, or holdup sensed by a detector.

ALARM DISCRIMINATOR — A device used to minimize or eliminate the possibility of false alarms caused by extraneous sounds or vibrations. It can be adjusted to provide alarm discrimination under any job conditions.

ALARM SIGNAL — An audible and/or visual signal indicating an emergency that requires immediate action, such as intrusion, fire, smoke, unsafe equipment conditions, equipment failure, reporting line tamper or failure, and so forth. In general, all signals are treated as alarm signals, although alarm signals are sometimes differentiated from circuit faults or trouble signals.

ALARM SYSTEM — An assembly of equipment and devices designed and arranged to signal the presence of an alarm condition requiring urgent attention, such as unauthorized entry, fire, temperature rise, etc.

AREA DETECTION — A technique for detecting an intruder's presence anywhere within a specifically defined, protected area, as opposed to detection at a specific point such as a door.

AUDIBLE ALARM — The term applies to any noise-making device such as a siren used to indicate an alarm.

AUXILIARY LOCK — A lock installed on a door or window to supplement a previously installed primary lock.

BOLT — That part of a lock which, when actuated, is projected (or "thrown") from the lock into a retaining member, such as a strike plate, to prevent a door or window from moving or opening.

BOLT THROW — The distance from the edge of the door, at the bolt center line, to the furthest point on the bolt in the projected position.

BOX STRIKE — A strike plate that has a metal box or housing to fully enclose the projected bolt.

BURGLAR-RESISTANT GLAZING — Any glazing more difficult to break through than the common window or plate glass, designed to resist burglary attacks.

BUTTRESS LOCK — A lock which secures a door by wedging a bar between the door and the floor. Some incorporate a movable steel rod that fits into metal receiving slots on the door and in the floor. Also called a police lock.

CAM LOCK — A simple cam-shaped latch, not requiring a key for its operation, usually used to secure double-hung windows. Also called a crescent sash lock.

CANE BOLT — A heavy cane-shaped bolt with the top bent at right angles; used at the bottom of doors.

CASE — The housing in which a lock mechanism is mounted and enclosed.

CASEMENT WINDOW — A type of window hinged on the vertical edge.

CENTRAL MONITORING STATION — A system in which the alarm signal is relayed to a remote panel located at the facilities of a privately owned protection service company.

CHAIN GUARD — An auxiliary locking device allowing a door to be opened slightly, but restraining it from being fully opened. It consists of a chain with one end attached to the door jamb and the other attached to a keyed metal piece which slides in a slotted metal plate attached to the door.

CUT — An indentation made in a key to make it fit a pin tumbler of a lock.

CYLINDER GUARD RING — A hardened metal ring, surrounding the exposed portion of a lock cylinder, which protects the cylinder from being wrenched, turned, pried, cut, or pulled with attack tools.

CYLINDER — The cylindrical sub-assembly of a lock.

DEADBOLT — The bolt must be actuated to a projected position by a key or thumb turn, and when projected is locked against return by end pressure.

DETECTION RANGE — The greatest distance at which a sensor will consistently detect an intruder under a standard set of conditions.

DETECTOR — Any device for detecting intrusion, equipment failure or malfunction, unsafe equipment operation, presence of smoke or fire, or any other condition requiring immediate action. Detectors include a means for translating the detected abnormal condition into some form of alarm signal – either a local or remote alarm, the latter over a reporting line, with or without electrical supervision.

DOOR CLEARANCE — The space between a door and either its frame or the finished floor or threshold, or between the two doors of a double door.

DOOR FRAME — An assembly of members surrounding and supporting a door or doors, and perhaps also one or more transom lights and/or side lights.

DOOR JAMBS — The two vertical components of a door frame called the hinge jamb and the lock jamb.

DOOR STOP — The projections along the top and sides of a door frame against which a one-way swinging door closes.

DOUBLE GLAZING — Two thicknesses of glass, separated by an air space and framed in an opening, designed to reduce heat transfer or sound transmission.

DOUBLE-HUNG WINDOW — A type of window, composed of upper and lower sashes that slide vertically.

DUTCH DOOR — A door consisting of two separate leaves, one above the other, which may be operated either independently or together. The lower leaf usually has a service shelf.

ENTRANCE DELAY — The time between activating a sensor and the transmission of an alarm signal by the control panel. This delay allows you to turn off your alarm after returning home without sending an alarm signal to the central station.

ESCUTCHEON PLATE — A surface-mounted cover plate, either protective or ornamental, containing openings for any or all of the controlling members of a lock such as the knob, handle, cylinder, or keyhole.

EXIT DELAY — This permits a person to turn on the alarm system and to leave through a protected entrance without causing an alarm.

FLUSH BOLT — A door bolt so designed that, when installed, the operating handle is flush with the face or edge of the door. Usually installed at the top and bottom of the inactive door of a double door.

FOOT BOLT — A type of bolt applied at the bottom of a door and arranged for foot operation. Generally the bolt head is held up by a spring when the door is unbolted.

GLAZING BEAD — A strip of trim or a sealant such as caulking or glazing compound, which is placed around the perimeter of a pane of glass or other glazing to secure it to a frame.

GRADE AA CENTRAL STATION — Grade A central station; Grade B central station: Underwriters Laboratories (UL) designations for different classes of central stations, based on degree of protection afforded and specific requirements for equipment, personnel, procedures, records, and maintenance. Requirements are outlined in the UL publication Standards for Safety, Central Station Burglar Alarm Systems, UL611.

GUARD PLATE — A piece of metal attached to a door frame, door edge, or over the lock cylinder for the purpose of reinforcing the locking system against burglary attacks.

HAND (of a door) — The opening direction of the door. A right-handed door (RH) is hinged on the right and swings inward when viewed from the outside. A left-handed door (LH) is hinged on the left and swings inward when viewed from the outside. If either of these doors swings outward, it is referred to as a right-hand reverse (RHR) door or a left-hand reverse (LHR) door, respectively.

HASP — A fastening device consisting of a hinged plate with a slot in it that fits over a fixed D-shaped ring, or eye.

HEEL (of a padlock) — That end of the shackle on a padlock which is not removable from the case.

HOLLOW CORE DOOR — A door constructed so that the space (core) between the two facing sheets is not completely filled.

HORIZONTAL SLIDING WINDOW — A type of window, composed of two sections, one or both of which slides horizontally past the other.

INACTIVE DOOR (or leaf) — The leaf of a double door that is bolted when closed; the strike plate is attached to this leaf to receive the latch and bolt of the active leaf.

JIMMY-PIN — A sturdy projecting screw, which is installed in the hinge edge of a door near a hinge, fits into a hole in the door jamb, and prevents removal of the door if the hinge pins are removed. Also known as pinning-the-hinge.

KEY IN-KNOB LOCK — A lock having a key cylinder and the other lock mechanism, such as a push or turn button, contained in the knobs.

LAMINATED PADLOCK — A padlock, the body of which consists of a number of flat plates, all or most of which are of the same contour, superimposed and riveted or brazed together.

LINE SEIZURE — Characteristics provided by the integral circuitry of tape dialers and digital communicators which "seizes" in-use phone lines to ensure transmission of emergency signals.

LINE SUPERVISION — Electronic protection of an alarm line accomplished by sending a continuous or coded signal through a circuit. A change in the circuit characteristics, such as a change in impedance due to the circuit having been tampered with, will be detected by the monitor. The monitor initiates an alarm if the change exceeds a predetermined amount.

LOCK PICK — A tool or instrument, other than the specifically designed key, made for the purpose of manipulating a lock into a locked or unlocked condition.

LOUVERED WINDOW — A type of window on which the glazing consists of parallel, horizontal, movable glass slats. Also called a jalousie window.

MEDICAL ALERT — A signal initiated by a person in need of medical attention, transmitted to a remote receiving station where information is kept relative to the individual's medical problem.

MORTISE — A rectangular cavity made to receive a lock or other hardware; also the act of making such a cavity.

MORTISE LOCK — A lock designed for installation in a mortise.

MOTION DETECTION — Detection of an intruder by making use of the change in location or orientation in a protection area as the intruder moves about.

NICAD: (Contraction of "nickel cadmium") A high performance, long-lasting rechargeable battery that may be used as an emergency power supply for an alarm system.

OPERATOR (of a window sash) — The mechanism, including a crank handle and gear box, attached to an operating arm or arms for the purpose of opening and closing a window. Usually found on casement and awning type windows.

PADLOCK — A detachable and portable lock with a hinged or sliding shackle or bolt, normally used with a hasp and eye or staple system.

PATIO-TYPE SLIDING DOOR — A door that is essentially a single, large transparent panel in a frame (a type commonly used to give access to patios or yards of private dwellings); "single" doors have one fixed and one movable panel: "double" doors have two movable panels.

PHOTOELECTRIC SENSOR — A device that detects a visible or invisible beam of light and responds to its complete or near complete interruption.

PIN TUMBLER LOCK CYLINDER — A lock cylinder employing metal pins (tumblers) to prevent the rotation of the core until the correct key is inserted into the keyway. Small coil compression springs hold the pins in the locked position until the key is inserted.

PIVOTED WINDOW — A window which opens by pivoting about a horizontal or vertical axis.

PROTECTED AREA — A term used to indicate the specific area being protected by a security system, the area under surveillance.

REMOTE ALARM — An alarm signal that is transmitted to a remote central monitoring station.

RESET — To restore the alarm to its original (normal) condition after an alarm signal.

RIM LOCK — A lock designed to be mounted on the surface of a door.

SENSOR — A device that is designed to produce a signal or other indication in response to an event or stimulus within its detection zone.

SHACKLE — The hinged or sliding part of a padlock that does the fastening.

SHUNT — To remove some portion of an alarm system from operation, allowing entry into a protected area without initiating an alarm signal.

SILENT ALARM — A remote alarm without any local indication that an alarm has been transmitted.

SLIDE BOLT — A simple lock operated directly by hand without using a key, a turnpiece, or other actuating mechanism.

SOLID CORE DOOR — A door constructed so that the space (core) between the two facing sheets is completely filled with wood blocks or other rigid material.

STRIKE — A metal plate attached to or mortised into a door jamb to receive and hold a projected latch bolt and/or deadbolt in order to secure the door to the jamb.

THUMB TURN — A unit which is gripped between the thumb and forefinger, and turned to project or retract a bolt.

UL-LISTED — Signifies that production samples of the product have been found to comply with established Underwriters Laboratories requirements. The manufacturer is authorized to use the Laboratories' listing marks on the listed products that comply with the requirements.

WINDOW GUARD — A strong metal grid-like assembly which can be installed on a window or other opening.

WIRE GLASS — Glass manufactured with a layer of wire mesh approximately in the center of the sheet.

ZONES — Smaller subdivisions into which larger areas are divided to permit selective access to some zones, while maintaining other zones securely and to permit pinpointing the specific locations from which an alarm signal has been transmitted.

Index